John Craven's
COUNTRYFILE
HANDBOOK

*For my grandchildren, in the hope that
our countryside will not change too much.*

John Craven's
COUNTRYFILE
HANDBOOK

BBC
BOOKS

This book is published to accompany the television series entitled
Countryfile, broadcast on BBC1.

Executive editor: Andrew Thorman
Series producer: Teresa Bogan
Producers: Andrew Tomlinson. Andrea Buffery. Barbara Lewis.
Production Manager: Hilary Jones

10 9 8 7 6 5 4 3 2 1

First published in 2010 by BBC Books, an imprint of Ebury Publishing.
A Random House Group Company. This edition published in 2012.

The Random House Group Limited Reg. No. 954009

Addresses for companies within the Random House Group can be found at
www.randomhouse.co.uk

A CIP catalogue record for this book is available from the British Library.

ISBN 978 1 849 90553 4

MIX
Paper from
responsible sources
FSC® C016897

The Random House Group Limited supports The Forest Stewardship Council
(FSC®), the leading international forest certification organisation. Our books
carrying the FSC label are printed on FSC® certified paper. FSC is the only forest
certification scheme endorsed by the leading environmental organisations,
including Greenpeace. Our paper procurement policy can be found at
www.randomhouse.co.uk/environment

Editing and additional research: Cavan Scott

Commissioning editor: Muna Reyal
Project editor: Laura Higginson
Copy-editor: Stephanie Evans
Design and illustrations: Robert Updegraff
Production: Helen Everson

Printed and bound by CPI Group (UK) Ltd, Croydon, CR0 4YY

To buy books by your favourite authors and register for offers,
visit www.randomhouse.co.uk

Contents

Introduction

Welcome to my guide to our great British countryside, based on the two decades I've spent travelling to every corner of it to present more than a thousand editions of BBC1's *Countryfile* programme. It's hard to believe that *Countryfile* was first broadcast more than 22 years ago – on 24 July 1988. The show replaced the *Farming Programme,* which had been on the air for 25 years, and promised a wider view of the great British countryside, reporting on rural affairs, conservation, farming and food issues as well as opening a window to its beauty and delights.

I wasn't there when it started (I was still presenting and editing *Newsround*) but I joined the team when it was one year old and haven't looked back since. Why would I? What other job would give me the opportunity to explore so much of the landscape, meet so many country folk and learn so much about our rural history and heritage?

These days, the countryside is more popular than ever – a fact not only reflected in the recent proliferation of rural programmes on television. Never before have so many people ventured out from our towns and cities and fallen in love with this wonderful (and largely free!) facility just beyond the urban boundaries. Never before have so many quit those towns and cities to start new lives in the countryside. And never before have traditional country folk faced greater challenges to their way of life.

Wherever I go, I meet people who are passionate about the countryside. That passion may have started with a weekend wander along a footpath or stream, or a visit to a farm shop or nature reserve, but as it develops the more they want to see, to understand, to connect.

Although around 80 per cent of the nation lives in busy urban areas, I've always believed that we Brits have the countryside in our genes – after all, only a couple of centuries ago, before the Industrial Revolution, most of our ancestors lived on the land. Those who moved to the new urban areas to work in factories still kept a connection with their roots through the food in their larder; they ate what was grown locally, when it was in season and they understood how the seasons worked.

Many 'townies' also relied on the countryside for a break from the dirt and depression of daily life, like the early ramblers who campaigned for the right to roam over hill and dale and the workers who flooded from London and other big cities into the fields to pick hops or soft fruit and cut flowers, taking a working holiday in the summer sun.

But for countless families, as decades passed, that link with their rural roots became broken – and what better time than now to restore it. There is an obvious danger in all of this though; we need to guard against looking at our countryside with rose-tinted glasses; with nostalgic fervour for the way it used to be. Or at least, the way we think it used to be – the bucolic rural scenes immortalised on millions of postcards, jigsaws and chocolate boxes.

Those places still exist of course, but the rural life that so many chase after has its own very real and current issues to deal with, be they affordable housing, the closure of village services or the threat of bovine tuberculosis that hangs over so many of our cattle farmers.

What I find so stimulating is the way these rural issues have steadily climbed much higher up the national agenda. When people start exploring them, start asking questions about what they see, those who truly share the countryside gene don't run away from them. Instead, they embrace the issues and, in some cases, are consumed by them. They throw themselves into conservation, fight to keep traditions alive and campaign to make a difference. You see it in their eyes, a proprietorial attitude that drives them to protect the countryside. They may not own the actual land (at least most of them don't) but they act as if they do. They realise how much we've let slip away over recent generations and what we're in danger of losing in the future.

I hope that this handbook will help you explore our rural roots and understand the lie of the land a little better; that it will be a useful companion for those pulling on their walking boots for the first time, while also including something new for those who've lived in the countryside all of their life.

It contains many of the lessons I have learnt over the years. You'll find here the human stories behind the landscape, from historic landmarks such as castles and bridges to those changes, which we now take for granted, brought about by the needs of agriculture – hedges, fields and woodlands. You'll discover how those habitats were created, how they are being cared for, and what types of wildlife they support. It's all too easy to forget that the landscape we think of as natural is a product of thousands of years of management and farming. Britain was originally covered in forests, bracken and wetlands. Many of the views we enjoy now are as man-made as city streets – but so much more enticing.

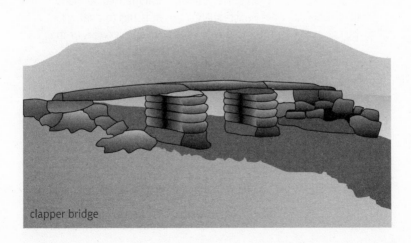

clapper bridge

Chapter by chapter, we'll explore these landscapes. We'll dip into village life, finding out how our places got their names (just why, for instance, should Pendle Hill really be called hill-hill hill?) and why some villagers still pull a plough into their local church at the beginning of the year or race carrying a bag of heavy wool on their back. We'll wander through farmland, finding out how agriculture is constantly changing and explaining what you'll see and hear. What do those sheepdog calls mean? Why do some animals have rings in their noses? And why are a growing number of farmers ploughing their land by moonlight?

We'll climb the wind-blown and rugged uplands, discovering how the fight for countryside access led to the creation of the National Parks while learning some age-old country lore along the way, such as how to tell what weather is on the way from clouds, flowers and birds. Then we'll head down to the rolling lowlands, checking as we go the rules for treating the countryside with respect, foraging for wild food and learning why we should give new English wines a try.

As the handbook comes to a close we are into the woods, identifying the leaves and trees, making sense of why rotten wood should be left alone to provide vital habitats, learning which wood is best for burning and how you could even buy a woodland of your own. Then finally we're out on the water, navigating through the tricky subjects of reintroducing lost animals such as the beaver, exploring our canals and celebrating the conservation successes of our otters and water voles.

As we journey around this land of ours together we'll step into history, find out how to identify some of our most iconic wildlife, including owls and butterflies, and delve into some of the big stories that affect everyday country life. I'll explain the facts behind our most controversial and contentious rural issues, from fox hunts and badger culls to wind farms and genetically modified food, providing you with the facts so that you can make your own mind up about some of these very real concerns.

The countryside has been a part of my life ever since I first got on a bike as a boy and cycled out of suburban Leeds into the surrounding Yorkshire Dales. I learnt something then that has stayed with me ever since – once the countryside bug bites you, it never lets you go. You can't help but want to be there and at the same time do all you can to make sure it is protected for the future. For some of us, the countryside is a wonderful place to visit, for others it's a way of life. For me, it's simply the best place on Earth to be.

John Craven

CHAPTER ONE

Villages and Market Towns

Just who exactly is a rural person?

Ever wondered just what makes you rural? How far out in the sticks must you live to qualify? Well, officialdom has come up with the answer. For administrative purposes, you are classified as rural if you live more than three miles from a state school, doctor or dispensing chemist. A dry definition, as you'd expect, and country dwellers can conjure up many better social, historical and emotional ones, but as a practical baseline it's not a bad start.

Other people have come up with different definitions over the last few years. The Commission for Rural Communities (CRC) – the government's independent rural advisory body – uses a community's population to gauge whether they are rural or urban. Settlements with fewer than 10,000 residents are considered rural, those with more are classed as urban.

If you accept this definition, it means that there are a lot more rural communities in the UK than there are urban ones. According to the 2001 census, there are 4,221 settlements with over 100 residents (the lowest number to be included in the census data). Of those, 3,460 have fewer than 10,000 residents and are therefore, according to the CRC, rural with only 761 considered urban.

Here are a few more facts for you:

❯ The average age in rural areas is 42, compared to 36 in urban areas.

❯ Two-fifths of country folk are aged over 50 and one in 12 is over 75.

> The USA's all-seeing Central Intelligence Agency officially views the UK as: 'a land of rugged hills and low mountains with rolling plains in the east and south east'. According to them, 10 per cent of our population is rural, with 23 per cent of our land arable.

The difference between a hamlet, village, town and city

A hamlet = a settlement traditionally without a church.

A village = a settlement traditionally with a church.

A town (or market town) = a settlement that has, at some point in its existence, been given the right to hold a market.

A city = a settlement that has been given city status by the monarch or parts of the British government. Contrary to popular opinion just having a cathedral doesn't automatically raise your town to city status.

All in the name

Ever wondered about the history of the place you live in, or the area you're visiting? There could be clues all around you, starting with its very name. The clues are often right there on the signposts, once you know what to look for. Here are some of the most common words you'll find in the names of British hamlets, villages and towns with a little about what they originally meant.

Aber-

As in Aberdeen (Aberdeenshire), Aberdare (Rhondda Cynon Taff) or Aberchirder (Aberdeenshire)

From an Old Celtic word meaning a confluence, where two bodies of water meet. Abergavenny in Monmouthshire, for example, is the point where the rivers Usk and Gavenny join.

Ard

As in Tollard Royal (Wiltshire), Armagh, originally Ard Mhacha (County Armagh) or Penarth, originally Pen Ard (Glamorgan)

Adapted from the Old Celtic word for high place.

Avon

As in Avonwick (Devon), Stratford-upon-Avon (Warwickshire) or Avonmouth (Bristol)

Avon comes from the Old Celtic word *abona* meaning, quite simply, river. This means that, rather amusingly, the many river Avons that run through Britain are all actually called the 'river river'!

In Welsh, the word for river is *afon* as can be spotted on countless Welsh signposts, pointing the way to such waterways as Afon Cegidog or Afon Clwyd.

Bal-, ball- or bally-

As in Ballachulish (Highlands), Ballymoney (County Antrim) or Ballynahinch (County Down)

From the Irish, Scots or Manx Gaelic word *baile*, which served the same purpose as -ton in English names, denoting a settlement, farm or, in later years, an estate.

-bury, burgh, borough or –berry

As in Avebury (Wiltshire), Westbury (Berkshire) or Aldeburgh (Suffolk)

In most cases, any of the many variations of bury usually come from the Old English *burh* meaning a fortified camp or stronghold. This is certainly true in places such as Canterbury in Kent or Salisbury in Wiltshire.

However, it may also be derived from *beorg* meaning hill or mound – where of course you may have also found a fortress (see pages 115–18). Silbury Hill in Wiltshire is the largest human-made prehistoric mound in Europe, rising 40 metres above the natural landscape.

-by

As in Derby (Derbyshire), Grimsby (Lincolnshire) or Sowerby (North Yorkshire)

'By' is another word for farm or settlement, this time from the Scandinavian or Old Norse. Danby in North Yorkshire is thought to have been originally a farm run by a Danish family, whereas Kirkby, a name found repeatedly all over the country, means simply 'a village with a church'.

Caher, caer, car or cair

As in Cardiff (Glamorgan), Caerwent (Monmouthshire) or Caterham (Surrey)

'Caher' comes from an Old Celtic word which itself is derived from the Latin *cathedra*, meaning throne. As the centuries passed, it became another name to indicate a hill fort or stronghold.

Charl or chorl

As in Charlecote (Warwickshire), Chorley (Lancastershire) or Charlton (London)

In the case of some settlements, the word charl or chorl came from the Old English word *ceorl* or *churl*, meaning a freeman, one of the 10 per cent of the population who farmed the land, paying rent to the local landowner or lord without being in his service. Such placenames are not to be confused with ones named after various folk called Charles, such as the towns of Charlestown in Derbyshire or Cornwall, which take their names from Henry Charles Howard, 13th Duke of Norfolk, and local businessman Charles Rashleigh respectively.

-chester, -cester or -caster

As in Chester (Cheshire), Manchester (Lancashire) or Silchester (Hampshire)

Any town ending with -chester would have been a place with fortifications, probably Roman. The original Old English word was *ceaster* from the Latin *castrum* meaning camp or fort. So Exeter was a 'walled city on the river Exe' and Godmanchester in Cambridgeshire would have been 'Godmund's fortress', named after a man of note.

-combe or Compton

As in Woolacombe (Devon), Combe Longa (Oxfordshire) or Ilfracombe (Devon)

Another rare case of the English borrowing a word from the Celtic language, namely *cwm*, meaning 'place of the valley'.

Creech or crook

As in Creech St Michael (Somerset)

The Old Celtic word *crug* meant hill. Over time the word crug was often replaced by 'church', leading to many places across the country becoming known as Churchill.

16

Cross or crouch

As in Crosby (Merseyside), Crossmyloof (Glasgow) or Crouch (Kent)

Cross or crouch in a placename – coming from the Old English *cruc* – either indicates that the settlement was founded on a crossroads or was a place known for a standing Christian cross.

-don or downs

As in Downend (Gloucestershire), Faringdon (Berkshire) or Downhill (County Londonderry)

From the Old English *dun* meaning high open land or, in some cases, hill. In Scotland the word is often associated with fortification. Confusingly *den* means valley.

Eccles

As in Eccles (Greater Manchester), Ecclefechan (Dumfries and Galloway) or Exhall, originally Eccleshale (Warwickshire)

A settlement that once held religious significance or surrounded a religious building, from the Latin *ecclesia*, meaning church.

-field

As in Sheffield (Yorkshire), Hatfield (various) or Macclesfield (Cheshire)

The inclusion of the word field isn't what we think of these days as enclosed areas of pasture or crops, but instead comes from the Old English *feld* meaning cleared or open land, former forest that had been felled and turned over to cultivation to feed the ever growing population. With time, communities would have popped up in the midst of this now arable land.

There are similar associations with leigh or ley (such as Leyland in Lancashire or Berkeley in Gloucestershire), coming from the Old English *leah*, meaning woodland clearing.

Ford or forth

As in Fordingbridge (Hampshire), Oxford (Oxfordshire) or Ampleforth (North Yorkshire)

A crossing in a river, shallow enough for people to pass (see page 234 on fording). In the north of England the word ford became *forth* as it was passed down the generations.

Ham

As in Hampton (southwest London), Hamstall Ridware (Staffordshire) or Ham (Kent)

Names including 'ham' usually mean one of two things, either a homestead or estate or, if derived from the Old English *hamm*, a meadow enclosed by a river.

Kil- or keil

As in Kilbarchan (Renfrewshire), Kilbirnie (north Ayrshire) or Kilkeel (County Down)

In Scotland and Ireland, the prefix 'kil' means church, so Kilmacolm near Glasgow means Church of my St Columba. In Wales the prefix 'llys' serves the same purpose.

Pen

As in Pendle (Lancashire), Penzance (Cornwall) or Pen-y-Ghent (North Yorkshire)

From the Old Celtic *penn* meaning end or head, the word changed over time to mean hill. Quite why the Anglo-Saxons often found it necessary to add the Old English *hyll* is unknown, especially when you get to places such as Pendle Hill, which can be translated as the hill-hill hill.

Strat-, -stret or street

As in Chester-le-Street (County Durham) Stratford-upon-Avon (Warwickshire) or Street (Somerset).

This one's quite obvious. Any variation on street comes from the Old English *strœt*, which was a corruption of the Latin *strata*, meaning paved way. It generally means that the place was near a Roman road or, in Stratford's case, was a ford that crossed the road.

-stōw

As in Stow-on-the-Wold (Gloucestershire), Stow Bardolph (Norfolk) or Stowmarket (Suffolk)

An Old English *stōw* was a place where people gathered, a meeting place. Bristol, for example, was once Brycg Stow meaning 'the place of assembly by the bridge'. Many of these assembly places were also linked to places of pilgrimage or worship, so Morwenstow in Cornwall is named after Morwenna, a local female saint.

Spital

As in Spitalfields (London), Spital (Berkshire) or Spital in the Street (Lincolnshire)

This can either denote a hospital or a place that gives hospitality, such as a monastery or religious house, taking its cue from the Middle English word *spitel*.

Stock or stoke

As in Woodstock (Oxford), Basingstoke (Hampshire) or Stoke-by-Nayland (Suffolk)

Most of the hundreds of places that have either stock or stoke in their name, come from the Old English word *stoc*, which means outlying farmstead or settlement. They were 'outlying' as they were secondary places, connected to a more important community such as Stoke Bardolph in Nottinghamshire, which was the outlying farm of the Bardolph family, while Stoke Poges in Buckinghamshire was a hamlet owned by the le Pugeis family.

However, there is a chance that a placename may mean something completely different if it derives from Old English *stocc* or *stoccen*, which relates to tree stumps or logs. Stokenchurch in Buckinghamshire, for instance, is the place of the church made of logs.

Sted or stead

As in Ashsted (Birmingham), Nurstead (Hampshire) or Hampstead (London)

Quite literally a place where people lived, from the Old English *stede*.

Stone or stan

As in Stonehaven (Aberdeenshire), Stonehenge (Wiltshire) or Stanstead Abbotts (Hertfordshire)

A case where the name 'does what it says on the tin'. *Stān*, the Old English word for stone, could indicate a place either where stone was plentiful or quarried, or marked with a standing stone.

Tre- or tref-

As in Trebetherick (Cornwall), Tresco (Isles of Scilly) or Trefaldwyn (Powys)

In Cornwall and some parts of Wales, finding a place bearing the prefix of Tre usually means that location was once a house or farm. Tredrizzick, near Padstow, means 'farm covered by bracken' while Tredegar in Gwent was originally 'the house of Tegyr'.

-wick

As in Wick (Somerset) Lenchwick (Worcestershire) or Smethwick (West Midlands)

From the Old English *wic*, this derivative usually indicates a group of buildings joined together by a common trade or product, usually related to farming. So we get Butterwick in Cumbria, Dorset, County Durham and Lincolnshire among others, meaning a farm where they make butter, or Shapwick in Somerset, which was originally a sheep farm.

Wick can also refer to a place known for the production of salt, such as Nantwich in Cheshire, or a farm that was owned by a larger settlement like Bathwick in Somerset, which would have been a farm linked to the city of Bath. However, if your -wick is on the coast or in Scotland it probably comes from the Old Norse word *vík*, meaning bay or creek.

Wold, weald or wealed

As in the Nottinghamshire Wolds, Stow-on-the-Wold (Gloucestershire) or the Weald of southeast England

A corruption of the Old English *wald* meaning high forest land, an area that was later cleared for agriculture. The Cotswolds are named after the sheep that grazed over these walds, a cot being a place you keep sheep.

-worth, -worthy or -wardine

As in Tamworth (Staffordshire), Bredwardine (Herefordshire) or Haworth (Yorkshire)

From the Old English *worthign* meaning enclosure, a worth was probably originally an enclosed dwelling or home.

The country calendar

The British countryside is alive with traditions and customs all year around. Some are repeated from village to village while others are unique to a specific location. Here are just some of the many celebrations that make up the country calendar – though you can be guaranteed that there are many more happening wherever you live.

6 January – Twelfth Night or Epiphany

Once far more important in our calendar than it now is, Twelfth Night is now only really known as the last day for taking down your Christmas decorations if you are to avoid bad luck. In the past, however, the end of the yuletide festivities was also an opportunity for a big party to mark the coming of Epiphany, a Christian celebration of the visit of the Magi to the Christchild. Today, many rural communities are reintroducing wassailing celebrations on this day when people revel around and make offerings to the oldest tree in the orchard in hopes of good harvest (see page 174).

6 January – The Haxey Hood

Two teams, one from the village of Haxey in Lincolnshire and the other from nearby Westwoodside, attempt to capture the 'hood' – a length of rope wrapped in leather – and steal it away to their local pubs. This mad free-for-all dates back to a 14th-century legend of a lady who lost her hood in the wind and was amused to watch labourers fight to retrieve it for her.

The first Sunday after Twelfth Day (7 January) – Plough Sunday

After the revelry of Twelfth Night, the farm labourers returned to work as the annual cycle of agricultural work began again. On the nearest Sunday, the plough – which was often shared among farms, would be decked with ribbons and dragged into the church to be blessed. Today, many communities still have Plough Sunday services, where they thank God for the farmers and pray for a good year on the land.

Meanwhile, if you go down to Whittlesey in Cambridgeshire on the weekend of Plough Sunday you can be sure of a big surprise. A farmer in a full-size bear costume made of straw is paraded around the village

21

by the 'plough-witches' who ask for money or sustenance. The custom used to occur in nearby Ramsey too, but died out in the 1950s. The origins of the bizarre tradition aren't known, but it's thought that it was to remind the locals about their dependence on the land.

2 February – Candlemas

Another Christian feast day that has slipped from the mainstream, Candlemas was the day when Mary was ritually purified 40 days after the birth of Jesus and presented her son to the Temple. In the countryside it was a significant day as it symbolised a halfway point in winter, between the winter solstice and equinox. It was an important date for farmers to check that they had enough animal feed to get them through the rest of the winter. Candles were, and in some cases still are, placed in every window and around the parish church in honour of Mary.

The first Monday after 3 February – Hurling the Silver Ball

A silver-coated ball is thrown into a large crowd of school children and passed from hand to hand until the clock strikes twelve noon. Whoever is holding the ball at that point wins the game. Hurling used to be a popular sport in Cornwall but now only really exists in the St Ives competition and a similar, if more boisterous, game played twice a year in St Columb. The latter version is played by adults and can get quite manic, so shopkeepers often barricade their windows and doors long before the ball is hurled.

Shrove Tuesday – Pancake Race

It's been years since I took part in a pancake race but in the market place at Olney, Buckinghamshire, it's a strictly women-only affair. Every year they line up wearing aprons, skirts and scarves and wait for the sound of the Pancake Bell, after which they run to the church gate, tossing their pancake all the way. The winner receives a kiss from the verger and treats from local shops. It's been going since 1445 and was once only open to housewives, although today any woman over 18 can take part.

It's not just the women who have all the fun on Shrove Tuesday. In Ashbourne, Derbyshire, and Alnwick, Northumberland, mass games of football are organised, sometimes played with up to 150 people on one team, while in Jedburgh, Roxburghshire, a game of handball is played through the streets.

The more heavenly minded might want to head to St Mary's Church in Wirksworth, Derbyshire, where they hold a traditional church clipping service. The congregation gather outside the church and surround the building, holding hands so that it is entirely encircled. Clipping probably dates back to old pagan ceremonies where people would hold hands around a sacred place to absorb power. However, when the practice was revived in the 19th century it came to symbolise the protection of the community. Only a handful of churches around the country still perform the ceremony on this and various other dates of the year, including Mothering Sunday. Quite often, children perform the act by dancing around the building holding hands.

Easter Monday – Hare Pie Scramble and Bottle Kicking

Bottle Kicking sees the village of Hallaton in Leicestershire taken over by a game to roll three barrels containing beer – the bottles in question – to either of two village boundary streams. The free-for-all is preceded by the sharing of a so-called hare pie (actually made of beef) that has been blessed by the vicar.

Only the foot-and-mouth crisis of 2001 temporarily stopped the centuries-old tradition although in 1790 a local vicar tried to ban the hare-pie festivities claiming they were unholy and pagan. Overnight a stark warning was daubed on the side of his house: 'No pie? No parson!'

Another popular Easter Monday custom requires the men of Gawthorpe in West Yorkshire, and various visitors, to carry a 50kg bag of coal on their back over 1,000 metres to be crowned the World Coal Carrying Champion (although these days both women and children also have their own coal-carrying competitions as well).

The second Monday after Easter – The Tuttimen Hocktide Festival

In days gone by, tenants paid their rent on Hock Day and Michaelmas. Today Hock Day is marked in Hungerford, Berkshire, by two 'Tuttimen', carrying poles decorated with flowers, ribbons and herbs, going from door to door to receive food, money or a kiss from the ladies of the house.

1 May – Mayday

The maypole is one of the most iconic images of village life and first turns up in records around the 14th century but, despite popular opinion, has never seemed to have any real connection to pagan rituals or fertility rites. Even so, the Puritans banned them in the 17th century, just in case. Certainly many people now include it in Beltane celebrations, the fire festival that marked the coming of spring in the pagan religions.

The custom of choosing a local young girl to be crowned as May Queen is again popularly thought to be as old as the hills, but is actually a Victorian invention, devised to recapture a sense of a 'Merrie Olde England' that never really existed.

There are a number of May Day festivals across the country from my particular favourite, the 'Obby' Oss of Padstow, Cornwall – where two men wearing twirling, flowing costumes meant to resemble hobby horses try to trap girls beneath their skirts – to Jack-in-the-Green dances performed by Morris sides who welcome this tall effigy covered in greenery to the village green before heading off to the pub.

Most people have also heard of the Cheese Rolling race at Cooper's Hill, Gloucestershire, which is traditionally held on the spring bank holiday in late May. Thrill-seekers chase a wheel of Double Gloucester cheese down the hill, risking life and limb to catch the dairy product – which can reach speeds of 70mph. The event is said to have been played out every year for two centuries although it was halted in 2010 due to health-and-safety concerns.

The nearest Thursdays to 12 May and 24 October – The Stow Gypsy Horse Fair

These two fairs – originally held on the feast of St Philip (12 May) and the feast of St Edward the Confessor (24 October) – were once sheep fairs associated with the Cotswold town of Stow-on-the-Wold. However, as the wool trade faltered they became horse fairs, attracting huntsmen, farmers and travelling folk. They still do and you can still spot many traditional painting wagons among the more-modern caravans.

Spring bank holiday – Woolsack Day

Similar to the World Coal Carrying Championship in Gawthorpe, the Woolsack Day race in Tetbury, Gloucestershire, sees competitors run with a 27kg sack of wool up and down a steep hill, either as part of a relay or solo. BBC presenter Tom Heap did really well when he took part on behalf of *Countryfile*.

Around 18 June – World Stinging Nettle Eating Championships

It's hardly an age-old custom but one that has become infamous in recent years – especially in the *Countryfile* offices, which has sent two of my colleagues, Ben Fogle and James Wong, to eat as many 60-centimetre lengths of nettles as they could in an hour. (Notice how, unlike Tom, Ben and James, I try to avoid most of these challenges!) The World Stinging Nettle Eating Championships is held at the Bottle Inn in Marshwood, Dorset, and originated when two farmers were arguing about whose land had the longest nettles. One claimed that his nettles reached 5 metres in length and said that if anyone else could produce a longer stem, he'd eat his nettles. Someone did, and the rest is – rather painful – history. For less radical ways of using nettles, turn to pages 169–71.

21 June – Summer solstice

The longest day of the year when the sun is at the highest point. Every year thousands travel to Stonehenge in Wiltshire, to witness the sun rise among the stones.

First week of July – Wenlock Olympian Games

In 1858, a local doctor in Much Wenlock, Shropshire, William Penny Brookes, was worried about the health of many of his patients – they were sitting around and drinking too much – so he organised the first Olympian Games in modern times in the small market town. As well as athletics, the games included cricket, quoits and a three-mile penny-farthing bike race. They are still held every year (not every four) and I once practised on a penny-farthing – but not for long! The reputation of the Much Wenlock Games spread and Dr Brookes helped inspire the setting-up of the international Olympic movement. Sadly he died four months before the first modern Olympiad was held in 1896.

Second Friday in August – The Burryman

No one knows exactly why a man dressed in flannel undergarments and covered from head to toe in wild burdock burrs is guided, arms held aloft, on a nine-mile hike around South Queensferry in West Lothian every summer. Some historians claim he is a symbolic scapegoat who was said to take the town's sins with him as he was plunged into the sea at the end of the day. For others he was a sacrifice to the sea gods or a form of fertility worship. Whatever the origins, all the locals agree that if he didn't make his annual rounds, disaster would hit the town.

First Friday in September – Crying the Neck

In many places in Cornwall, most notably in Penzance, the end of the harvest is celebrated by Crying the Neck. The final part of the wheat crop is collected and a farmer holds a sample of it aloft crying out: 'I 'ave 'm. I 'ave 'm.' The other reapers reply 'What' 'ave 'ee?', to which the farmer answers, 'A neck, a neck.' The neck of wheat is traditionally plaited into some form of corn dolly, which is ploughed back into the soil or fed to the farm's best animal to bring another good harvest. The celebrations are usually concluded with Cornish pasties and cider.

First Monday after 4 September – Abbots Bromley Horn Dance

On Old St Bartholomew's Day, or Wakes Monday, the Staffordshire village of Abbots Bromley and its surrounding areas are treated to a visit by six men carrying a pair of hefty reindeer antlers and a motley crew including a man in drag (playing Maid Marian), a fool, a boy carrying a crossbow, another carrying a triangle, a hobby horse and an accordion player. The antlers, which are believed to be over a thousand years old, are kept in the local church (St Nicholas) for the rest of the year until they are called upon once again. Where they came from is a mystery. There were no reindeer in England a thousand years ago, although some say that Scandinavian settlers brought the antlers here. Did the immigrants also bring the custom with them? Nobody knows for sure although the dance may have its origin in the age-old belief that dressing in the skin of your quarry before a hunt protected you from harm and promised good hunting.

Third Saturday in September – World Gurning Championships

As part of the annual Egremont Crab Fair in Cumbria, locals pop their head through a horse brace known as a braffin and try to pull the ugliest faces possible. The origins of this bizarre ritual may have something to do with the crab apples that give the Fair its name. One bite of those sour fruits can leave you pulling the most peculiar of faces. Much to her embarrassment the lovely Michaela Strachan competed a few years ago and while the *Countryfile* cameras looked on, she was crowned world champion!

5 November – Bonfire Night

While the rest of the country are 'oooing' and 'aaaahing' at the sight of fireworks, the people of Ottery St Mary in Devon watch one another carry barrels soaked with tar around the streets. Just to make things a little more dangerous the barrels are set alight! It's all said to have started with a ritual to frighten away evil spirits but the prospect of carrying a flaming barrel would certainly scare me!

Not that far away, in the village of Shebbear, a one-tonne monolith is turned over to the sound of a discordant peal from the church bells. The reason? The Devil himself is said to be trapped beneath the stone and the villagers don't want to see him escape.

23 December – Tom Bawcock's Eve

A local legend tells of one particularly bad winter in Cornwall where the fishermen of Mousehole were kept from going to sea by atrocious weather. The villagers were facing starvation as food supplies had been exhausted, so, to save them all, Tom Bawcock took his fishing boat and risked life and limb by heading out into the storm. He returned, against all odds, with a boat full of fish and Mousehole was saved. Every year the village is decked out in lights in honour of Tom's bravery. *Countryfile* has joined in the celebrations and I helped to bake Mousehole's unique dish – the Stargazy pie, with the fish heads poking out of the pastry, looking skywards.

24 December – Tolling the Devil's Knell

Every Christmas Eve, the bell ringers of Dewsbury, West Yorkshire, head to All Saint's Church and ring the tenor bell once for every year since Jesus' birth. The ceremony is timed to perfection so the last note is heard at midnight. The custom began in the 15th century and is said to signify the belief that the Devil's fate was sealed the moment Christ was born. Ever since it was revived in 1828 the knell has been tolled, other than on the rare occasions where the bell was being cast or during the Second World War, when all church bells were silenced.

26 December – Boxing Day

Traditionally known as St Stephen's Day, Boxing Day is marked by fox-hunts up and down the country, known as Boxing Day Meets. Of course, in these days of the ban on fox-hunting (see page 177) no actual foxes are pursued. Instead an artificial trail is put down for the hounds but people come from far and wide to see the spectacle.

Ten things you didn't know about thatched roofs

Village scenes full of beautifully thatched cottages adorn many a box of fudge or chocolates, but how much do you actually know about thatching?

1. We've been thatching roofs in Britain for at least 4,000 years, since the Bronze Age.

2. The process was developed as the building materials of the time, which included walls made from wattle and daub with cruck beams, couldn't take much weight. Thatch was the perfect solution.

3. Originally thatchers worked with whatever material they could get their hands on: flax, grass, sallow, sedge or straw. In the south of England, long wheat straw became the norm whereas in the north, heather was the thatch of choice, especially in Scotland.

4. A thatched house was a poor man's house. The rich could afford stone and therefore had houses that could withstand heavier roofs.

5. The industry began to decline when the railway network started to spread across the country in the 19th century. Suddenly, cheap slate could be transported from Wales and tiled roofs began to grow in popularity.

6. Today, most surviving thatched roofs are maintained with water reed, long straw and combed wheat reed.

7. At first the thatch is tied into bundles and laid on to the beams, where it's secured with rods. A secondary level is laid across this and then reinforced with a further ridge layer to provide structural support.

8. All thatched roofs should last at least 15 years. After that it's down to the skills of the thatcher and the materials used. If it is laid well a long-straw thatch will last between 15 and 35 years, while wheat reed will probably need replacing after 40 years. In some cases, thatched roofs made from superior Norfolk reed have lasted up to 55 years before being replaced.

9. Every year around 50 thatched cottages burn to the ground. About 90 per cent of these are the result of chimney fires, prompting annual reminders from the fire service for people to clean their chimneys. In the last couple of years the numbers have been creeping up to 70-odd disastrous fires every year. Experts blame this increase on the increased use of wood-burning stoves being fitted by inexperienced homeowners. Wood-burners run much hotter than the old traditional open fires and some elderly chimneys can't cope with the heat as they only offer about 7 centimetres of protection between the flue and the thatch.

10. Some thatchers are now growing their own thatch from medieval seeds gathered from old thatched roofs. Because most modern wheat isn't needed for thatching it has become weaker and less useful to the thatcher over time, so artisans trying to ensure the craft's survival are starting to turn back the clock.

How to tell the difference between a swallow, swift, house martin and sand martin

I'm lucky because I often get to see the first bursts of spring several times a year. I've filmed blossoms and buds appearing in Cornwall and weeks later watched the same thing happening in northern Scotland. However, when I'm back home the sure sign that spring has arrived is sitting in my garden and watching swallows and house martins perform their amazing aerobatics in the sky above. All over the country villagers will be joining me in turning their eyes to the skies to spot these summer visitors, especially the house martin, which is particularly attached to village life thanks to its habit of nesting in the eves of, well, our houses.

Do you know how to tell the difference between a swallow and a martin, or a swift for that matter? There are a few tricks I've picked up over the years to help me identify them.

> Does it have red cheeks, a white underside and a long forked tail? It's a swallow.

> Does it look entirely black, have a pale throat, narrow wings and looks a bit like a sickle when in flight? Also, is it making a piercing screaming noise when it's high in the sky or flying around buildings at dusk? It's a swift.

> Does it show a white top rump when flying and have a shallow forked tail? Is it nesting in the eaves of houses? It's a house martin.

> Is it reasonably small with brown plumage and a shallow forked tail? It's a sand martin.

swallow

swift

house martin

sand martin

Where our food comes from and what the label means

These days we're all a little more aware of what we're eating. We want to support local, responsible producers, eat more seasonally and reduce the air miles our food has taken to reach us. The last few years have seen animal-welfare groups and celebrity chefs alike campaigning for better conditions for our farm animals, insisting that happy animals produce better meat. While the jury is still out on that one, consumers are left with a confusing array of labels and types of meat that can be utterly bewildering. We are asked to choose between standard or free-range chickens, battery or barn-reared eggs and outdoor- or indoor-reared pork. And that's just scratching the surface. Here's a helpful guide to which meat standard is which.

Chickens

Standard broiler chicken
Around 774 million chickens – 90 per cent of the national flock – are reared according the Red Tractor's Assured Chicken Production guidelines. Standard chickens are raised in barns to a maximum of 19 birds per square metre. To put that in context it means that one chicken lives in a space about three-quarters the size of an A4 piece of paper. They must be kept in conditions appropriate to twilight or better for eight hours a day and most are slaughtered at five weeks old.

Freedom Food chicken
To qualify for the RSPCA's standard of animal welfare no more than 15 indoor-reared chickens must be kept per square metre – the equivalent of a space 15 per cent bigger than an A4 piece of paper – be given better lighting and bales of straw, perches or even footballs to play with. Freedom Food chickens are slaughtered at seven weeks old.

Free-range chicken
Free-range chickens must have access to outdoor conditions for at least half their life, living as natural a life as possible. At present, however, there is no limit to flock size meaning that it is possible for stocking

densities to be as high as standard birds. Free-range chickens are slaughtered at eight weeks old.

Organic chicken

All organic chickens are free range with a recommended flock size of 500 birds, although the standard does allow up to 1000 birds if further conditions are met. Organic chickens must spend two-thirds of their life outdoors and will be given feed containing no more than 10 per cent non-organic material. Organic chickens are slaughtered at 10 weeks.

Eggs

Caged or battery hens

These birds are kept in small wire cages with a minimum of 550 square centimetres per bird. More than 50 per cent of all eggs bought in Britain are from caged birds. Cages of these type are to be banned in Europe in 2012 and replaced with so-called enriched cages. This will allow each hen the slightly improved conditions of 750 square centimetres and a perching and scratching area.

Barn hens

These hens stay inside but at stocking levels of no more than nine birds per square metre. They have access to nests and perches. Four per cent of eggs sold in Britain are barn-hen eggs.

Free-range hens

To be classed as free range, the hens must have continuous daytime access to open-air runs that are mainly covered with vegetation or pasture. In the EU, every hen must be allowed at least 4 square metres of space. Forty per cent of all eggs bought in the UK are free-range.

Organic hens

To be labelled organic, the hens must be free-range, fed on organic food and raised on organic land. They have twice as much indoor space as standard free-range hens.

All egg-producing hens, except organic, can have their beaks trimmed to prevent them pecking each other. A ban on all UK beak trimming was due to take place in 2011, but this has been postponed.

Pigs

There is a whole host of labels and classifications relating to pig production. At present there is no legal requirement to display this information.

Indoor bred

Pigs that are reared indoors from the moment they're born to the moment they're slaughtered. While giving birth, sows can be confined in farrowing crates. This accounts for around 60 per cent of British pigs.

Outdoor bred

Pigs that are born outside to non-confined sows and then brought inside for fattening after around 4–6 weeks. Some 27 per cent of pigs in the UK are outdoor bred.

Outdoor reared

Ten per cent of British pigs are outdoor reared, meaning they live out in the elements for the majority of their lives, and are brought in eight weeks before slaughter to fatten up.

Free range

Free-range pigs are born, reared and fattened outside, with some shelter for sleeping. Three per cent of British pigs are free-range.

Red Tractor and Quality Standard pork marks

The bare minimum in UK pig-welfare standards. Farrowing crates – metal cages that prevent the sows crushing their piglets by confining them in a narrow space – are allowed as is tail docking to stop piglets biting each other. Pigs must be given materials such as straw to root around in. Ninety-two per cent of all British-produced pork is covered by these schemes.

Freedom Food

Pigs raised to the RSPCA welfare standards may be reared indoors or outdoors. The Freedom Food label guarantees that they have solid bedding and that they haven't been subjected to farrowing crates or castration.

Organic

To qualify for Soil Association certification, pigs must be reared outside and be allowed to root. Neither tail docking nor castration is allowed. The pigs must also be fed a diet free from genetically modified (GM) food.

Cows and sheep

Neither beef nor lamb is graded to distinguish between free range or indoor reared as most British cattle and lambs are reared outside with access to pasture. Some supermarkets do mark their meat as being from livestock that is 'grass-fed' or given 'access to pasture' just to make sure. The Soil Association's organic status also insists on access to outdoor pasture.

What's the difference between lamb and mutton?

In the past lambs born in spring and slaughtered after Christmas were classed as mutton but these days it's a question of age. Lamb is generally meat from sheep reared for between five months to one year and mutton is meat from sheep that are over two years old. If you've looking for meat reared between one and two years you need to ask for hogget, although that's difficult to find.

In days past, mutton was one of Britain's most popular meats. In 1861, that Victorian domestic goddess, Mrs Beeton, declared that: 'Mutton is, undoubtedly, the meat generally used in families. And, both by connoisseurs and medical men, it stands first in favour, whether its fine flavour, digestible qualifications, or general wholesomeness be considered.' After the Second World War, however, mutton fell from favour. When rationing was lifted people wanted to explore other meaty alternatives – most of which needed shorter cooking time. The fall in the value of wool also hastened its disappearance from our tables as it became cheaper for farmers to slaughter lambs rather than keep them for unprofitable wool production. In recent years, various celebrity chefs and even the Prince of Wales have thrown their weight behind mutton. Today only around 200 British farms, butchers, restaurants and abattoirs serve or sell mutton although the number is gradually increasing year on year.

Protected food names

Every foodie knows that Parma ham hails from Italy and Champagne is produced and bottled in France. There's a good reason for this. PDOs (or Protected Designation of Origin) came into force thanks to European Union legislation back in 1993. If your produce is lucky enough to be granted PDO status, no one else in Europe can imitate it unless their product is produced, processed and prepared in the geographical area in question. Between them France and Italy have 300 local delicacies protected in this way.

Of course, some people think this is another case of the European parliament interfering in 'our' food. In 2005, Judy Bell of Shepherds Purse cheeses faced an expensive rebranding exercise when the European Court of Justice ruled that the name feta cheese could only be used by producers in certain areas of Greece. Shepherds Purse had been producing Yorkshire feta for years. After a prolonged battle with the European Union their Greek-style cheese is now known as Fine Fettle Yorkshire cheese.

So is this just a case of needless bureaucracy and red tape? Not according to the British producers striving to achieve PDO or its close relation PGI (Protected Geographical Indication, which certifies that the product must be produced or processed or prepared in the designated area). Here are just a few of the current protected food names in Britain.

Yorkshire Forced Rhubarb

Designated as a PDO in 2010

Forced rhubarb is grown indoors in massive sheds and is traditionally harvested by candlelight. The process was discovered by accident when a London gardener knocked a pile of soil over his rhubarb and discovered that the stems shot upwards at a quicker rate searching for the light. Now only indoor rhubarb growers in the famed West Yorkshire Triangle of Leeds, Bradford and Wakefield can use the name Yorkshire Forced Rhubarb.

Melton Mowbray Pork Pie

Designated as a PGI in 2009

A genuine Melton Mowbray pork pie must be produced in the vicinity of the Leicestershire town and the meat needs to be grey like roast pork not pink like cured pork. As its designation is only PGI, however, the meat doesn't need to be local, as there aren't enough pig farms around Melton Mowbray.

Arbroath Smokie

Designated as a PGI in 2004

If you love your smoked haddock, only fish smoked over hardwood fires within a 5-mile radius of Arbroath on the east coast of Scotland can be called an Arbroath Smokie. Robert Spink, owner of one of the 12 remaining smokeries in the town, applied for the designation after he noticed a product smoked on electric grills in a major supermarket using the name.

Cornish Clotted Cream

Designated as a PDO in 1998

Cornish Clotted Cream, produced in Britain's most southwesterly county using milk from Jersey, Guernsey and Friesian cattle was the 500th designated product in Europe to be given the PDO marque.

Blue Stilton cheese

Designated as a PDO in 1996

Blue Stilton can only be made in the counties of Derbyshire, Leicestershire and Nottinghamshire. Only six dairies are currently licensed to make the cheese. Originally Stilton was produced with raw milk, but the PDO stipulated that Stilton can only be made with pasteurised milk. This meant that cheesemaker Joe Schneider discovered that his Stilton made the original way with unpasteurised milk couldn't be called Stilton even though his dairy operates in Nottinghamshire. Joe's solution? His cheese is called Stichelton, after the archaic name of the town where Stilton was first churned.

Jersey Royal potato
Designated as a PDO in 1996

First cultivated by a farmer named Hugh de la Haye in the Bellozanne Valley, this waxy tuber was originally known as the Jersey Royal Fluke. It can now only be grown on the island, where it accounts for 70 per cent of Jersey's agriculture. At present it's the only fresh product to be protected in the UK.

West Country Farmhouse Cheddar cheese
Designated as a PDO in 1996

It was too late for Cheddar cheese when the PDO designation was created: 'Cheddar' was already being produced in too many countries for a PDO to be granted. This rather long-winded name is the compromise. West Country Farmhouse Cheddar cheese can only be made using milk from cows reared and milked in Somerset, Dorset, Devon or Cornwall, to the traditional recipe and aged on the farm for at least nine months, maintaining the link to the farmer.

Five products pending protection:

➤ Craster kipper

➤ Cornish pasty

➤ Traditional Cumberland sausage

➤ Jersey butter

➤ Cornish sardine

The biggest problems facing rural communities

For *Countryfile*'s twentieth anniversary we carried out a poll to try to find out what people thought the greatest single threat to the future of the countryside over the next twenty years. To make it more balanced we interviewed people from both urban and rural areas. Here are the results:

Issue	Total Percentage	Percentage of Urban People	Percentage of Rural People
1 Lack of affordable housing	26	26	25
2 The effects of climate change	20	20	16
3 The need for renewable energy	14	14	14
4 The cost of producing food	13	13	16
5 Over-development in the countryside	10	9	12
6 Loss of rural services	6	5	7
7 Threat to wildlife and habitat	4	3	5
8 Animal welfare	2	2	1
9 State of the sea	2	2	1
10 Animal disease	1	1	1

Anyone who understands country life knows that the number-one threat – lack of affordable housing – is obvious. It brings with it so many problems, everywhere you go. As I travel up and down the country I hear the same story: villages and towns where house after house has been sold to city folk wanting a weekend country retreat or to newcomers intending to commute. The Commission for Rural Communities (CRC) estimates that 800,000 people have moved to rural areas from towns and cities in the last decade. Old country folk complain that for the first time in their lives they no longer know their neighbours, who leave for work as the sun is rising and arrive home after it has set. The phrase dormitory town is used time and time again to describe this modern phenomenon.

The loss of community spirit is sadly only one result of living in a dormitory town or village. As people search for their perfect country home in idyllic surroundings, the price of housing is pushed artificially high to the point that the locals can't compete.

The number of young people moving to towns and cities because of lack of jobs or, if they are working, the lack of rural housing within their income range is probably unprecedented since the Industrial Revolution. According to the CRC the exodus has now reached around 200,000 young people leaving the countryside every single year.

Community services in peril

The problems soon snowball. The lack of local, young families leads to village schools becoming undersubscribed and either closing or combining, resulting in children having to travel long distances to receive their education. Shops, pubs and post offices are likewise underused. Once they were at the very hub of rural Britain, now they are a threatened species; you can search for miles and not find one. With fewer local people to support them, and commuters stopping off at supermarkets on the way home, many local services are closing. Post offices have been particularly hit. In the last ten years, one in three rural post offices have pulled down the blinds on their counters for ever. At the time I'm writing this, figures have just been released that show that, in 2009, the rate of closure had reached two for every day of the year. Other figures show that 54 country pubs and 33 village shops go out of business every month.

Rural businesses may also face another problem in our increasingly digital world. While 60 per cent of our urban areas can receive high-speed cable-linked broadband, only 1.5 per cent of villages and hamlets can do the same, a crippling state of affairs for many small businesses or people wanting to work from home.

One particular group of country folk is hardest hit because rural services are disappearing – pensioners. Often retired people don't have cars and bus services are limited, so they rely increasingly on relatives and good neighbours to help with their shopping and other needs. The problem is going to get worse because it's reckoned that in ten years time one in every four villagers will be over 65 – and many of the younger people who before would have kept an eye on them will have left for the suburbs.

And yet the rural population boom doesn't show signs of slowing down. By 2028, the Office for National Statistics is expecting to see the urban population increase by 9 per cent; in rural areas it is set to rise by 16 per cent as successful urban dwellers look to the countryside for a better quality of life. The National Housing Federation claims that in the past five years it has seen the number of local people on waiting lists for affordable rural homes rise by 47 per cent from 507,757 to 750,000.

There are various schemes across Great Britain to build affordable housing in the countryside, either to buy or rent. There are also properties being built that offer split ownership between a tenant and the local housing authority. Over time, the tenant buys a share of the property, to give them that all-important foot on the property ladder. Yet, in many cases such well-intentioned schemes face opposition from locals who don't want any new builds affecting the prices of their own properties.

Back from the brink

I consider myself lucky that, where I live in Oxfordshire, we still have a shop, a junior school, a bus service, a post office (two half days a week) and three pubs. But, I realise we are among the very fortunate. Even so, as I continue on my travels around the countryside I am told of the inspiring stories of communities who are bravely fighting the tide.

Some time ago I was in the lovely village of Cerne Abbas in Dorset and was told what happened when the only local shop was about to close. A villager stood up during a church service and urged everyone to lend the shopkeeper enough money to keep the business going, and within a couple of days £12,000 had been raised. The shop was restocked, the locals pledged to use it (which clearly they had not been doing) and within a short time the loans had been repaid. Now, the shop is thriving.

There are other tales with a happy ending: in one village, Gunnerside in Swaledale, North Yorkshire, the King's Head pub was in desperate need of repair and on the verge of closure so locals rallied round to clean and tidy the place, and get it back in business. Elsewhere pubs have reopened with split personalities to drum up more trade – lounge bars are also shops and sometimes even post offices. And in Suffolk a post office came back to life thanks to a local benefactor who left £500,000 in his will to the village church. The church was able to purchase the post office and reopened it two years after it had closed.

The reality is that country people now have to fight to keep the things that once were taken for granted. Another 10,000 affordable houses in rural areas over the next ten years would certainly help. And if we are lucky enough still to have our shop, pub, post office or bus service, we should make use of it – then we can't blame ourselves if it goes.

CHAPTER TWO

Fields and Farmland

How big is an acre?

Few words are more synonymous with the British countryside than 'acre'. For centuries this simple word has defined how our landscape is measured. Many of us first heard it as children, thanks to A. A. Milne and the adventures of Christopher Robin and Winnie the Pooh in the Hundred Acre Wood, which still exists in the Ashdown Forest in East Sussex. Like many thousands of adults and children, I've walked through it and thrown sticks from the replica of the Bridge at Pooh Corner!

The acre is woven into our rural history but how did it come about and how can anyone who doesn't actually own one envisage its size? The first record of it was as an early English word 'aecer', which meant an open field of no particular measurement – not much use if you want to work out how much land you had.

Later an acre became the area that one man and his ox could plough in one day. That was rather vague and varied from region to region depending on the soil type – light, sandy soil would have taken less time to work than heavy clay for example. Edward the First (1239–1307) took time off from hammering the Scots to try to standardise it, coming up with a measurement of 40 rods long by 3 rods wide (a rod is about 5^1/$_2$ yards).

But there were still variations across the country and the measurement finally became fixed as an easily remembered figure:

1 acre = 1 furlong (660 feet) x 1 chain (66 feet)
or 4840 square yards

If you're still struggling, here's how to impress if the subject crops up in conversation or a pub quiz. An acre is roughly two-thirds the size of a football pitch, although pitches can differ. My favourite is that an acre is the amount of space needed to park 200 cars – but, there again, it just depends how good you are at parking!

Of course, everything changed when metrication came along and an acre suddenly became 0.4047 of a hectare.

$$1 \text{ hectare} = 2.47 \text{ acres}$$

But the 'old currency' is so strong that many country folk still talk and think in acres. To Christopher Robin and all of us, the Forty Point Four Seven Hectare Wood just isn't the same.

Hedges and borders

There isn't much natural about the current British countryside. Although many people think our green and pleasant land is as it has always been, once it was either covered by dense forest or submerged under water, making travel inland difficult other than via the river systems. Man changed all that. Around five thousand years ago our Neolithic ancestors began to clear the forest by burning to cultivate the soil, and herding animals whose grazing prevented the trees from recolonising. Over centuries of farming, the landscape – the lowlands in particular – was altered beyond all recognition and is now almost entirely artificial.

In the process we created one of the country's most distinctive features – the humble hedgerow. It's been called our biggest, greatest nature reserve and I like to think of it as the stitching in the patchwork quilt that is lowland Britain.

Today there are approximately 506,000 miles of hedgerow – that's nearly 20 times the circumference of the earth. Impressive as that figure sounds, it's not half as much as there used to be, a decline that conservationists are urgently trying to halt. But before we can find out why, we need to know how the hedgerow came into being.

Why hedges were planted

There are four main reasons why hedgerows were planted:

1. To mark ownership boundaries. The majority of our hedges today were planted between 1720 and 1840 when the open fields of old were enclosed to create farms. Some, however, are even older than this and are actually the edges of ancient woodland left behind when the trees were felled. It's estimated that some hedges in Devon and Cornwall are more than 800 years old. The very fact we call them hedges may indicate they date back even further than that. It's likely that the word comes from the Anglo-Saxon *haeg* or *gehaeg*, meaning enclosure. If that's the case it would mean that we started planting hedges around a millennia ago.

2. To keep livestock in or out of a field.

3. To provide shelter from the elements for crops, animals and farm workers alike.

4. To provide a sustainable source of firewood.

Why they were dug up again

Quite simply, farming outgrew the small enclosures system. After the Second World War, the need to produce more food meant that fields had to be enlarged. The latter half of the 20th century also brought with it larger machinery that needed more room to manoeuvre. Increasing mechanisation meant that fewer people were employed on farms and as maintaining miles of hedgerows was both time-consuming and labour-intensive, they became even more surplus to requirements. In 50 years we lost over 50 per cent of our hedgerows. You can't blame farmers though – they were being offered tempting government grants to grub up hedgerows.

Grubbing up hedges wasn't just to make way for industrial-scale agriculture. Between 1925 and 1939, a thousand miles of hedges were removed every year for urban development and since 1945 a further 700 miles a year have been taken out. Motorways, reservoirs and military installations meant more hedges had to go. While 120,000 miles of hedgerow were lost to farming between 1945 and 1970, non-agricultural projects caused a further 20,000 miles to disappear. Thankfully today, the trend is gradually being reversed and, ironically, farmers are now encouraged to plant new hedges as part of agri-environmental schemes that bring in welcome grants. Work is also being done to investigate how wood trimmed from our hedgerow system can be used as a biofuel to help combat climate change, the wood being used in either woodburning stoves or chipped for biomass boilers. The hedge, it appears, is here to stay.

Birds

Our feathered friends benefit most from hedgerows, which make a good substitute for disappearing woodland and prove to be a bountiful source of food. As well as producing berries and seeds, shrubs are a veritable larder of tasty insects. Hedge shrubs come into flower earlier than forest trees such as beech, chestnut and oak; so the early bird can feast on bumper supplies of insects in spring. Then, as the seasons progress, hedgerow trees start to lay on a feast. A single oak tree can support 284 species of insects, and the humble hawthorn can be home to 149.

▶ Where there are insects there are also mammals, which means that hedgerows make rich hunting grounds for owls and kestrels while sparrowhawks will be keeping an eye out for smaller birds.

▶ Hedgerows are invaluable for rare and common birds alike, from yellowhammers (*Emberiza citrinella*), whitethroats (*Sylvia communis*), bullfinches (*Pyrrhula pyrrhula*), dunnocks (*Prunella modularis*), robins (*Erithacus rubecula*) and chaffinches (*Fringilla coelebs*).

▶ Untrimmed hedges and hedgerow trees act as songposts for birds such as blackbirds (*Turdus merula*) and song thrushes (*T. philomelos*) who use the perches to advertise their presence and establish their territory in the breeding season.

▶ Studies have shown that birds prefer untrimmed hedgerows; you find twice as many birds on a hedge that's 4 metres high than one that is just 2 metres high. It's common sense really. Birds nesting in taller trees and shrubs will be less vulnerable to ground predators and unkempt shrubs will contain more berries.

Five reasons why our hedgerows are so important

They are living history

Some of the oldest hedges were planted to separate our historic counties or to mark parish boundaries. They can contain outstanding veteran trees kept alive by careful hedge maintenance over the years. In fact, that maintenance itself is part of our social history, a centuries-old craft passed down from generation to generation. Every region of the country has its own particular way of laying hedges, which adds to the area's distinctiveness. See page 53 for more on regional hedge styles.

They provide food for free

For many it's just a childhood memory, but is there anything more pleasurable than berry picking from hedgerows on a late summer's day? Of course, while providing us with miles of berries for jams, hedgerows also provide valuable food, for many birds (see pages 70 and 164).

They protect the land and crops

Hedges act as valuable windbreaks for crops and also help reduce erosion on vulnerable soils. If sited strategically they can also prevent flooding and reduce pollution, capturing water that may contain chemical waste from pesticide and fertiliser, filtering it so it doesn't end up in the water supply.

They shelter game birds

Gamekeepers find hedgerows particularly beneficial as they provide sheltered corridors for pheasants and partridges to move around the farm. Partridges in particular rely on hedgerows. Partridges like to nest in hedgerow verges, but, being jumpy birds, they don't like to be in the line of sight of neighbouring pairs. The more hedgerows a farmer has to provide privacy for breeding pairs, the most nest territories can be established on the land, and the bigger the farmer's stock will be.

They are one of Britain's most significant wildlife habitats

It's estimated that our hedgerows provide homes for 1,500 different types of insect, 600 species of plant, 65 different types of mammal and 30 species of bird.

Hedges do have to be managed, however, and conservation groups recommend that farmers only trim their hedges every three to four years, allowing the trees to increase in height by 10cm every time the hedge trimmed. Where there are specific reasons for trimming hedges annually, farmers are encouraged to trim one side only, leaving the other bushier to provide the all-important cover and food.

Mammals

> As you'd expect, the hedgehog (*Erinaceus europaeus*) nests and hibernates in hedges around farmland, foraging for worms and invertebrates around the roots. They often share their hedgerow home with other mammals such as bank voles (*Myodes glareolus*), badgers (*Meles meles*), stoats (*Mustela erminea*) and the UK's smallest mammal, the pygmy shrew (*Sorex minutus*).

> The hazel dormouse (*Muscardinus avellanarius*) got its common name from the Victorians who found the little mammal hibernating and brought them home as pets for their children. They would have made pretty bad nursery companions though: they sleep all day and hibernate from October to April. When they're finally awake, they much prefer climbing trees to being cooped up in a cage and are very susceptible to extreme weather conditions.

As the timid dormouse doesn't like moving across open land, hedgerows form an important network of routes that allows the population to move around the countryside to breed. Even the smallest gap in a hedgerow can cause a dormouse to turn back and can lead to isolated, therefore, unsustainable families.

> Bats use hedgerows as aids to navigation. These flying mammals use tall (ideally 3 metres high) and wide hedges as flight paths, nipping back and forth between their roosts and hunting areas. Taller trees act as signposts in the dark, offering familiar landmarks to help the bat find its way home. If the wind picks up too much when they're on the wing, the bat can also nip into the hedge for a spot of shelter, and find a tasty insect snack while it waits.

Insects

▶ Bumblebees love hedgerows. Many species like to nest in bushy vegetation while others favour holes and burrows that have been abandoned by small mammals. Hedgerows can provide both environments. It is thought that bumblebees, like bats, also use hedgerows as natural motorways, complete with foraging service centres on route for a spot of mid-flight sustenance. Farmers wanting to give the bumblebees a helping hand on their land try not to trim hedges more than once every two or three years and, when they do, avoid cutting them back between March and September when the bees are making their nests. There's a sound financial reason for all this. Bumblebees are one of our most prolific pollinators and are estimated to be worth £200 million to the British economy owing to their helpful habit of pollinating our crops.

▶ More than 20 of Britain's lowland butterfly species breed in hedgerows, including the brimstone (*Gonepteryx rhamni*), whose caterpillars flourish in hedgerows containing buckthorn, or the holly blue (*Celastrina argiolus*), which, as you'd expect from the name, heads straight for holly or ivy. Hedges are vital to some of our most endangered butterflies, such as the once-widespread brown hairstreak (*Thecla betulae*), which lays its eggs on blackthorn, whereas the pearl-bordered fritillary (*Boloria euphrosyne*) uses hedgerows as important source of nectar. Like the blackbird, some butterflies use hedges as a way of marking their territory, alighting on taller trees to let visiting butterflies know that they've flown on to someone else's patch.

▶ To help butterfly conservation, responsible farmers try to avoid cutting back hedges immediately after harvest so that the flowers remain to support overwintering butterflies.

▶ While a spider scuttling through a house may send some running from the room, even the most devout arachnophobe would have to admit that there is something quite beautiful about seeing the early morning dew caught, jewel-like, in the webs of hedgerow spiders. Our most common hedgerow spider is the diadem or cross spider

(*Araneus diadematus*) with a series of white dots making up a cross on its yellow or grey abdomen, while the money spider (*Linyphia triangularis*) uses hedgerows as a take-off point for a spot of ballooning. They spin a line of thread that rises on currents of hot air allowing them to travel up to 100 miles on the wind.

Reptiles and amphibians

> You're probably used to seeing them in ponds, but the great crested newt (*Triturus cristatus*) makes use of ditches beneath some hedgerows to move one territory to another.

> Toads spend half the year out of water, and the damp, rotting piles of leaf litter found at the bottom of hedges make an ideal place for them to hibernate over winter. The constant supply of slugs and snails helps too.

> Britain's only venomous snake, the adder (*Vipera berus*), finds shelter in hedgerows, as does our largest reptile, the grass snake (*Natrix natrix*), which feeds on the toads it finds there as well as the odd mouse or small bird. The highly secretive slow-worm (*Anguis fragilis*) can also sometimes be found burrowing deep into the ground beneath hedges to hibernate. This legless lizard is often mistaken for a snake.

Typical hedgerow shrubs and trees

Ash (*Fraxinus excelsior*)

Blackthorn (*Prunus spinosa*)

Buckthorn (*Rhamnus catharticus*)

Crab apple (*Malus sylvestris*)

Dog rose (*Rosa canina*)

Dogwood (*Cornus sanguinea*)

Elder (*Sambucus nigra*)

Gooseberry (*Ribes uva-crispa*)

Hawthorn (*Crataegus monogyna*)

Hazel (*Corylus avellana*)

Holly (*Ilex aquifolium*)

Field maple (*Acer campestre*)

English oak (*Quercus robur*)

Privet (*Ligustrum vulgare*)

Rowan (*Sorbus aucuparia*)

Silver birch (*Betula pendula*)

Spindle (*Euonymus europaeus*)

Grey willow (*Salix cinerea*)

Did you know . . .?

If you see a row of tall, gappy trees, you're probably looking at an ancient, unmanaged hedge. Over time, if they're not cut back, hedgerows will grow out of control, the tree and shrubs competing for space. The battle will always be won by the trees that will grow so tall they block out the light for the smaller shrubs. The shrubs die out and you're left with the victorious trees standing proud.

How to work out the age of a hedge

There's a country method for estimating the age of a hedge called Hooper's rule.

1. Take a 30-metre stretch of hedgerow.

2. Count how many species of shrubs are in the hedge.

3. Multiply the number of species by 100 and that figure gives you the approximate age of the hedge.

So how does that work? Well, it's thought that a new species of shrub establishes itself every 100 years, so if your section of hedgerow contains two different species it's around 200 years old. In other words, the more species found within one stretch of hedge, the older it is. If you're ever lucky enough to find a hedge containing over ten species, you may be looking at one of the oldest in the country – around 1,000 years old.

There is a slight snag. If your hedge has been planted in the last 20 years, chances are it was planted with a number of different species of shrub so Hooper's rule only applies to hedges dating back before 1990 or thereabouts.

How a hedge is layed

Laying a hedge isn't just a case of planting a line of trees and shrubs and hoping for the best. Hedge-laying is an ancient and skilled craft and the style of hedgerow varies depending on where you are in the country. There are around 30 different regional styles in the UK, the most common one being the standard or Midland bullock. This thick and sturdy hedge-laying style was developed to withstand the weight of heavy livestock leaning against it. The side of the hedge facing the livestock in the field is known as the 'far side' while the opposite or 'near side' is often banked with a slight ditch.

Step 1

When the hedgerow trees or shrubs have reach around 3.5 metres in height, the lower branches on the near side are removed. Once this is done, the trunk is cut through near to the ground at a 45-degree angle. The hedge-layer is careful to leave enough of the trunk uncut so that the sap can flow and the tree doesn't die. This process is known as pleaching.

Step 2

The cut or pleached trunk is then bent and interwoven between a row of vertical 1.5-metre-tall hazel or ash stakes driven into the ground a metre apart. These hold everything in place and give some stability.

Step 3

Long rods of hazel, willow or ash are tightly woven, rope-like, along the top of the hedge between the stakes, again to help stabilise the structure and prevent the bent trees from springing back up. Over time these binding rods rot away, but by then the new growth will mean that the pleached trunks will remain where they are.

Step 4

After unwanted branches have been removed, the hedge is left to grow, with new shoots springing up from the cuts in the trunks. Over time the growing hedge will be trimmed to form an A-shape, thicker at the base and thinner at the top.

Other significant styles

The Devon hedge

This tightly packed hedge is layed on top of a raised bank of earth. The bank usually forms the barrier against livestock while a double row of bushy pleached hedges on top keeps lambs secure. Devon is said to have more hedges than any other county, mainly due to its large size: around 20 per cent of the species-rich hedges left in Great Britain. Many a motorist visiting these parts has got a nasty shock when, steering into the side of a hedge to avoid an oncoming vehicle, they discover they've hit a solid bank.

The Somerset hedge

Two rows of stakes, one on either side of the hedge, hold the pleached trunks in place. This particular style of hedging makes a good barrier for sheep.

The Yorkshire hedge

Instead of topping a hedge with woven rods, a straight, softwood rail is nailed to the top of the stakes, creating a type of fence. This style of hedge is usually used in fields that rotate between arable use and sheep farming. It requires a couple of years free of livestock to establish itself, but once it has grown it can easily withstand sheep.

Combating soil erosion

It's almost too obvious to say but soil is one of the main building blocks of life. Without fertile soil, nothing can grow and if nothing can grow, food sources become scarce. We take it for granted. After all, soil has always been there, and it always will remain, right? Unfortunately, many people doubt that simple belief because of an unprecedented rise in soil erosion.

Soil erosion is a natural process that takes place all around the world. Soil is moved from location to location by wind or water. However, it isn't a process that should happen too fast and when it does, largely helped along by inappropriate use of the land, it can have disastrous effects. If the fertile topsoil, or humus, vanishes quicker than it can be replenished the result is land that has no agricultural value and people soon start talking of food shortages and soaring prices.

That's a conversation that's happening among scientists right now. It's estimated that worldwide 75 billion tonnes of soil are lost every year through erosion and around 80 per cent of the planet's farmland is now either moderately or severely eroded. Some areas of the world are worse than others. In China soil is being lost 57 times faster than natural processes can replace it, while in Europe the figure stands at 17 times faster. It's not just our crops that are in danger. Soil acts as a valuable carbon sink, so the more that is lost, the more greenhouse gases are released. At present Britain's soil is thought to contain more carbon than all of Europe's forests put together. The trouble then is that as the planet gets warmer, more topsoil is stripped away, either by desiccation or flooding, and we become locked into a vicious circle. It's scary stuff. Some scientists are even predicting that unless something drastic is done to stop the loss, European farming soils, Britain's included, could vanish within six decades.

There are other effects. Sediment from soil erosion can find its way into water-storage reservoirs, limiting their effectiveness and increasing the risk of floods. Water courses can also be affected. The biodiversity of our rivers suffers as eggs laid by fish in riverbeds are smothered by sediment, starving them of oxygen, while the general quality of the water risks being reduced, requiring more treatment before it is fit for consumption. On land, over time, sediment causes roads and footpaths to become slippery, making travel hazardous, and if drains fill with eroded soil flash floods can result.

It's all the stuff of nightmares, but when you see the facts in black and white, it's easy to see why so many governments around the world are beginning to take the risks seriously and why farmers are being asked to take steps to prevent soil erosion. This can be as simple as contour tillage, the practice of ploughing across gradients rather than up and down the slope (although this isn't always possible) or, once a crop is harvested, leaving the stalks to bind the soil. Such measures are not without problems of their own: those stalks can also provide overwintering sites for pests. Some plants, such as maize, are also particularly known for causing erosion. The maize crop, used widely in animal feed, is harvested late in the season using heavy machinery that compacts the ground, meaning that water struggles to percolate through the soil. The result is more surface run-off taking with it vital nutrients and topsoil. To make matters worse, a lot of maize is grown on sloping land, which compounds the problem. Farmers are therefore being encouraged to grow varieties that can be harvested earlier in the year and to avoid obvious erosion hotspots when planting the crop.

Steps such as these make good financial as well as environmental sense for our farmers. Figures from the Department for Environment, Food and Rural Affairs (DEFRA) suggest that, the wider problems notwithstanding, soil erosion is costing the agricultural industry £9 million every year through lost production.

What can be done?

As with all environmental concerns on this scale, it's sometimes difficult to see what individuals can do about it, but there are a few steps you can take in your local area to help fight soil erosion, either in the countryside or your own garden.

1. Join an environmental or conservation group and help plant ground cover, trees and shrubs, the roots of which will help bind the soil, making it less likely to be washed or blown away.

2. Plant hedges, windbreaks or build dry stone walls (see pages 122–4). Trees, shrubs and walls reduce the strength of the wind, preventing it whipping over open land and taking soil with it.

3. When walking make sure that, wherever possible, you try to stick to the paths to help prevent their edges erode away.

4. In your gardens, cover your soil with mulch. This keeps it damp and therefore more difficult for wind or water to strip away.

5. Use edging, such as stones or bricks. These cut down run-off water, which can carry topsoil away with it.

Did you know . . . ?

One of the most striking examples of the effectiveness of a windbreak is provided by the gardens of Tresco in the Isles of Scilly. When merchant banker Augustus Smith was appointed as Lord Proprietor of the Islands in 1834 he found Tresco to be an unmanageable wilderness. He set about planting a windbreak of Monterey pines to protect the landscape from the Atlantic winds and today Tresco is home to beautiful, incredibly fertile, sub-tropical gardens.

Types of farming

Roughly 70 per cent of the UK is used for agriculture. We are therefore reliant to a large degree on the farming community for the way our countryside looks and how it is used. It's worth examining how different types of farming make different demands on the land.

1. Conventional farming

Conventional farming operations rely on artificial chemicals to act as fertilisers. While the majority of mixed farms use manure from their animals' sheds to provide their fields with a first hit of nitrogen, phosphates and potash to help crops, even they will fall back on chemicals to help nourish the soil throughout the agricultural year. Additionally, they will spray pesticides, herbicides and fungicides to keep the crops healthy and free from pests and weeds.

Around 350 different pesticides are currently permitted in Britain and farmers use an estimated 4.5 billion litres of the stuff. Not that pesticides are simply sprayed willy-nilly. Chemicals of all types are expensive and hit the farmer's bottom line, cutting into the profit margin. Some environmentalists are concerned that there may be long-term effects of pesticide residues in our food and water supply, but many conventional farmers argue that chemicals are necessary if they are to grow enough food to meet the demand from the public and compete in a fierce global market.

One of the most controversial aspects of conventional farming is the intensive system, growing as many crops or rearing as much livestock as possible per unit of land. Throughout this book you will come across arguments from environmentalists that modern methods are having a negative impact on our wildlife, animal-welfare standards and the environment. However, for many people intensive farming is the only way to feed the planet's ever increasing population. The world population is expected to grow from 6 billion today to 8.5 billion by 2060. That's an awful lot of extra mouths to feed.

The last ten years have also seen an overwhelming demand for cheap, affordable food and lots of it. Furthermore, we are now looking to our farmers to help combat climate change and to produce biofuels, leaving less space for food production.

Since the 1960s, intensively managed farming and improved yields together have allowed a 75 per cent increase in food production worldwide, although some claim that this level cannot be sustained over long periods of time.

2. Genetically modified (GM) farming

As part of that bid to increase food production GM farming looks to modify plants (and potentially animals) genetically to produce crops that will grow faster, be stronger and be able to withstand the effects of global warming, survive in harsher conditions, or be immune to the effects of specific diseases.

The 1990s and early 2000s saw huge campaigns against the introduction of GM farming in Britain with some elements of the media labelling it 'Frankenstein food', which pro-GM scientists say was mere scaremongering. Those fighting against GM worry that such foods may damage the health of both humans and animals. Other concerns are that GM crops may be harmful to beneficial insects or that they might contaminate nearby non-GM crops. Organic farmers are particularly concerned about this, arguing that their organic certification would be affected.

Supporters of the science point out that millions of North Americans have been eating GM crops for over 10 years without ill effect although the more cautious feel it may be too soon to tell. Thousands of acres of North American farmland produce GM crops – mainly maize and soya – meaning that most meals consumed in the States contain some genetically modified content. Supporters argue that before any GM food actually finds its way to your plate it would have been through far more rigorous tests and analyses than conventional crops.

Europe has so far been highly conservative in its approach to GM. Only two products have been cleared to be grown in the EU – Monsanto MON 810 maize, cleared in 1998, and the Amflora potato, cleared as recently as March 2010. However, it's important to note that the starch from this potato, for which it is grown, is only used for processes such as animal feed and making paper. Direct human consumption is not permitted. Although Britain has yet officially to back GM production, it is increasingly a grey area. For example, pig farmers regularly buy food pellets for their animals from the United States, pellets that more often than not include GM produce. So, if we eat the meat from animals that have been fed GM produce are we not already consuming genetically modified food ourselves? This is one hot potato that will be continue to be juggled for years to come.

3. Organic farming

One of the first pieces I ever did for *Countryfile* asked the question of whether organic farming had a future. Twenty years ago it was still seen as being quite freaky – all sandals and hippies. Today, of course, it's far more mainstream, worth an estimated £1.6 billion to the economy. Amazingly, the same doubts over its future still exist, especially when money is tight and people start to wonder if they can afford premium prices for organic food.

Quite simply, organic farming is a system of agriculture that is carried out to a set of legally defined standards that exclude the use of chemical pesticides and fertilisers. Instead, age-old practices such as crop rotation are utilised to keep the soil rich in nutrients and natural pest controls are put into place as an alternative to pesticides. Therefore, organic farmers claim that their produce is more environmentally sound and sustainable. And, after all, until a century ago nearly all the world's farms were organic. As organic farming is not reliant on chemicals, supporters say that it will survive any peak-oil crisis. Furthermore, no GM crops are allowed in an organic system and it requires higher standards of animal welfare including more space for livestock. Unless absolutely necessary, antibiotic treatment of animals is avoided.

Worldwide the organic standard is governed by various bodies. In the UK, the main standard is that of the Soil Association, based in Bristol. Farmers pay to have their methods monitored and products certified as being organic. Once they've achieved this they can display one of the governing bodies' logos on their labelling. Farmers can also register with the Organic Farmers & Growers and the Organic Food Federation.

Critics of organic farming claim that the system requires far more space than conventional farming to produce the same amount of food and therefore they doubt whether an organic system could ever meet modern food demands. There have also been calls for the organic bodies to consider whether organic food that is transported over large distances should be stripped of its environmentally friendly status. There is the argument that it's far greener to buy non-organic, but locally produced food rather than organic produce from abroad, or even the other end of the country, which takes its toll on the environment in food miles.

4. Biodynamic farming

If the people I interviewed twenty years back considered organic farming slightly wacky, what would they have made of biodynamics? At its heart, biodynamic farming follows the same principles as organic but also tries to incorporate even greater biodiversity and – most radically – the phases of the moon. Produce is grown, harvested and in some cases eaten according to astrological lunar cycles, the farming calendar being dependent on how the moon is moving through the twelve constellations of the zodiac. According to this holistic system, the best time to sow or reap your crops is when the moon is ascending – and the upper part of the plant is apparently bursting with vitality – or descending, when all that vigour is down in the roots.

Biodynamics isn't exactly new. It was developed over 80 years ago by an Austrian philosopher and scientist, Rudolf Steiner. There's a spiritual side to the process as biodynamic farmers embrace the concept that plants are a living link between the earth, air and the cosmos as a whole. Therefore, they only feed their plants and animals using natural means, eschewing chemicals and, in some cases, even treating their livestock with homoeopathic medicine.

As you would expect, all of this clean living comes at a price. Biodynamic produce, which has started to appear in the big supermarkets, can cost up to 20 per cent more than non-organic produce.

5. Hydroponic farming

I recently watched a new type of hydroponics system in action while just a few yards away orangutans swung from trees and elephants sprayed themselves with dust. But my location wasn't as exotic as it sounds: I was standing in Paignton Zoo in Devon. Hydroponic cultivation can be practised anywhere because it doesn't need soil – just water and nutrients. It's being increasingly used in greenhouses to grow tomatoes and salad leaves all year round.

What makes the system at Paignton different is that plants are grown in rotating trays that are stacked high in custom-made buildings. Computers monitor the crops, ensuring that they receive exactly the right amount of sustenance – and the crops are protected from changes in the weather, pests or natural disasters. In a hydroponics unit, even seasons have no bearing on production.

This modern take on the Hanging Gardens of Babylon is seen by some researchers as a radical answer to the question of how we are to grow enough food in a world of diminishing natural resources. While the revolutionary facility at Paignton Zoo, developed by a British firm, is only feeding the animals at present – producing 11,200 plants per crop in an 100 square metre machine using only 5 per cent of the water required by conventional methods – some have suggested that we could see tower-block farming springing up in the hearts of cities using similar systems. At present, no hydroponically grown crops can be classified as organic due to the distinct lack of soil. Researchers are now looking to see how existing farm buildings on conventional farms could be converted to hydroponics units.

Diversifying to survive

The past twenty years have seen British farming change beyond all recognition. Our farmers have had to cope with financially crippling animal diseases, the lowest food prices in modern history and increased competition from imports. While many farmers have closed their gates for good in the face of such problems, others have looked at alternative means of bringing in money and balancing the books. Farming is in their blood so they will try anything to save their business and that often means trying something completely new.

The *Farm Business Survey 2008/2009*, released by DEFRA in January 2010, revealed that over half of England's 57,000 farms have now diversified in one way or another, bringing in an additional income of around £300 million.

My fellow *Countryfile* presenter, Adam Henson, runs a popular tourist attraction on his Cotswold farm. When his dad, Joe, launched the farm park project featuring rare breeds in the early 1970s his neighbours frowned upon the enterprise. Today such schemes are proving to be the lifeblood of many farms. Some are still linked with agriculture, others are a radical departure, but all seem necessary in the current climate.

Let's have a look at the main ways in which farms are diversifying:

Farmers' markets

The growth of the farmers' market has been one of the great successes of the past decade. It's hard to believe that little over a decade ago the concept was unheard of in the UK. The trend started in the United States, specifically California, which today has half the population of the UK but twice as many farmers' markets. Before the boom hit Britain, I travelled to the Golden State to report on one of the markets for *Countryfile*. It was held just off Rodeo Drive in Hollywood and our researcher was devastated to learn she'd just missed George Clooney picking up his weekly fruit and veg. The farmers' market is a thriving sector that's still growing. Ten years on, some North American supermarkets are giving up space in their car parks and even in their food halls to local producers.

Over on our side of the pond, the first official farmers' market opened in Bath, Somerset, in 1997. Perhaps *Countryfile* can take a little credit for getting the movement off the ground, because our report created a great deal of interest. Nationally there are now more than 550 farmers' markets bringing in an estimated £220 million a year. Most markets operate once or twice a month although there are moves across the country to try to increase the frequency to make it easier for people to use the markets more regularly. And North America is again ahead of the game. Some US farmers' markets are opening in the evening so people can visit straight from work.

Farm shops

Farms have always sold direct to the public, even if it's only a few eggs over the farm gate or pick-your-own strawberries. However, the past decade has seen an explosion in farm shops – units on the farm property that sell the farm's wares direct to locals. While some are still simple huts with wobbly tables and the bare minimum of modern tech, others are competing with the high street with state-of-the-art, purpose-built or converted buildings. The very best have integrated butchers, cafés and restaurants, and an intimate knowledge of where your food has come from. At present it's thought that there are over a thousand farm shops in operation.

Farm festivals

In 1970, Somerset farmer Michael Eavis organised the very first Pilton Pop Festival on his land – and I was there, reporting the goings-on for BBC1 TV's local news show, *Points West*. The headliners were glam-rockers Marc Bolan and T. Rex while the 1,500 festival-goers paid £1 for their tickets and got some free milk thrown in. Fast forward 40 years as the festival – now known as Glastonbury, of course – is an annual highlight of the music scene and big business with 170,000 people passing through the gates.

How local is local?

The growing popularity of farm shops has raised one problem. How can you be sure that your shop – or your farmers' market for that matter – is the genuine article? Can people just jump on the bandwagon and start advertising their wares as 'farm fresh' or some such claim? The answer is yes. The most noteworthy example of this came in 2007 when Heinz brought out its range of 'Farmers' Market' soups, and you can't walk down a supermarket aisle without seeing the faces of farmers grinning from the labels of apparently local foods.

The National Farmers' Retail and Markets Association (FARMA) reports that there has been an increase in the number of retailers that have no link to an actual farm. Similarly, anyone can start up a market and brand it as a farmers' market.

To help avoid people being duped into thinking they're buying farm produce, FARMA is introducing two schemes over the next year or so. The Genuine Own (GO) scheme certifies that the produce on a farmers' market stall comes directly from a farm, while the Genuine Own And Local (GOAL) badge is given to farm shops that can prove that their produce is sourced from their own farm and neighbouring producers.

Glastonbury is not the only farm-based festival. Dumfries and Galloway's annual Wickerman festival, named after the cult horror film, takes place in a natural amphitheatre on Jamie Gilroy's cattle and sheep farm while Lounge on the Farm attracts thousands of music-lovers to Merton Farm in Kent. The Farm Festival held at Gilcombe Farm, Bruton, Somerset, is another annual music festival. It was launched in 2004 as a charity event and is seen as an alternative to overtly corporate operations such as Glastonbury.

Adventure farms

Urbanites have long used the countryside as a way to relax and unwind from the stresses and strains of city life: walking, riding, bird watching and sailing to catch a valuable breath of fresh air.

Not all leisure pursuits offered on UK farms are so tranquil these days as more and more adrenalin junkies, thrill-seekers, extreme-sports fanatics and stag-parties head for the fields. The high-octane activities now on offer include:

> Aerial woodland walks

> Archery

> Blind driving courses

> Bushcraft

> Canoeing

> Clay pigeon shooting

> Falconry days

> Go-karting

> Hallowe'en ghosthouses and festivals

> Horse boarding

> Human table football

> Indoor climbing

> Mazes

> Mountain biking

> Mountain boarding

> Off-road 4x4 driving

> Paintballing

> Quad bike tracks

> Raft building

> Zip lining

Farming unusual animals

Old MacDonald may have had pigs, cows and geese on his farm, but these days he could add a whole cast of new, surprising animals to his nursery-rhyme roster. Here's just a few:

Alpacas and llamas

Around three thousand alpacas (*Vicugna pacos*) were introduced to the UK in the early 1990s and have become a firm favourite at agricultural shows up and down the country. Their numbers have since swelled to around 30,000 in Britain. Hailing from Peru, Bolivia and Chile, the animals are farmed for their strong, silky wool, which is said to be as luxurious as cashmere and warmer than sheep's wool.

A charming feature of alpacas is that they make a noise rather like humming.

A close relation of the alpaca, the llama (*Lama glama*), is also now kept on UK farms. Being larger pack animals, llamas are mainly seen as tourist attractions as enterprising farmers offer visitors the unique experience of walking the British countryside alongside a llama who carries their gear and picnic. A couple of llamas by the names of Gilbert and George once lived in the paddock next to my cottage and seemed to spend most of the time fighting each other. Perhaps it's their in-built aggression that makes them very good at protecting sheep – put a llama in with a flock and it'll see off any potential predators.

Bison

Cattle farming may sound more traditional, but bison farmers insist that the bovine is a relative newcomer to the British Isles. It's certainly true that bison (*Bison bonasus*) did roam the plains of ancient Britain, but were hunted to extinction here some five thousand years ago. While a herd of the shaggy creatures is always guaranteed to bring in the sightseers, the real money is in the flavoursome meat. Richer and sweeter than beef and lower in fat and cholesterol, a bison steak will give you around 35 per cent more protein than beef, meaning that you're likely to eat around a third less.

Many people confuse bison with buffalo. It's not surprising as both beasts are related but the water buffalo (*Bubalus bubalis*) comes from

Asia whereas bison are from North America and Europe. Yet buffalo are also reared in Britain now, their creamy milk making lovely mozzarella cheese, which is low in cholesterol.

Camels

The ships of the desert are some of the most recent additions to British farms, with herds established in both Cornwall and the Gloucestershire Forest of Dean. The camels (*Camelus bactrianus*) are mainly used for trekking – the sight of a train of camels carrying holidaymakers along the bleak Goonhilly Downs on the Lizard Peninsula has to be seen to be believed – although when the beasts moult, their wool can be pulled off by hand and spun into yarn.

Crocodiles

In 2006, a farmer in East Anglia set up Britain's first crocodile farm. Andy Johnson from Church Farm in Oldhurst, Cambridgeshire, also farms, cattle, pigs and lambs, but decided to start his reptile operation as he wanted to produce home-grown *Crocodylus* to undercut the market value of illegally supplied crocodile meat. The production of the mild-flavoured meat, high in protein and low in fat, does present the farmer with the odd problem. Three years after they arrived on his farm the toothy beasts measured up to 3 metres long and weighed up to 190 kilos and had quickly outgrown their pool.

Ostriches

The sight of an ostrich (*Struthio camelus*) on a British farm may still cause you to do a double take, but the giant, flightless birds have been farmed here since the late 1980s. The largest birds on the planet have been domesticated for 150 years, mainly in South Africa, although at first it was to supply prized ostrich feathers for the fashion industry. The British market is largely based around meat production. The red meat is tender but strongly flavoured, and contains little in the way of fat. There's another tasty secondary product as well. One ostrich egg is roughly the equivalent of 24 hen eggs, weighs 2 kilos and takes up to 90 minutes to hard boil. Once cooked, it will retain its heat inside the shell for two hours although you'll need something a little stronger than a teaspoon to crack into it – a domestic drill is more likely to break into it. It's not a cheap meal though. On average an ostrich egg will set you back £15–20 in a supermarket.

Getting the name right

Most people who love the countryside can tell a cow from a pig and a duck from a goose, but do you know your gib from your queen or your jack from your jill? Here's a list of the most common animals in the British countryside, the terms to use if they are male, female or young, and their descriptive and often humorous collective nouns.

Animal	Male	Female	Young	Collective noun
badger	boar	sow	kit or cub	a cete of badgers
bat	male	female	pup	a colony or cloud of bats
beaver	male	female	kit	a colony or family of beavers
bee	drone	worker (unless the queen)	larva	a grist, hive or swarm of bees
bird	cock	hen	chick	a flock of birds
boar	boar	sow	piglet, shoat or farrow	a sounder or singular of wild boar
butterfly	male	female	caterpillar	a rabble of butterflies
cat	tom (or gib if neutred)	queen	kitten	a clowder of cats
cattle	bull	cow	calf	a herd, drove or drift of cattle
chicken	cock (if older than one year), cockerel (if younger than one year)	hen	chick	a brood, clutch, run or peep of chickens
crow	cock	crow	chick	a murder of crows

Animal	Male	Female	Young	Collective noun
deer	buck or stag	doe or hind	faun	a herd, leash or mob of deer
dog	dog cur, sire (if parent) or stud (if breeding)	bitch	pup	a pack or kennel of dogs
donkey	jackass	jenny	colt or foal	a pace or herd of donkeys
dove	cock	hen	squab or chick	a flight, dole or plague of doves
duck	drake	duck	duckling	a raft, paddling or bunch of ducks if on water; a team, bed or flock if in flight
eagle	tiercel	hen	eaglet	a convocation or con-gregation of eagles
falcon	tiercel	falcon	chick	a cast of falcons
ferret	hob	jill	kit	a business of ferrets
fox	reynard, tod or dog	vixen	cub, kit or pup	a skulk or leash of foxes
frog	male	female	tadpole or pollywog	a knot or army of frogs
goose	gander	goose	gosling	a gaggle of geese
grouse	cock	hen	chick	a covey of grouse
hare	buck or jack	doe or jill	leveret	a down or husk of hares
hawk	tiercel	hen or haggard	eya or chick	a cast, kettle or boil of hawks
hedgehog	boar	sow	hoglet, pup or piglet	an array of hedgehogs
heron	cock	hen	chick	a sedge or siege of herons

Animal	Male	Female	Young	Collective noun
horse	stallion or stud	mare or dam	foal, colt (male), filly (female)	a stuff, string, field, herd, remuda or stable of horses
mole	boar	sow	pup	a labour of moles
mouse	buck	doe	pup	a mischief or nest of mice
otter	dog	bitch	cub	a bevy or romp of otters
owl	male	female	chick	a parliament of owls
ox	steer or ox	cow	stot or calf	a yoke of oxen
peafowl	peacock	peahen	chick	a muster or an ostentation of peafowl
pig	boar	sow	piglet, shoat or farrow	a herd or trip of pigs
pigeon	cock	hen	squab	a kit or flock of pigeons
rabbit	buck	doe	kitten, kit or bunny	a leash, nest, trace or warren of rabbits
rat	buck	doe	pup, pinkie or kitten	a mischief of rats
seal	bull	cow	pup	a herd, pod or harem of seals
sheep	ram or tup	ewe or dam	lamb	a flock of sheep
squirrel	buck	doe	pup	a dray or scurry of squirrels
swan	cob	pen	cygnet	a game, bank or tem of swans
turkey	tom	hen	poult	a rafter of turkeys
weasel	dog, buck, jack or hob	bitch or jill	kit	a gang, confusion or pack of weasels
woodpecker	cock	hen	chick	a descent of woodpeckers

The strange case of the disappearing farmland birds

In many ways British birds have a lot to thank farming for. Before agriculture took hold of our landscape you would have been hard-pressed to spot skylarks, lapwings and corn buntings in the sky, let alone hear their heart-warming songs. The wild woods that covered the land would have kept them hidden from sight. When our early ancestors felled the woodlands and created a patchwork of open farmland they effectively set free the species we now know as farm birds. Suddenly there were acres upon acres of new land providing the kind of food or shelter these birds needed and their numbers flourished. Over the centuries, linnets, yellowhammers and turtle doves were the constant companions of farmers.

Then, in the latter half of the 20th century everything began to change. Their songs began to disappear from the air and sightings became fewer with every passing decade. In 1999, the then-Labour government decided they had to act, and set a target to reverse the national decline in farmland birds by 2020 using a variety of environmental schemes. The success or failure in this task would be measured against the controversial Farmland Birds Index. Nineteen birds, as chosen by the British Trust for Ornithology (BTO), would be used as a barometer. Originally 28 species were identified as farmland birds using the definition of species 'feeding in open farmland during the breeding season, even though they may nest in woods or hedges'. Six species were immediately rejected as they were considered too rare or limited to specific regions to be useful as part of a nationwide survey. These were the hobby (*Falco subbuteo*), quail (*Coturnix coturnix*), Montagu's harrier (*Circus pygargus*), corncrake (*Crex crex*), stone curlew (*Burhinus oedicnemus*) and cirl bunting (*Emberiza cirlus*), while the red-legged partridge (*Alectoris rufa*) and pheasant (*Phasianus colchicus*) were removed as they were introduced, not native, species. Finally, the barn owl (*Tyto alba*) was dropped due to a lack of annual population data.

This left the 19 birds that now make up the index:

1. Kestrel (*Falco tinnunculus*)

2. Rook (*Corvus frugilegus*)

3. Jackdaw (*C. monedula*)

4. Whitethroat (*Sylvia communis*)

5. Corn bunting (*Emberiza calandra*)

6. Reed bunting (*E. schoeniclus*)

7. Yellowhammer (*E. citrinella*)

8. Skylark (*Alauda arvensis*)

9. Linnet (*Carduelis cannabina*)

10. Goldfinch (*C. carduelis*)

11. Greenfinch (*C. chloris*)

12. Tree sparrow (*Passer montanus*)

13. Yellow wagtail (*Motacilla flava*)

14. Grey partridge (*Perdix perdix*)

15. Turtle dove (*Streptopelia turtur*)

16. Stock dove (*Columba oenas*)

17. Woodpigeon (*C. palumbus*)

18. Lapwing (*Vanellus vanellus*)

19. Starling (*Sturnus vulgaris*)

And what of the results? Well, according to the Farmland Birds Index, other than the period 1994–2004 when things seemed to stabilise, the presence of these species has plummeted to an all-time low, with numbers hovering around a drop of 53 per cent since 1966.

Organisations such as the RSPB have been quick to link this decline to changes in agriculture. These include:

The loss of mixed farming

In the past the majority of farms raised both livestock and arable crops, providing both open nesting sites and feeding areas for the young. By farmers specialising one way or another, it's argued that valuable habitats have been lost for farmland birds as well as other species such as the brown hare (see pages 79–80).

The switch from spring to autumn sowing of cereals

This means that most farms that sow cereals in autumn have lost overwinter stubble, which provides food and shelter for birds between harvest and mid-February.

An increase in the use of chemicals in agriculture

More intensive farming methods

Some conservationists claim that the drive to produce more intensively grown crops has meant the grubbing up of hedgerows (see pages 45–6) to create larger fields, drainage of important wetlands to create more arable ground and the habit of ploughing closer to the edge of a field to increase the area in production.

The subject of margins became increasingly high profile in 1992 where, as part of the Common Agricultural Policy (CAP), the EU decreed that farmers set aside an area of land to slow production and reduce the European food-mountains. In the first year of the scheme 15 per cent of all cropped farmland was required by law to be left for wildlife, although that figure dropped to 10 per cent by the year 2000 and in 2008 the scheme was scrapped altogether. Conservationists were appalled as in their view the set-aside land had proved to be a valuable source of wildlife habitat. For a while it looked as if DEFRA would establish its own compulsory set-aside to prevent Britain's 1 million acres of it being ploughed up and put back into production. Instead, the government decided to back a voluntary scheme.

The Farmland Birds Index has attracted its detractors over the years. Some farmers argue that the 19 birds are too arbitrary and don't provide a sufficiently wide picture to be used as an indicator of farmland biodiversity. As the majority are in decline, they say that it paints too black a picture. Instead those farmers would like to see a list of birds that overwinter on farmland such as the pink-footed goose or golden plover. And where is the sparrowhawk, they ask, or the magpie, buzzard, gull, swallow, collared dove, green woodpecker and grey heron, all species that are believed to be on the increase?

Others claim that the reason for the decline of the 19 birds on the index is that they are increasingly victims of predators, either by mammals, such as the grey squirrel and badger, or birds such as sparrowhawks and magpies. Then there's climate change – is that taken into account when crunching the data?

Whichever side you are on, this is a debate that won't be going away any time soon – unlike, it seems, some of our favourite farmland birds.

The five most endangered farmland birds according to the Farmland Birds Index

1. Turtle dove *(Streptopelia turtur)*

Declined 88 per cent between 1970 and 2007 and 66 per cent between 1995 and 2007. A small increase was recorded in 2008-9 but the species is still in overall decline.

The true love of 'The Twelve Days of Christmas' fame may struggle to gather that many turtle doves these days with numbers of the dainty bird at a dangerous low. Its distinctive and calming purr is no longer a familiar sound of the countryside and some scientists have claimed that it will vanish from our shores within the next two decades unless the decline is reversed. What is particularly baffling about the blue-grey dove with chestnut and black wings is that the population is crashing even on farmland specifically managed for wildlife. The Game and Wildlife Conservation Trust has suggested that the lack of weed seeds – the mainstay of a turtle dove's diet – on modern farmlands means that the birds aren't breeding in the numbers of the past. It appears that today's doves have a shorter breeding season and produce half the number of clutches per pair that they used to. To make matters worse, crop failures or habitat loss in the sub-Saharan African plains where the birds overwinter may also be having an adverse effect.

2. Grey partridge *(Perdix perdix)*

Declined 89 per cent between 1970 and 2007 and 45 per cent between 1995 and 2007

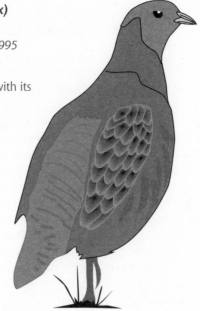

This dumpy and cagey game bird, with its orange head and chirricking call, is said to spend only 3 minutes a day in flight. Once widespread on arable lands as well as rough pasture and even sand dunes, its decline has been linked to the loss of hedgerow verges, where the bird nests, and the loss of winter stubble and food, due to changes in sowing practices and the use of pesticides. The lack of nest sites with adequate cover is thought to be causing more chicks to be lost to predators.

3. Corn bunting *(Miliaria calandra)*

Declined 89 per cent between 1970 and 2007 and 30 per cent between 1995 and 2007

Another victim of the loss of winter stubble, the stout male corn bunting was once known for its promiscuity and was so prevalent and well-fed that it was known as the 'fat bird of the barley'. Today, while they can still be seen in southern and eastern England, they have largely disappeared from Wales and northwest England, a decline that has been mirrored throughout northern Europe. As with the grey partridge, increased used of pesticides and herbicides has severely cut the numbers of insects and weeds gathered by the bunting to feed their young.

4. Yellow wagtail *(Motacilla flava)*

Declined 71 per cent between 1970 and 2007 and 24 per cent between 1995 and 2007

This beautiful green and yellow ground-nesting bird is a summer visitor to Britain. Once a common sight hopping at the feet of grazing cattle, it has been subject to a decline since the 1980s. Interestingly, when the yellow wagtails first return in April from overwintering in Africa they make straight for autumn-sown crops to nest and by June, when the crops have grown too long, the birds switch to non-cereal crops such as potatoes, field beans and peas. Unfortunately, crops such as field beans don't offer much in the way of cover, leading to high levels of predation. Potatoes, however, are ideal, thanks to their loose canopy of cover, which provides easy access for the parents and helps conceal the nest. It's estimated that the yellow wagtail needs to have two nesting attempts every year if they are to break out of their decline. However, at present, around 59 per cent of nesting attempts fail, mainly due to predation.

5. Linnet *(Carduelis cannabina)*

Declined 57 per cent between 1970 and 2007 and 24 per cent between 1995 and 2007

Once incredibly popular as a caged bird on account of its beautiful song and striking crimson breast and forehead, the linnet is a gregarious bird, which nests in colonies in shrub, gorse, bramble or hedgerows. As of 2007, linnet numbers have shown some signs of stabilising although there has been no indication that they are approaching their levels of distribution of 40 years ago. The improved conditions are thought to be linked to the wide-scale introduction of oilseed rape on British farms.

Songs of success

All is not lost for British farm birds, as one recent success shows. In 1989 the cirl bunting faced extinction. Its distribution range was once right across southern England, but only 118 breeding pairs survived.

The Cirl Bunting Species Recovery Programme, led by the RSPB and co-funded by Natural England, worked with farmers in the West Country to provide year-round food and shelter for the black and yellow marked bird. Around 60 hand-reared chicks have been relocated from Devon to Cornwall every year to help the bunting increase its range and in 2009 it was revealed that there are 862 breeding pairs, a 25 per cent increase on the last major survey in 2003.

While this programme is only limited to two counties in one corner of the country, it does show what can be achieved in the right conditions. And it's not alone. Thirty years ago the population of the stone curlew imploded until by 1986 only 160 breeding pairs remained. Whereas the stone curlew, with its piercing yellow eye, once nested in grassland, the changing countryside meant that it had to find shelter in sugar beet and onion crops. The birds' impressive camouflage proved too good and the farmers who regularly ran over the nests with their tractors didn't even know they were there. Two conservation projects – one in the Breckland area of Norfolk and Suffolk and the other on Salisbury Plain – have seen numbers reach 350 pairs and rising.

Meanwhile, the population of the shy and retiring corncrake hovered just above 400 pairs in 1993. Today there are about 1,100 pairs. Surveys are under way to see whether this relative of the moorhen has begun to spread from sites in the west of Scotland – no easy task as the reclusive corncrake will do anything to avoid being spotted, happy to skulk around in long vegetation. Sometimes the only way of knowing that a corncrake is near is to listen for the males belting out their peculiar 'crek crek' call, described by some as sounding like a credit card being dragged across a plastic comb. Bizarre as the call is, it must be music to the ears of those who thought they were witnessing the disappearance of the species from Scotland.

How to tell a hare from a rabbit

Britain boasts two main species of hare. The mountain hare (*Lepus timidus*) is our true native, having existed in these islands since the ice age. Now limited to the uplands of Scotland and Ireland, its coat changes colour in winter, turning white to provide perfect camouflage against the snow (apart from the tips of its ears that remain stubbornly black). In summer, it may appear a bluish grey, leading it also to be known as the blue hare.

However, the brown hare (*L. europaeus*) is the one most of us recognise. Possibly introduced to Britain by the Romans from the plains of Asia, it is an animal of myth and legend. Numbers are thought to have been seriously affected by the same changes in agriculture that appear to have done so much damage to our farmland bird numbers (see page 70). In the late 19th century there were estimated to be 4 million brown hares in Britain, but just over 100 years later that number has dropped to 80,000 and there are fears that they may become locally extinct in some areas, such as the Southwest. Scientists believe that this drastic decline could be attributed to the fact that hares do not store a huge amount of fat in their sleek bodies and need to feed all year. To find the right food throughout the year the hare needs a mosaic of different habitats, which have become increasingly rare in the modern, intensive world of farming: former grasslands have been converted to crop land and the switch to autumn sowing means that there is a dearth of food in spring. There's also the rather gruesome news that baby hares, or leverets, are often mashed by farming equipment where they rest.

So, while sighting a hare was always an honour, it is now becoming a rarity. If you do catch a glimpse of this elusive creature running across a field how can you be sure that you're spotting a splitting hare and not a common bunny? Here's a handy checklist:

Rabbit	Brown hare
Body length = 40cm max	Body length = 65cm max
Can weigh up to 2kg	Can weigh up to 4kg
Grey-brown in colour	A warmer golden brown with a white belly
Relatively short ears	Longer ears (twice the length of their heads), tipped with black
Dark brown eyes	Light brown eyes that appear almost yellow
Shorter legs mean that rabbits move in jerky, low bouncing hops	Longer, stronger legs mean hares bound off into a faster run, zig-zagging across a field to confuse predators
Run with their tail up, showing its light underside	Run with their tail down, showing its black upper side
Can run at a fairly respectable 20mph	Can reach speeds of up to 45mph (it's not called haring along for nothing!)
Live underground in warrens, accessed by a hole 15–20cm wide	Live above ground in shallow depressions known as forms
Can be often seen in daytime	Rest during the day; best chance for a sighting is at dawn or dusk
Baby rabbits (kittens) are born below ground, naked and blind	Baby hares (leverets) are born above ground, covered in fur, eyes open and ready to run
Tend to live in groups	Tend to live solitary lives

rabbit

hare

More hare-raising facts

▶ Hares and rabbits aren't rodents. They're actually part of the mammalian order known as Lagomorpha.

▶ Both hares and rabbits eat their own droppings. And before you wrinkle your nose in disgust, it's a matter of waste-not, want-not. The droppings they produce in the day are softer so that they can eke out that very last ounce of nutrition by having a second helping, while droppings produced at night, being harder and squeezed of any last drop of goodness, are left behind.

▶ For more of a chance of spotting a hare, head to Suffolk, Norfolk or Cambridgeshire because approximately half of Britain's brown hares live in East Anglia.

▶ The phrase 'mad as a March hare' comes from their frenzied springtime mating rituals, in which brown hares can be spotted on their hind legs, boxing furiously at each other. The breeding season actually starts in February and lasts through to mid-September but the March antics are more noticeable for the somewhat prosaic reason that the crops are shorter and you can see what they're up to and the slightly racier reason that it's usually during March that the females become more interested. As the female comes into oestrus or on heat she will start to attract more attention, which leads to the boxing matches. But don't be fooled into thinking you're seeing two males fighting over her. What you're actually seeing is a female, fed up with being pursued by a male, turning around and trying to land a left or, for that matter, right hook on him. The male, eager to defend himself, will rear up and be forced to box with the female he's been fixated with. Eventually, a persistent male will wear down her resistance and nature will take its course. Once the deed is done, that's it for the male; he has no part in rearing young and shoots off to find another female to mate – and possibly box – with.

▶ The Easter Bunny was in fact originally a hare. The word Easter comes from the name of Eostre, the Anglo-Saxon goddess of spring and fertility, whose favourite animal was a brown hare. Over time children were told that the hare laid the brightly coloured eggs that they were sent out to collect on the morning of Easter Sunday in celebration of the return of spring. Modern birders believe that there may have been some confusion between eggs found in the shallow nests on the ground made by lapwings and the fact that hares rest in similar forms. Maybe our ancestors really did think that hares laid eggs.

Either way, as with much of our pagan heritage, the Christian church turned everything on its head and the holy hare became something to be feared and avoided. Instead of being a sign of a benevolent goddess, the Christians declared that hares were witches transformed into the form of a cursed animal to escape capture from the righteous or to suck cows dry of their milk. It was also believed that if a pregnant woman clapped eyes on a hare her baby would be born with a cleft lip and palate – hence the archaic term 'hare lip'. The only way she could save her unborn child from disfigurement was to rip the dress she was wearing on the unfortunate day.

The bad luck didn't end on dry land. If a sailor or fisherman were foolish enough to say 'hare' while at sea, the boat and crew were surely doomed.

Badgers and bovine TB

The only wild animal in the UK with its own Act of Parliament to protect it is *Meles meles* – the Latin term for a creature better known to you and me as the badger. One result is that numbers have soared in recent years to around 300,000, so badgers can hardly be called endangered. But the Protection of Badgers Act 1992 cannot save them from their worst enemy – the driver. Every year, one in six badgers is killed on our roads.

Those deaths are accidental but badger numbers would plummet further if many cattle farmers had their way. They want them culled because they blame badgers for passing bovine tuberculosis to their herds. This chronic infectious disease can also strike at deer, goats, dogs and cats but it's the disastrous effect on cattle that makes the headlines. If just one animal fails the regular compulsory skin test for TB, the entire herd is 'shut down' – the farmer is not allowed to move any cattle on or off their land. Infected animals have to be isolated and destroyed – around 40,000 of them a year – which costs us taxpayers a whopping £100 million in compensation.

It is heartbreaking for farmers to see fine animals, often the result of generations of careful breeding, being taken out. They can't trade in their cattle until the standstill is lifted, so pedigree breeders are out of pocket by many thousands of pounds in lost business. Dairy farmers, though, are still able to sell their milk as long as it is pasteurised.

Movement restrictions are only lifted after the herd has had two subsequent tests, sixty days apart, which prove negative. All farmers can do after that is keep their fingers crossed it doesn't return; but if the tests are positive the misery continues. *Countryfile* viewers discovered just what it's like living with the tensions of bovine TB when my colleague Adam Henson saw his cattle hit by the disease on his Cotswold farm.

It reached its peak back in the 1930s when half the national herd was infected. Compulsory testing and slaughter saw it drop to only 1 per cent but now it's back with a vengeance. Worst hit is the Southwest of England, which has dairy cattle and badgers in large numbers, so can that be more than just a coincidence?

Does the disease go round in circles from one species to the other or is it transmitted directly from badger to cow? These are questions still to be answered but research has shown that, following a cull of badgers, some animals flee the area of the cull and begin to be affected in surrounding areas that previously had been free of TB.

I've seen one estimate that half the badger population would need to be eliminated to secure even a small reduction in the disease. Be that as it may, many farmers – and the National Farmers' Union – are convinced culls are the only way to control the spread. The Welsh Assembly, which has devolved powers over agriculture, approved a cull which would start in Pembrokeshire. But in July 2010 it was halted before it began by the Appeal Court in Cardiff, after The Badger Trust questioned its extent and effectiveness. In England, the coalition government looks set to overturn previous policy on culls, despite the Department of Environment, Food and Rural Affairs saying in 2009 that it would not sanction a cull and instead earmarking £20 million to develop a vaccine against bovine TB. But coalition ministers say there will now be culls and a statement from Downing Street said: 'As part of a packet of measures, we will introduce a carefully-managed and science-led policy of badger control in areas with high and persistent levels of bovine TB' This complex and controversial issue is, unlike the badger, by no means black and white.

The pros and cons of a badger cull

For:

⟩ Badgers do indeed carry bovine TB and pass it on to cattle.

⟩ A scientific review of the subject, carried out in 1997 by Professor John Krebs, concluded that there was 'compelling' evidence that badgers transmitted infection to cattle. At the time, however, he did add that the effectiveness of a badger cull was by no means certain so recommended a series of random trials.

⟩ Former government adviser and chief scientist Sir David King has joined the ranks of leading scientists in saying that while 'cattle controls remain essential … in certain circumstances and under strict conditions, badger removal can reduce the overall incidence of TB in cattle'.

▶ The current series of testing and slaughter of infected cattle has done nothing to halt the rise of the disease.

▶ The cost of compensation to the taxpayer continues to rise year on year.

▶ Vaccines for badgers are seen by many as difficult and costly to administer. The badger would have to be caught by farmers and vets to administer the drug, which lasts for 12 months, after which recapture is necessary to administer a booster. A pilot vaccination scheme was due to be launched in Devon, Gloucestershire, Herefordshire, Staffordshire and Worcestershire, but will now only take place near Stroud, Gloucestershire from July 2010 and last for 5 years.

▶ Oral vaccinations are expected to be available from 2014. A cattle vaccination is not expected to be available until 2018 at the earliest and many farmers believe this will be too late.

Against:

▶ Activists claim that a cull only makes the badger a scapegoat while the main problem will always be cattle-to-cattle transmission of the disease.

▶ Many believe that to kill thousands of animals that are protected by law is unethical. The Protection of Badgers Act 1992 makes it illegal to kill, injure or take badgers or interfere with a badger sett.

▶ The introduction of compulsory tests and slaughter of infected cattle all but eradicated the disease in the 1950s. Some argue that by improving the systems, the same outcome could be achieved.

▶ Campaigners cite the 10-year study by the Independent Scientific Group (ISG) on TB in cattle, which concluded in 2007 that, although badgers play a significant part in spreading the disease, a wide-scale cull would make no meaningful contribution to controlling it. The trials, which cost £50 million and saw 11,000 badgers culled, indicated that instead of controlling the disease it merely spread the problem in surrounding areas, as disturbed badger groups broke up and spread the disease into non-infected areas around the trial zones. However, further analysis of the ISG report has shown that the cases of TB within the trial zones have continued to fall since the trials came to an end and are now 54 per cent lower than the surrounding areas.

> Instead of a cull, money should be invested in vaccines and practical ways of keeping cattle and badgers apart, including electric fences.

Meanwhile, this timid creature much loved by millions continues to bumble around the countryside in search of its main food, earthworms – it can eat up to 200 a night – though it is also partial to grubs, insects, cereals, fruit and small mammals including rabbits, hedgehogs, mice and rats.

Badgers follow long-established pathways on their nightly forays and return (vehicles permitting) to their homes of interlinking underground tunnels known as setts. They live in social groups and are good parents who will defend their cubs at all costs.

Though the Act of Parliament gives badgers a level of protection denied to many other wild species some unscrupulous so-called 'sportsmen' defy the law to catch and kill them. They send terriers into a sett with radio transmitters on their collars so when the dogs confront a badger, the men know where to dig. They pull it to the surface, often using a pair of large specially made tongs, and then either kill it on the spot or sell it on for a session of 'badger baiting', where the animal is put into a small pit and attacked by dogs. The badger doesn't stand a chance but they are brave creatures and put up a fight to the death, often inflicting horrendous injuries on the dogs. Badger baiting is a cruel left-over from medieval times that was outlawed nearly two hundred years ago, yet in the 21st century there are still people willing to pay good money to watch this appalling spectacle. The RSPCA has set up a team of undercover inspectors determined to track down these gangs of baiters and bring them to court.

Other creatures that can cause problems down on the farm

Rabbits (*Oryctolagus cuniculus*)

They may be one of the country's favourite pets but the rabbit is an eternal headache for our farmers. Said to have been introduced by the Normans in the 12th century for their fur, the humble cottontail soon proved the old cliché of 'breeding like rabbits' to be true and rapidly spread throughout the country, helped by the gestation period of just

30 days and litters numbering between two and eight kittens at a time.

Current estimates put the British rabbit population at 35 million and growing at an annual rate of 2 per cent. But why are they such a problem for farmers? Well, consider this. Ten rabbits can eat the same amount of food as one adult sheep, chomping their way through pasture, grassland, crops and even young trees. Considering how many rabbits we now have, it's little wonder that they cause millions of pounds-worth of damage on our farms. And, in the words of one famous bunny, 'That's not all, folks'. Rabbit warrens can cause land erosion, injury to animals who trip and fall and damage to expensive farm machinery. Taking everything into account, rabbits are fair game on farms all year around. Poisoning is not allowed, so many are shot, netted or gassed, while ferrets and falcons are often used to control numbers.

The 1950s saw a more extreme solution. To stop rabbits working their way through valuable post-war crops the myxomatosis viral disease was released and decimated the rabbit population. However, the resourceful rabbit came bouncing back and numbers have almost completely recovered.

Crows (*Corvus corone*) and magpies (*Pica pica*)

Carrion crows are considered a real threat to both ground-nesting farmland birds and livestock, especially young lambs. The large black birds feed on the eggs and chicks of such birds as lapwings, redshanks, grouse, pipits and partridge, and have also been known to injure or kill new-born lambs, pecking out their eyes, sometimes even before the creature has died.

Shooting the highly intelligent crow is legal as is the use of a Larsen trap. This is a cage with two compartments, each with its own spring door. One compartment contains either food or a decoy bird and the second is kept open until a crow enters, sits on the perch and the door shuts behind it. The trap is completely legal as long as the decoy bird is provided with clean water, food and shelter and the trap is checked every day.

The Larsen trap is also an exceptionally effective way of capturing magpies, a species that has been the subject of a population explosion in rural areas in recent years. Like crows, the distinctive black and white birds are said to feed on the eggs and young of ground-nesting birds, presenting a threat to many game-bird farms. It is legal to shoot magpies or destroy their nests.

A number of animal-rights charities are campaigning to ban the use of Larsen traps, declaring them to be inhumane, as they can be used to trap birds of prey and place the decoy bird under undue stress.

Rats (*Rattus norvegicus*)

Rabbits have nothing on the rat when it comes to breeding prowess. A single pair of rats can produce 800 offspring every single year and the UK population is thought to be around 60 million – that's nearly one rat for every person! The rodent commonly blamed for spreading the Black Death in the 14th century can still carry a number of serious diseases including E. coli, foot and mouth disease, tuberculosis, salmonella and Weil's disease. The majority of these can be passed on in either their urine or droppings – and rats produce a lot of both: every year one rat produces 5 litres of urine and 14,600 pellets, many of which can end up in animal or even human food.

On the subject of food, it's been estimated that the British rat population consumes 200 tonnes of food every day, food that otherwise could end up on the human plate, and by gnawing through electricity cables, the rodents are believed to be responsible for starting one in every two farm fires.

Rats are legally killed in just about any manner possible, be that poisoning, shooting, traps, gassing and by ferrets.

Fox (*Vulpes vulpes*)

Probably one of the most controversial animals in all of Great Britain, let alone the countryside, the fox is still seen by many farmers as being a major agricultural pest. Said to take lambs, piglets and game birds, the fox is most associated with killing chickens and many a farmer has arrived too late to find his hens have been slaughtered. Foxes kill more birds than they can eat at one time and so if one gets into a chicken run it will kill every chicken it can get its paws on and then leave the corpses on the ground. Two main reasons have been given for this apparent blood lust. The first is that when a fox comes upon a bountiful source of food it will kill as much as possible and then carry away the carcasses to bury and eat later. But it can only cope with one body at a time and it is often disturbed by the farmer. The other explanation is that the fox kills restrained prey because it isn't sure how to deal with animals that don't run away. Killing more than you need isn't a habit limited to foxes. Hyenas, shrews, mink, weasels and leopards all perform the same gruesome trick.

As for lambs, the figure is much lower. It's estimated that less than 2 per cent of them are killed by foxes in England and Wales every year.

Legally foxes can be shot but not killed by poison, gas or hunted with packs of hounds (see pages 177–80). The Hunting Act 2004 does allow the use of a single terrier below ground to dig out foxes 'for the purpose of preventing or reducing serious damage to game birds or wild birds which a person is keeping or preserving for the purpose of their being shot'.

It has to be noted that not all farmers see foxes as pests and some actively encourage them as a way of seeing off rabbits.

Dos and don'ts for walking near livestock

Almost every year at least one story about an unfortunate rambler being trampled by cattle hits the headlines. It's true that angry or curious cows can cause problems, but millions of walkers co-exist with their bovine neighbours without incident by following some simple rules:

Do

▶ move quickly and as quietly as possible.

▶ walk around the edge of a field rather than through the middle of the herd.

▶ warn animals that you're there if you're approaching from behind. A calm whistle or word will be enough but try not to startle them.

▶ avoid going into fields with cattle if you are walking a dog. Cows are skittish around dogs and during spring and early summer, when most are rearing calves, may well attack any dog near their young.

▶ keep dogs under control on leads if you do walk near livestock. On open country and common land you must keep your dog on a lead no longer than 2 metres between 1 March and 31 July and all year around near farm animals.

▶ let go of the lead if threatened by cows. A dog will easily outrun the cow so let it go and make your way out of the field as quickly but calmly as possible. Only when you're clear of the cows should you call for your dog. If it comes to you when there are still cattle around there's a chance you could be trampled.

▶ clap your hands firmly if cattle and ponies are blocking your way. Usually this will be enough to get them to move out of the way, but if they don't, never try to force your way through. Find another route around instead.

▶ break up large groups of people. These can appear threatening to cattle so split yourselves up before walking near livestock.

Don't

▶ get between a cow and her calf and never, ever pet a calf, no matter how appealing it looks.

▶ run if you startle a herd of animals. They might stampede.

▶ go into a field with a solitary bull. Usually bulls are OK if they're in a field with cows but don't take any chances.

▶ feed farm animals. Feeding will encourage them to come up to people, which can cause problems in future.

▶ stop near animals with open bags. They may think the bags contain food.

▶ leave pushchairs unattended. Cattle especially are inquisitive and may approach a pushchair and rummage through its contents, whether or not your child is in it!

What do sheepdog calls mean?

I can watch a shepherd driving a flock of sheep with his trusty sheepdog for hours. By 'sheepdogs' we usually mean border collies although there are many different breeds such as the Welsh collies, bearded collies, huntaways and kelpies. Whatever the breed and wherever you go in the countryside, most working dogs are controlled by use of some familiar phrases, which have been called out over our countryside for generations.

But what do they mean? What instructions is the shepherd giving? Here's a handy list of what the farmer says and the dog hears!

Walk up
Walk towards the sheep.

Come-bye
Move around the sheep in a clockwise direction.

Away
Move around the sheep in an anticlockwise direction.

Time now
Keep going slowly.

Steady
Keep going slowly.

Get back
You're getting too near the sheep. Back off.

Lie down
Stop or lie down (depending on the training).

Stand
Stop or lie down.

Look back
Leave those sheep; now look around for another group to work.

That'll do
Your work is finished; come back to me.

Coats of many colours

As the year draws near to its end, farmers begin planning for lambing in the spring. The gestation period of a ewe is 5 months so around November the female stock will be introduced to an eager ram or tup.

Before they are let in to serve the ewes, the ram is fitted with a harness around their chest complete with a raddle – or coloured marker to you and me. When the ram mates with a ewe, the marker leaves a stain on the wool on her back so that the farmer knows that nature has taken its course.

Ewes come into heat every 13–19 days so the colour of the marker is likewise changed every couple of weeks, typically going through a sequence such as yellow, then green, red, blue and finally black. If, by Christmas, the ewe is covered by a whole host of colours, it may indicate that she is infertile. And, of course, if the ewe falls pregnant the colour on her rump lets the farmer know who the proud father is.

'A ring at the end of its nose, its nose'

When the owl and the pussycat needed a ring for their impromptu wedding they were lucky enough to find a pig willing to sell for one shilling the ring at the end of his nose. But what was it doing there in the first place?

The first record of a ring being inserted into a pig's nose dates back to the Middle Ages. Swineherds were given permission to graze their pigs in royal forests between Midsummer's Day and 12 January – on one condition. Pigs have very powerful snouts and can easily churn up the ground in the search of food. Ringing the nose discouraged the porcine plunderer from rooting too deeply, thereby protecting young trees from damage. Over time the practice of pig ringing became widespread to protect valuable crops from being dug up and to prevent pools of stagnant water forming in the muddy troughs their foraging leave behind. The job of ringing pigs provided a lucrative sideline for the village blacksmith who soon became proficient at handling squealing and wriggling beasts.

Pig-ringing is still a part of modern farm life for some although these days an experienced farm-hand or vet will administer the rings – two or three small ones in the top of a sow's snout or one larger one in the case of a boar.

Some farmers, however, believe that ringing is cruel and will cause the pig unnecessary pain. The Soil Assocation's standards for organic pork ban the practice outright as it feels that pigs should be allowed to follow their noses and root whenever they want.

Bull ring

As everyone knows, bulls are powerful creatures that need to be handled carefully. Some bulls have rings placed in their noses between 9 and 12 months of age by either a trained dairy worker or vet. A handler then uses this ring in a number of ways to get the bull to do what he or she wants, exerting pressure on the sensitive area of the nose. Sometimes this can be as simple as feeding halter ropes through the ring. A ring staff can also be used, a wooden or steel staff topped with a snap that clips on to the bull's ring.

These days, ringing is largely reserved for bulls that are going to be shown at livestock exhibitions or country shows.

Horses

Britain is a horse-loving nation, but while these magnificent creatures were once working animals, the use of mechanical horsepower has meant that the majority of the 1.3 million horses in the UK are kept for pleasure or sport. Some heavy horses still help plough fields or pull carts, but, as we shall see their numbers are dwindling.

Let's look at some key British horse facts:

> Some 2.1 million people ride once a month or more, a figure that is up from 1.4 million in the late 1990s.

> Around 49,000 foals are born annually.

> Since 2005, every horse, donkey and pony in England and Wales has been required by law to have its own passport. The passport costs £20 but can save the owner a hefty fine if they don't register their animals. Horses without a passport can't be moved from place to place, sold, exported or slaughtered for human consumption – not that horsemeat is a big worry in the UK.

> In the space of a year, 4.3 million people take to the saddle. That's 7 per cent of the entire British population.

> There are 720,000 horse owners in the UK, of which 65 per cent have more than one horse, and 15 per cent own more than two.

> It costs as much to buy a horse as it does to keep it every year thereafter. New horse sales bring in over £400 million.

> As a nation, we spend £700 million on riding lessons every single year.

> Roughly 19,000 equestrian businesses operate in the UK, employing 28,000 people.

> The equine industry is said to be worth £4 billion to the economy.

> Of the total land in Britain, over 400,000 hectares (1.2 million acres) is used to maintain and produce horses.

> Racing horses is Britain's second most popular spectator sport after football. Around 6 million of us go to the races every year, with 1,500 race meetings held at Britain's 60 racecourses. The total number of individual races is around 9,000.

> The horse charity World Horse Welfare claims that 35–45 per cent of British horses are obese. Being overweight can cause a horse to have heart and lung problems, a diabetes-like condition and lameness.

From the horse's mouth: useful words and phrases

Aside If you ride aside, you ride with both legs on one side of the horse. Also known as sidesaddle.

Astride Riding with one leg on either side of the horse.

Breaking a horse in Mounting a horse for the first time to train it to respond to your commands and become accustomed to being ridden.

Bolt When a horse suddenly tries to run away.

Cob A stocky, short-legged horse, perfect for everyday riding, but not of particularly fine breeding.

Colt A male horse under four years of age.

Cross-country A horse-riding event when a rider has to complete a cross-country course including roads, jumps and obstacles within a set time.

Dam A foal's mother.

Draught horse A heavy or working horse (see page 100).

Dressage From the French for training, a competition where riders perform a series of complicated manoeuvres that are graded by judges. Dressage is the only Olympic sport in which men and women compete equally.

Equine A horse or things pertaining to a horse.

Farrier A professional who cares for horses' feet (see page 97).

Foal A horse under the age of one year.

Forelock The part of the mane that falls between the ears on to a horse's face.

Gait The way a horse moves. There are four main gaits, depending on speed. Horses walk at around 4mph, trot at around 8mph, canter (or lope) at between 10 and 16mph and gallop at between 25 and 30mph.

Gelding A castrated male. Unless a male is to be used for breeding they are castrated to improve their temperament.

Hinny The offspring of a horse stallion and a jenny.

Paddock A fenced area of pasture where a horse is kept, with either a surface of grass or earth.

Hand A measurement used to work out the height of a horse. A hand is roughly (10cm) or the width of a grown man's hand, hence the name.

Horse An equine over 14 hands high.

Indoor school A building, usually a barn, used for riding lessons.

Livery stable A business that horse owners pay to stable and look after their animals.

Mare A female aged four years or over.

Maiden A racehorse that is yet to win a race.

Mule The offspring of a jackass and a horse mare.

National Hunt racing The official name of jump racing. The National Hunt season runs from mid-October to the end of April.

Piebald A horse with patches of black and white colouring.

Point to point An amateur steeplechase organised by the local hunt.

Pony An equine under 14 hands high.

Show jumping A sport in which the rider and horse must jump over or between various obstacles.

Sire A foal's father.

Skewbald A horse with patches of brown and white colouring.

Steeplechase A horse race that involves leaping over a series of fences.

Stud farm An establishment that breeds horses.

Sound A healthy horse with no lameness.

Stallion A male horse aged four or over that hasn't been castrated.

Tack Horse-riding equipment including saddle and bridle.

Withers A horse's shoulders.

Yearling A horse of either sex between one and two years old.

The farrier

There used to be an old saying in farming, which still rings true today: 'No foot, no horse.' Whether it's the agricultural work of days gone by or the riding and sport of today, if your horse has weak or damaged feet you won't be able to use it. While every book on grooming ever written advises riders and workers to check a horse's hooves twice daily, the equine world has relied on another figure to make sure that their horse's feet are in top condition: the farrier.

Just a hundred years ago every village would have had its own farrier, and although the profession had dwindled throughout the 20th century, the rise in the popularity of horse riding has resulted in something of a revival. In twenty years the number of farriers has increased from around 2,500 to 3000. Back in the 19th century, a horse-owner would take their animal to the farrier's forge, although these days it's usually the other way around, the farrier travels to the clients to shoe their horses and check the overall health of the all-important hooves. The forge is now a portable gas oven that can be taken from stable to stable. It is used to heat the iron shoe so that the farrier can manipulate it to fit the hoof perfectly. The red-hot shoe is held against the lower surface of the hoof, making a mark that will show whether any alterations need to be made, and it is then hammered out on the anvil. This process will be repeated until the farrier is satisfied that the shoe fits and it is cooled in water. It is then attached to the hoof using seven nails driven in at an angle, before excess growth is trimmed with cutters and smoothed. Shoeing a horse is a precise procedure, but doesn't hurt the animal. The horn of the hoof is such a bad conductor that they don't feel the heat and the farrier's extensive training will mean that the nails are driven into areas that will cause no pain. Young horses may at first be spooked by the smoke and noise, but become used to the procedure with time.

Why horses need shoes

But why do we shoe horses in the first place? After all, wild horses never needed to be shod, moving with ease over different kinds of terrain with bare hooves. The constant movement and variety of surfaces travelled meant their hooves were smooth and hard.

Then we came along and domesticated them. We stored our horses on soft pastures or bedding, which meant they were walking less. Consequently their hooves became softer, and then we expected them to carry riders or tow heavy loads over harder terrain. So, horseshoes are attached to reinforce the hoof, protecting the horse from any pain as it shoulders the load.

A brief history of shoeing

Not that this is a modern phenomenon. Some historians believe that the Egyptians first shod their horses some 3,000 years ago to improve their durability. Mosaics found in Pompeii show horses being shod and iron relics dating from AD 481 that resemble modern horseshoes have been found in the Netherlands. The practice is thought to have been introduced to Britain by the Normans in 1066.

The meaning of the word farrier itself has changed over time, shifting from a horse doctor to, in the last couple of centuries, someone who shoes horses. It possibly derives from Henry de Ferraris, who was William the Conqueror's Master of the Horse.

The clients of a modern farrier will include racehorse stables, which require lightweight shoes, and other professionals such as show-jumpers and dressage teams. They will also deal with recreational ponies and hunts that generally require more of a tidy up and pedicure rather than reshoeing. And it's a constant task. A horse's hoof can grow between 3 and 5 millimetres per month, depending on their level of activity, health and nutrition. If the hoof grows too long, it will become fragile and cracked. Uneven hooves can cause the horse to become lame and walk in an abnormal manner, so regular visits from the farrier are essential.

Additionally, a farrier checks for infection or disease, treating hooves as necessary. It's all skilled work, as there's also a danger of making a horse lame if the trim of a shoe throws them off balance. For these reasons, by law, no-one can call themselves a farrier unless they are authorised by the Farriers Registration Council.

It's fascinating to watching a farrier shoe a horse, a true example of a great craftsman at work – or should I say great craftsperson, as there are a growing number of female farriers taking up the hammer and nails.

Lucky charm

No-one really knows why people hang horseshoes on the wall to bring good luck. There is some evidence that the practice may have originated in Ireland. It's believed that farmers nailed a horseshoe above the doors of the stables to protect their horses from demons, witches and things that go bump in the night. If you wanted to do it right, the horseshoe had to be attached by three nails, each hammered three times in honour of the Trinity.

Depending where you are in the country, some people hang the shoe upright in a 'U' shape so that no good luck escapes, while others prefer it with the two prongs pointing down, so that the beneficial luck pours down on you.

Know your working horses

Is anything more evocative than seeing heavy horses working the land? It conjures up images of days gone by and a different pace of life. Once draught horses were everywhere, bringing in the harvest and ploughing the fields in rural areas or hauling coal and delivering milk or beer in the cities. It's thought that up to the First World War around 2.8 million draught or heavy horses worked in agriculture in the UK. Today the number is something around 5000 and falling fast. Are heavy horses heading to extinction? Are they doomed just to be anachronistic oddities at country shows and museums? I hope not and there are valuable jobs that they still carry out. Here are the four main species of heavy horse that you'll see today.

Shire horse

Colouring: Grey, black, brown or bay with white on the feet and legs.

Characteristics: A long and lean head, well-set eyes and Romanesque nose. The shire horse has a thick neck and muscular frame, with distinctive silky feathering on the legs.

Size: Stands between 16.2 and 18 hands (168–83cm).

Origin: Probably brought to Britain by William the Conqueror in 1066.

Historic uses: Because of their sheer size, shire horses were used in medieval battles as living tanks transporting warriors in suits of armour that were too heavy for native horses. As the nature of war changed, and armour was no longer required, neither was the shire horse although that wasn't the end of the story.

The shire horse started to be used on farms for tasks that, in the past, would have required oxen. These included ploughing and transporting heavy loads such as timber. Shires were also a usual sight towing barges along British canals and were at home in the city as much as the countryside. By the early 1890s carrier firms were using 19,000 horses in London alone and a further 3,000 heavy horses were in use by the capital's brewers – a large proportion of which would have been shires. But the invention of the internal-combustion engine and the increasing use of motor vehicles and tractors in the 20th century meant that once again the shire was to become surplus to requirements and started to disappear from our roads and fields.

Present uses: You can still find shire horses in smallholdings and some woodlands, where machinery would struggle to find a path through sensitive areas. Perhaps the most famous shire horses are the four drays used to deliver beer barrels to the pubs of Devizes for the Wadworth brewery.

Status: At the turn of the 20th century there were around 6,000 breeding pairs. Today there are only 3,500. Some experts fear that the shire horse may become extinct within a decade unless a new breeding programme is put into place. Usually up to 300 female shire horses of breeding age are required annually to replenish those too old to breed. At present all the UK can manage is 200 per year.

Clydesdale

Colouring: Black, bay, brown or roan. Most have white legs and some have white on the stomach.

Characteristics: A straight nose, large ears, a long, arched neck and slightly sloping shoulders. The Clydesdale has a short back, muscular hindquarters and feathered legs.

Size: Stands between 16 and 17 hands (162–74cm).

Origin: A native breed of Scotland, founded in Lanarkshire; named after Clydesdale, the original name of the area. It was bred in the 18th century from native Lanarkshire mares and Flemish stallions to improve the weight of the animal.

Historic uses: At their height, the Clydesdale was exported around the world, from North and South America to Australia and New Zealand. Back home, they were used for the usual agricultural labours, as well as pulling milk floats and, in the north, towing coal skips.

My great-uncle Alf was a coal merchant and his Clydesdale was called Sam. As a very small child I would be allowed to fill Sam's feed-bag and, as a treat, I was sometimes hauled up onto his back. He was a gentle giant and to me seemed as big as an elephant.

Present uses: These days most Clydesdales are kept for either breeding and showing, although some are still used to pull advertising carts for breweries and, like the shire, are sometimes employed in forestry.

More recently, Clydesdales have begun to appear in dressage arenas and are being ridden more and more, with crossbreeds even becoming show jumpers.

Status: Classed as vulnerable by the Rare Breeds Survival Trust, there are currently around 350 breeding Clydesdale mares in the UK.

Suffolk Punch

Colouring: Various shades of chesnut. And that's not a spelling mistake – traditionally chesnut is spelt with no 't' after the 's' when referring to this breed.

Characteristics: The Suffolk has long-muscular shoulders and surprisingly short legs for such an impressive body. The legs are clean of the feathers seen on a shire horse, which historically proved handy in Suffolk's thick clay soil.

Size: Stands between 16.1 and 17.2 hands (165–78cm).

Origin: 'A Suffolk Punch,' says William in Charles Dickens' *David Copperfield*, 'when he's a goodun, is worth his weight in gold.' For centuries that sentiment was certainly true. The Suffolk is Britain's oldest breed of horse. Dating back to before the 16th century, the bloodline of every Suffolk alive today can be traced back to one horse – a stallion foaled in 1768, known as Crisp's Horse of Ufford. This original horse, also called the 'foundation sire', was smaller – standing at only 15 hands (152cm) and was said to have had particularly poor hooves. Improved breeding sorted out this shortcoming and increased the breed's size.

Historic uses: Bred specifically to be 'low and stout' the Suffolk Punch's powerful stamina proved to be ideal for farming work, especially ploughing, but despite being exceptionally popular in its native East Anglia it only started to spread across the country in the 1930s. By then it was too late. The coming of motorisation hit these majestic beasts hard, and slaughterhouses were soon filled with the sad sight of Suffolks waiting for the inevitable.

Present uses: Today Suffolks are mainly used as show animals, although they carry out some draught and environmental work. Recently, the Suffolk Wildlife Trust used the horses to pull drilling rigs across a sensitive wetland environment as part of a project to provide much needed habitat for the rare great raft spider.

Status: The Suffolk's darkest hour came in 1966 when only nine foals were born. The Suffolk Horse Society – the oldest horse-breed society in the UK, formed in 1877 – went into action and the breed, which had numbered in the thousands just 100 years before, was saved from extinction. However, its numbers are still a worry. There are now only around 480 Suffolks in Britain, with fewer than 300 registered breeding females.

Percheron

Colouring: Usually grey or black. Some have white markings on their legs or heads, although in breeding circles any excessive amount of white is frowned upon. The older the horse, the lighter its coat becomes.

Characteristics: The Percheron's small-to-medium ears, large eyes and broad forehead betray its likely Arab origins. Its legs are free from feathering and its chest wide.

Size: Stands between 16.2 and 17.3 hands (168–80cm).

Origin: The origins of the Percheron are lost in time, but records of this ancient breed exist from the 8th century, placing the breed in a district of Normandy known as Le Perche. Local legends suggest that the horse was first brought to the area by Moorish invaders around AD 700. Other stories tell of them being bred from the horses that helped the Romans invade Brittany.

Historic uses: Although Normans may have brought Percherons to England in 1066, the British population was established in the late 19th century when stock was brought in from America and Canada to pull omnibuses in the larger cities including London, Manchester and Birmingham. During the First World War the breed became a popular choice for agricultural work. Farmers who had been called up to serve in France were impressed with its power and ability to work in muddy conditions as well as on hard surfaces, and so started to import them to work the fields.

Present uses: As well as becoming a popular show or riding horse, Percherons can still be found in logging operations, manoeuvering in tight spaces that a machine requiring a 4-metre access area would never handle.

Status: There are only around 200–250 registered Percherons currently in Britain. Because of these small numbers, breeding is carefully controlled. The British Percheron Horse Society has 12 active stallions on its books that serve between 30 and 40 mares to produce up to 35 foals per year. To guarantee that the gene pool remains strong, breeders ensure that it is not the same 40 mares that are put to the stallion each year.

CHAPTER THREE

The Uplands

Britain's National Parks

These days it's all too easy to take our National Parks for granted, but there was nothing easy about their creation. They are the result of over a century of struggle and campaigning by people who cared deeply about preserving some of Britain's truly special places for the nation. Between 1600 and 1860 a series of Parliamentary Enclosure Acts had allowed half of England's countryside to be fenced off. There was growing concern that the majority of the land was in private hands and that most ordinary people were denied access. Here are the key moments that led to the birth of the National Parks.

1810 – William Wordsworth describes the Lake District as 'a sort of national property, in which every man has a right and interest who has an eye to perceive and a heart to enjoy'.

1872 – In the United States, Yellowstone, the world's first National Park, is established in the states of Wyoming, Montana and Idaho.

1876 – The Hayfield and Kinder Scout Ancient Footpaths Association forms and campaigning begins to give common people the right to roam the countryside, escaping the confines and pressures of the city in their free time.

1884 – The first Access to Mountains and Moorland Bill is proposed to Parliament but fails to win support.

1895 – The National Trust for Places of Historic Interest or Natural Beauty is established. Its charter, according to its founder, Octavia Hill, is to protect the countryside 'for the everlasting delight of the people'.

1899 – The UK Gamekeepers' Association forms.

1908 – The second Access to Mountains and Moorland Bill fails.

1925 – The public are given the right to access urban common land in England and Wales 'for air and exercise' in the Law of Property Act.

1926 – As the Access to Mountains and Moorland Bill fails for a third time, the Council for the Preservation of Rural England is formed (now known as the Campaign to Protect Rural England or CPRE).

1931 A government inquiry recommends that National Parks would be a benefit to the country and that an Authority should be established to identify key areas.

1932 – After members of the Lancashire branch of the Communist-inspired British Workers' Sports Federation are thrown off Bleaklow, a peak just north of Kinder Scout in Derbyshire, a 20-year-old mechanic by the name of Benny Rothman leads 400 walkers to trespass on Kinder Scout. They are met by a band of gamekeepers but, after a scuffle, continue on their way and are joined by fellow trespassers from Sheffield. Victorious, they return to Hayfield, where the police are waiting. Benny and five other leaders are arrested and charged for 'riotous assembly'. Sixty years later, I met Benny at the foot of Kinder Scout and he recalled for me in a *Countryfile* interview that epic day that helped kindle the campaign for rural access. 'We did it', he told me, 'because we wanted everyone to be able to experience the wonders of our uplands, not just a few privileged landed gentry.'

Weeks after the Kinder Scout confrontation a second mass trespass, this time at Winnats Pass, between Castleton and Edale, is organised and more than a thousand ramblers take part.

1935 – Various walkers associations across the country amalgamate to form the Ramblers' Association (now known simply as the Ramblers) and a conference, chaired by Norman Birkett, once again calls for a National Park Authority.

1938 – The Standing Committee on National Parks publishes *The Case for the National Parks*, in which they state 'without sight of the beauty of nature the spiritual power of the British people will be atrophied'.

1939 – The Access to Mountains and Moorland Act is finally passed.

1942 – The government's Scott Report accepts that Britain needs National Parks, although the Second World War slows progress.

1949 – The National Parks and Access to the Countryside Act is passed, establishing the National Park Authority and plans for 10 parks for public enjoyment. Lewis Silkin, Minister of Town and Country Planning, proclaims that 'at last we shall be able to see that the mountains ... moors ... dales ... and tors belong to the people as a right and not as a concession. This is not just a Bill. It is a people's charter .... With it the countryside is theirs to preserve, to cherish, to enjoy and to make their own.'

1951 – Britain's first-ever National Park – the Peak District – is designated. Today it is the second most visited National Park on the planet, only pipped to the post by Mount Fuji in Japan.

Did you know ... ?

It's a common misconception that the National Parks are made up of public land. Each Park is largely owned by private landowners or organisations such as the National Trust and of course the thousands of people who have their own homes within the National Parks. The 15 National Park Authorities may own the odd spot of land, but it usually doesn't amount to much.

Our National Parks in numbers

Name	Year of designation	Area (sq km)	Highest point (m)
Brecon Beacons	1957	1,344	Pen y Fan 886
Broads	1989	305	Bath Hills 12
Cairngorms	2003	3,800	Ben Macdui 1,309
Dartmoor	1951	953	High Willhays 621
Exmoor	1954	694	Dunkery Beacon 519
Lake District	1951	2,292	Scafell Pike 978
Loch Lomond and the Trossachs	2002	1,865	Ben More 1174
New Forest	2005	570	Telegraph Hill 167
Northumberland	1956	1,048	The Cheviot 815
North York Moors	1952	1,434	Urra Moor 454
Peak District	1951	1,437	Kinder Scout 636
Pembrokeshire Coast	1952	621	Foel Cwmcerwyn 536
Snowdonia	1951	2,176	Snowdon 1085
South Downs	2010	1,624	Blackdown 280
Yorkshire Dales	1954	1,769	Whernside 736

Coastline (km)	Population	Annual visitors (million)
0	32,000	3.8
2.7	5,721	5.8
0	16,000	1.48
0	34,000	2.5
55	10,600	1.4
23	42,200	8.3
58	15,600	2.1
42	34,400	Not available
0	2,200	1.7
42	25,000	6.3
0	38,000	10.1
418	22,800	4.2
60	25,482	4.27
14	120,000	Not available
0	19,654	9.5

Other land designations you'll find in the countryside

Area of Outstanding Natural Beauty (AONB)

The AONB is another category of protected landscape in England, Wales and Northern Ireland. The official definition of an AONB is 'a precious landscape whose distinctive character and natural beauty are so outstanding that it is in the nation's interest to safeguard them'. The areas are designated by Natural England and the Countryside Council of Wales. Not all AONBs are open to the public, as many of them are made up of privately owned land, on which planning permission is tightly controlled and sustainable land management is generally encouraged. There are currently 49 AONBs in England, Wales and Northern Ireland (for Scotland see NSA below).

National Nature Reserve (NNR)

There are around 400 National Nature Reserves in the United Kingdom. Originally brought into being at the same time as the National Parks, NNRs were conceived as outdoor laboratories, ideal for examining British wildlife. Their role has grown over time. While not all NNRs are open to the public, the large majority offer access and some, like the Stiperstones in Shropshire or the Giant's Causeway in County Antrim, Northern Ireland, are major tourist attractions. They have to be managed carefully: the designated bodies, including Natural England, hold the right to strip a NNR of its classification if it isn't managed appropriately. These reserves are the cream of our Sites of Special Scientific Interest (see page 113) and the best examples of our natural habitats.

National Scenic Area (NSA)

The NSAs are currently Scotland's only national landscape designation and are granted to areas 'of outstanding scenic value in a national context'. In essence they are the equivalent of the AONBs of England, Wales and Northern Ireland. There are 43 NSAs in Scotland, designated by Scottish Natural Heritage.

Site of Special Scientific Interest (SSSI)

The UK's 7,000 SSSIs are incredibly important places but you'd never guess it from the title, which suggests sites that only interest boffins! Yet they are significant to us all because they are where you'll find nationally important wildlife habitats or geographical features. I think a much less bureaucratic, much more involving name is needed for these gems, which can be smaller than an acre or cover thousands of acres.

Restoring British meadows

It's one of the most glorious and rare sights in rural Britain, but never in a million years would you guess it from its official classification: MG3 *Anthoxanthum odoratum – Geranium sylvaticum* grassland. OK, 'geranium' is a bit of a clue, but if you sweep away the dusty Latin, what reveals itself, in simple English, is something close to the heart of every country lover – an upland hay meadow.

Nearly all of our meadows vanished after the Second World War. In a bid to grow more food, farmers were being encouraged to spray their meadows with fertilisers. That produced vast amounts of silage as winter fodder but ended a centuries-old tradition.

Grass used to be mown towards the end of summer and left in stacks to dry so it provided hay for livestock in winter. But grass for silage can be cut more than once a year and fermented, literally pickling away, to preserve it. It's a quicker, more economically efficient process. So out went haymaking, haystacks and that evocative smell of new-mown hay that drifted from field to field. Out, too, went the yellow, white and blue drifts of wildflowers that gave the meadows their distinctive appearance. Instead they have been replaced by a uniform green for the last sixty years or so. But ever so slowly, hay meadows are making a comeback.

There's a long way to go. There are currently only around 1,000 hectares (2,500 acres) of hay meadows left but schemes such as the Hay Time projects in the Yorkshire Dales and the North Pennines are seeing that these grasslands again feature in our uplands. Seed is harvested from species-rich donor sites in a cut of freshly made hay. This is then taken to carefully selected receptor sites and strewn over the fresh grass. As the hay dries, seeds from the donor site fall and establish themselves in the new field. It's a deceptively simple but extremely effective process. It also means that there are homes again for such wonderfully named species as wood cranesbill, great burnet, pignut, bugle, marsh hawk's beard, yellow rattle and lady's mantle – up to 120 species in one field.

Donor farmers receive payment for the seeds and receptor farmers can qualify for higher grants for managing hay meadows under agri-environment schemes. Everyone wins – farmers, Mother Nature and the visitors who can once again witness the glory of an English meadow on a summer's day.

Burning heather

At various points in this book I advise against starting fires in the countryside but for many land managers fire is an important tool. For thousands of years country folk have burnt the heather on our uplands to control its spread and, since the 1850s, to help manage their game-bird stocks. Centuries ago in Scotland fires, known as muirburn, were also lit to clear wide areas of open land so that farmers could spot wolves creeping up on their animals. Obviously, this isn't much of a problem these days but there are other reasons for an annual burn. Left unmanaged, heather grows into a dense mat of thick, woody stems that support little wildlife, offer little in the way of nutrition for grazing livestock and impede moorland farming practices. And so, every year, gamekeepers and farmers head out to the uplands to start controlled fires, burning back the deadwood and recycling the nutrients in the ash. Buds near the ground, which had previously been covered by moss and vegetation, now find themselves exposed to the sun and new growth is encouraged. Blazes are planned on a strict rotation so that a well-managed moorland is home to a diverse mosaic of heather and other plant life, in various stages of their lives. This mix of ages also provides an ideal habitat for grouse that feed on young heather shoots and nest in older heather, which provides essential cover. As grouse tend not to travel great distances, it makes sense for gamekeepers to create an environment for them that covers all their needs in a relatively small area.

Just as there are shooting and fishing seasons, there are also burning seasons, to ensure that the burn is timed for when the heather is dry, the ground beneath – often peat – is wet and the winds light but constant. It's also timed to avoid causing problems for other species such as ground nesting birds.

In England, Wales and Scotland the burn season is from 1 October to 15 April in the uplands and from 1 November to 31 March in lowland areas, while in Northern Ireland it runs from 1 September to 15 April. Heather can be burnt outside these dates but landowners need to apply for special permission and that is hard to come by. There are also strict guidelines for a controlled burn, including checking the wind direction before igniting the heather – to reduce any risk to roads, private property and wildlife – and ensuring there are enough people on hand to control the flames. Fires certainly should never be left unattended. Many fire chiefs also ask that landowners contact them before starting a burn so they can be prepared if something goes wrong. It also means they can identify controlled fires when concerned members of the public call to say they've spotted a blaze in the heather.

In some upland areas, such as Wales, the tradition of burning heather has been replaced with mowing, which is seen by some as being less hazardous to wildlife, but unless your patch of moorland is particularly level, the mechanical option is more difficult and in some cases more expensive.

Castles and strongholds

Over the past few years I have presented the BBC2 series *Castle in the Country*, first with Nikki Chapman and later with Gloria Hunniford. We've explored some of Britain's grandest homes including Burghley House, Castle Howard and Floors Castle. However, long before these marvellous edifices were constructed, the countrymen of Britain defended themselves from attack using earth, wood and stone. Let's have a look at how the British castle evolved over time and explain some of those names you'll spot on your map.

Dykes

One of the earliest forms of defence, dykes were being built in Britain seven centuries before the Romans turned up and continued to be constructed into the Middle Ages. They were simple affairs consisting of two main components – a deep trench and a high ridge of earth piled up above it. Some were small but others, like Offa's Dyke on the English/Welsh border, stretched along for over a hundred miles, so while the concept was simple the actual process of building a dyke took an awful lot of organisation and a vast amount of labour.

Such was the effort of creating these larger defences that legendary names began to be given to them, as if to indicate that only a god or mythical creature would have the strength to construct one. So we have Devil's Dyke on the South Downs and Wansdyke (literally Woden's dyke) across the Marlborough Downs in Wiltshire. As the god of gods for the Anglo-Saxons before their conversion to Christianity, Woden was obviously a busy deity because there are a multitude of Grim's Ditches over the British Isles: Grim, meaning hooded one, was one of Woden's many names, and his dykes can be found in Wiltshire, Oxfordshire, Berkshire and elsewhere.

Hill forts

The Bronze and Iron Ages ushered in new crafts and skills as the human race flourished and established itself into larger tribes and communities, which then found new ways of killing each other. The weapons developed during these periods meant the rich and powerful had to defend themselves from attack – and the answer was to head for the hills!

Over two thousand hill forts from this period have been discovered in Britain. These enclosed areas had a number of uses. Tribes would meet in them to trade and form alliances. Some were dwelling places, while others provided a safe place for retreat while under attack. The forts provided shelter in the hardest of winters and gave the local powers-that-be a high vantage point from which to keep watch over their territory. They were also formidable signs of power. An impressive hill fort was a symbol of the prosperity of a particular tribe and its king. With hill forts came a more feudal and, as the population of Britain grew, more violent way of life.

Living within the ramparts of a hill fort wasn't easy. Being high on a hill, the thatched buildings huddled together for protection against the fierce elements – and so too, I imagine, did the people within.

The age of the hill fort in England came to an end with the arrival of the Romans – and the last stand of King Caractacus, leader of the British resistance, took place at a hill fort on top, legend has it, of the Malvern Hills. I've stood on the spot, called British Camp, and it's easy to imagine the scene as the Romans with their superior forces and equipment raced up the steep hillside, stormed the walls and captured the fort. Caractacus escaped but was later taken prisoner and sent to Rome in chains. But he was allowed to address the senate and made such an impression that he was pardoned.

Back in Britain, communities abandoned the forts and moved to the new Roman towns in the valleys below. In Scotland and Ireland, free from Roman influence, life on the hill remains unaltered with some hill forts still being built in the Emerald Isle a thousand years later.

The most notable Iron Age fort in England is Maiden Castle in Dorset. Built in 600 BC on the remains of a Neolithic settlement, the ramparts enclosed an area roughly the size of 50 football pitches and provided home and security for many hundreds of people. In AD 43, the fort was taken by Roman legionnaires and its inhabitants moved to nearby Durnovaria, modern-day Dorchester.

Roman forts

As you'd expect, when the Romans built forts during their occupation they were considerably more organised than their British predecessors. Whereas the Iron Age hill forts were usually oval, and dependent on the lie of the land for their shape and size, the Romans weren't going to allow anything to dictate what their forts looked like. Whatever the landscape, the Roman forts were largely rectangular and eminently practical. Housing up to 800 men, they were surrounded by a ditch and protected by a rampart of earth and stone topped by stockades of timber posts. Within the walls access was by means of two straight roads, which crossed the interior, and the entire fort and its surroundings could be surveyed from watchtowers that stretched 9 metres into the air. In later years, before the legions pulled out of England to defend Rome from the Visigoths, the wooden forts were being replaced by stone and the Roman equivalent of concrete made from volcanic material, rubble and lime.

Often a civilian settlement, known as *vicus*, sprang up alongside the fort, largely due to the fact that Roman soldiers were well paid and needed something to spend their cash on. Wherever there were Roman soldiers, traders weren't far behind.

One of the most impressive remains of Roman occupation is found on Hadrian's Wall in Northumberland. Housesteads Roman fort (originally known as Vercovicium meaning the 'place of effective fighters') is maintained by English Heritage and visitors get the chance to poke around its granaries, gatehouses, hospital and even latrines.

Motte-and-bailey castles

Before the Norman Conquest, castles as we know them today were largely unheard of in England. The first attempt to construct a European-style motte-and-bailey castle came in 1051 when French craftsmen arrived to build one for Edward the Confessor. However, squabbles between the builders and the locals (nothing's new!) caused the project to be abandoned before anything substantial was erected.

When William the Conqueror arrived on the scene he brought with him the practice of castle building, starting with Pevensey on the southeast coast. Two decades later, the English countryside was already becoming littered with them.

Unlike the hill forts of old, which utilised the natural advantage of height, motte-and-bailey castles could be built on any landscape, and because they were elevated on an artificial mound of earth the Lord in question could, well, lord over his land and defend from on high. The motte referred to the mound itself, usually around 5 metres high, on which sat the wooden keep or lookout surrounded by a wooden wall known as the palisade. Many of these mounds remained when the castles were subsequently rebuilt using stone and they exist to this very day.

At the foot of the mound, lay the bailey, a courtyard, enclosed by a second palisade. Here you would find the living quarters of the lord and his people. The motte would be linked to the bailey by means of a ladder or walkway, which could be easily destroyed if the bailey were attacked and occupied.

Attacking a motte-and-bailey castle was no easy job. The entire structure was surrounded by a water-filled ditch (the moat). Maurauders would have to get across the moat, storm the gate or the palisade, work through the defences of the bailey, scale the sides of the motte, which were purposely steep so that they couldn't be climbed on horseback, break through the gate and take the keep. To make matters worse, all the time the attacking party would be bombarded by stones and arrows from on high. Of course they could try to burn the keep down, but flaming arrows (beloved by Hollywood movie makers) were useless as the longbow hadn't been invented and so the keep was well out of range. Furthermore, the Anglo-Saxon weapon of choice was a heavy battle-axe. Imagine lugging one of those up a motte while stones rained down on you, slipping and sliding on the steep, muddy slopes that were often soaked from above during a raid.

The best way to attack was to lay siege to the castle, but as a lot of Norman fortresses had extensive food and water stores, their enemies would have to wait a long time for those within the walls to starve and surrender.

Many fine examples of motte-and-bailey castles can still be seen in the UK including Castle Rising in Norfolk, Berkhamsted Castle in Hertfordshire and, of course, Windsor Castle in Berkshire. Sometimes the castle is long gone but the motte (or tomen as they're known in Wales) remains. One such is the 8-metre high heap at St Clears, which still dominates the village in Carmarthernshire, South Wales.

Other earthworks

Barrows

These giant heaps of soil or rocks in the landscape are burial sites that date back to Neolithic times. Round barrows housed the remains of individuals of note, say the chieftain and tribal leaders, and were built over the body, skeleton or ashes of the deceased. With time, the dead were accompanied by a little meat or grain and a mug of liquor to give them sustenance in the afterlife, along with weapons and even the odd dog in case they fancied a spot of postmortem hunting. Some round barrows were grouped together in barrow crematories, possibly where individuals of the same family were buried together.

Long barrows, on the other hand, were larger mass graves, often with numerous chambers within. They still make for impressive sights in the landscape, such as the 108-metre long Pimperne Long Barrow in Dorset, thought to be the largest in the country, or the 73-metre West Kennet Long Barrow in Wiltshire. Unchambered barrows were heaped upon the remains of many important folk in one go – communities often 'saved up' their dead relatives until there were enough corpses to bury – while chambered barrows were opened time and time again.

It's quite usual to see rows of trees along the top of both round and long barrows. This was the handiwork of 18th- and 19th-century landowners who sought to improve the beauty of their estates, unaware that they would cause so much trouble subsequently for archaeologists wanting to explore these early burial mounds.

Fogou

One of the great mysteries of the late Iron Age are the *fogous* or 'fuggy holes' of south Cornwall. A Cornish word pronounced *foogoo*, meaning cave, a fogou is a subterranean passage that was created by tunnelling out a trench and lining its walls with dry stone walling and popping giant slabs over the top to form a roof. There are currently twelve surviving fogous known in Cornwall but what we don't know is why they were built. Most fogous are found near settlements and theories about their purpose range from shrines to bolt holes during attack or places to store food. The latter seems to be supported by the fact that they were often built to face the prevailing wind and, as they have an opening at both ends, could act as a wind tunnel for drying meat.

Of course, there are also more preternatural explanations, ranging from the idea that they were places of ritual to, more outlandishly, the home of goblins and spirits. There are numerous tales about the Pendeen fogou: one about a bunch of boys who ran screaming from its depths and vowed never to utter a word about what they saw, and another about the ghost of a woman in white who appears on Christmas morning with a red rose in her mouth.

One of the best-preserved fogous is found within the Trelowarren estate on the Lizard Peninsula. While no-one knows why Halliggye was built, the fogou has had many roles over the years. It was used as an ammunition store during the Second World War and today it is an important habitat for the horseshoe bat.

Souterrain

The Scottish or Irish equivalent of a fogou and equally enigmatic.

Toot-hills

These hills were used as lookouts in times of crisis. At the first sign of danger, 9th-century 'tooters' would charge up the hill to keep a look out for raiders. Sometimes there was even a watchtower or house (known as a *totaern*) on hand to provide a bit of shelter. Depending on where you are in the country, these hills also appear on maps as tot-hills, touts or tuttles.

Dry stone walls

Dry stone walls are in no way unique to Great Britain – they are found in around 35 other countries including Australia, Canada, France, the United States and even Nepal – but nowhere shares our concentration. Our countryside is criss-crossed with 180,000 miles of dry stone walls and they've been built here for a very long time. Some archaeological digs have found remains of walls some 4,000 years old.

Styles of wall change from county to county, and sometimes even between individual dry stone wallers, but the basic principles of building a dry stone wall remain. I've tried my hand at it and quickly realised that these everyday features of our countryside are nothing less than works of art. Selecting the right stone for the right place comes as second nature to a skilled professional but I had to be shown where each one should go – and it can be back-breaking work.

A dry stone wall is actually made up of two separate, interlocking walls, bound together at regular intervals by a long 'through stone'. First the waller digs a shallow trench in which to lay large, heavy base stones. Then the wall is built up, the stones getting gradually smaller so that it narrows to the top, where large, flat stones and a series of upright capping stones finish the top. Smaller stones and pebbles, hammered carefully in to keep everything together, fill the gaps between the two walls.

It's a slow, painstaking process – the average waller constructs about 3 metres a day using about 3 tonnes of stone. And they're never out of work, as there are many miles of walls that need either building or restoring. Luckily today, a number of organisations, among them the conservation volunteers trust, BTCV, and the National Trust, also run dry-stone-walling volunteer schemes to help take the strain.

But why bother with such an archaic craft? Surely there are more modern methods that can take the place of the old dry stone wall? Well, here are six reasons why the dry stone wall is probably always going to be here to stay.

Six reasons why Britain loves dry stone walls

1. They're incredibly durable

Properly built, a dry stone wall can last well over a hundred years, with only a little maintenance.

2. They're local and sustainable

Originally, early farmers cleared their fields of stones and piled them at the side of the land to mark boundaries. Today, the majority of dry stone walls are built using local stone by local craftsmen. The stones largely haven't had to be transported miles and there's no factory churning out bricks, meaning that they're actually incredibly green. What's more, when they're rebuilt the stones are often recycled, the wall builder dismantling the old wall, grading the stones according to size and then reconstructing it using the exact same materials.

3. There's no mortar or cement

The weight of the stones and the way they're packed into a complex three-dimensional jigsaw means that there's no need for cement. When you consider that the cement industry is said to emit more carbon dioxide than every airline on the planet, the environmental benefit of not using it in dry-stone-wall construction speaks for itself.

4. They add distinctive character

Every region has its own version of the dry stone wall depending on the type of stone available. For example, in Scotland – where the process is known as dyking – the granite used in dry stone walls is heavy and difficult to work with, so walls in the Highlands often feature huge boulders at the base. In Cornwall, slate is used in a herringbone pattern supported by earth packed into any spaces, while in the Cotswolds the local, distinctively coloured limestone is softer and easier to work with. Head north and the walls of Derbyshire and North Yorkshire are constructed from coarser sandstone and have a more irregular appearance than in

South Yorkshire where the millstones used are so rectangular they almost look like breeze blocks.

5. They're a haven for wildlife

Many plant and animal species make their home in dry stone walls. Reptiles favour a dry-stone abode and adders in particular use them as a place to feed in spring, nest in autumn and hibernate in winter. Coal tits, tree sparrows, robins, redstarts and wrens all nest within the cavities and can be joined by voles, mice, shrews and toads. Some of our native flora also thrive on dry stones walls, and you'll often find lichens (see page 205), mosses and ferns growing between the rocks as well as plants such as saxifrage (Saxifragaceae) and even certain cabbages (Cruciferae).

6. They provide vital windbreaks

While hedges are often more appropriate in lowland areas (see page 44), dry stone walls can withstand the harsh winds of the uplands and many a hiker spots livestock using the walls as a shelter from a cruel gale. Sheep have learnt another trick. After a downpour they often huddle beside a dry stone wall and let the draughts whipping through the gaps between the stones dry their fleeces like a gigantic hair-dryer.

Did you know . . . ?

Sometimes you'll come upon a dry stone wall that features openings in the bottom half of the wall. These are known as 'sheep creeps' and, as the name suggests, they act as an underpass for sheep to crawl through to get from one field to another.

Wild camping

For many, sleeping beneath canvas is one of the countryside's greatest pleasures, although for the majority of us it's limited to official campsites. Others long to get back to basics, pitching their tent without the luxuries of a well-stocked shop, toilet block and hot showers. However, what's known as wild camping is illegal in most of England, Wales and Northern Ireland. We may have the right to roam (see page 144) but not pitch our tent anywhere we want. Of course, you may find a landowner who is willing to let you camp on their land, but the rule is: ask first.

The exception to the rule is Dartmoor. Wild camping is enshrined in the Dartmoor Commons Act 1985 amendment to the National Parks and Access to the Countryside Act 1949. Article 6 states that you can camp if you:

▷ Stay within areas marked as public access – a large proportion of Dartmoor is restricted due to military manoeuvres.

▷ Set up camp at least 100 metres away from a public road or enclosure.

▷ Use a tent (caravans aren't permitted).

▷ Stay less than two consecutive nights in the same spot.

Scotland is also a different kettle of fish and you're free to wild camp in any areas other than around:

▷ Building sites

▷ School grounds

▷ Houses and buildings

▷ Quarries

▷ Golf courses

▷ Sports fields that are in use

▷ Areas where admission charges are required

Again you are required to camp at least 100 metres away from a road.

The Wild Camping Code

If you are lucky enough to find somewhere to camp in the wild (and have full permission) there are some basic principles to bear in mind:

➤ If you're camping in a group, keep it small.

➤ Be considerate to others.

➤ Leave the area as you found it. Carry out everything you carried in.

➤ Never leave any litter.

➤ Bury your toilet duties using a trowel, but make sure they are 30 metres away from water.

➤ Never bury sanitary towels or tampons. Animals can be attracted by the pheromones and dig them up. Take them with you.

➤ Only light a fire if you have express permission to.

➤ Never disturb the environment or change the habitat where you camp.

How to predict the weather using nothing but clouds

Millions of people tune into *Countryfile* not just to watch the latest features on rural life and outdoor activities but also to catch the weather forecast for the week ahead. I always reckon that, with its isobars and detailed information, it's the best forecast anywhere on television – and I've certainly always relied on it when I'm deciding what to wear for my next shoot.

Even so, the elements can surprise us all when we're out in the wilds and conditions can worsen within minutes. Many of our films have almost been ruined by wind, rain and snow – but I can't recall one ever being called off because of the weather. We just have to plod on, like anyone else working outdoors – only we have to keep talking even when the wind is whipping away our voices and the cold is having a serious effect on our smiles! Rain plays havoc with lenses and spray from a choppy sea can put a camera out of action. Still, it's better than an office job!

Mother Nature also provides her own clues to what the weather for the day ahead will hold. The clues are often in the clouds so it always pays to keep 'a weather eye' on the sky.

There are ten basic types of cloud, each classified by their shape or their height in the sky, and grouped into three families that share certain characteristics: stratus clouds are layered, cirrus are wispy or hair-like, cumulus are fluffy and heaped together. Let's look at each of those in turn.

The stratus family

Stratus clouds hang low and can be white but are often grey blankets, blocking out the sunlight. Fog is a form of stratus cloud, clinging to ground level. They bring with them a considerable risk of rain or even snow.

Nimbostratus clouds are dark, low and ominous. The clue is in their name: *nimbus* is Latin for rain. You should prepare yourself for persistent showers that can last for days.

Altostratus clouds form at around 2,500 metres, classed therefore as medium cloud. Usually they resemble a sheet of grey but if they continue to darken you can be sure you're in for fairly continuous rain within two days.

Cirrostratus clouds are high and spread wide across the sky, often casting a halo around the sun or moon. They indicate that rain isn't likely at that moment, but could forewarn of downpours within a couple of days. This type of cloud can also be included in the cirrus family.

The cirrus family

Cirrus clouds take their name from the Latin for a tuft of hair and form wispy, white trails between 5,000 and 12,000 metres in the air. These are good clouds to spot if you're hoping for fair weather, indicating that high pressure and dry, sunny conditions are on the way.

Cirrocumulus clouds remain high in the sky, in a sequence of wavelike globules. In winter they usually indicate that the weather is going to be dry, if cold, and may be a sign that thunder will be heard. This type of cloud can also be included in the cumulus family.

The cumulus family

Cumulus clouds are the clouds of picture books – flat at the bottom and round and fluffy at the top. They also usually mean that you're in for fair weather, although you may feel the odd drop of rain. Glider pilots in particular love these clouds – they're the sign of good thermals.

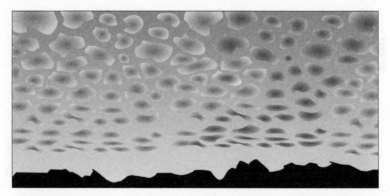

Altocumulus clouds usually form at around 2,500 metres and look like small puffs of heaped white or greying clouds, like a stack of pancakes or a spread-out fleet of UFOs. Wake up to these on a summer's morning and you could be in for thunder in the afternoon. They could also mean that colder weather is on the way and things could deteriorate over the course of the next day.

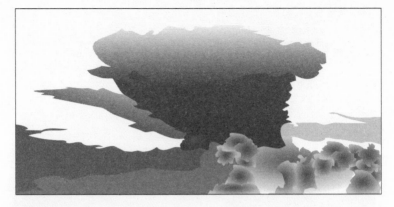

Cumulonimbus clouds are a bad sign: massive, heaped formations that can reach from low to high altitude and are curiously anvil shaped at the top. They bring with them heavy rain, hail, thunder and lightning.

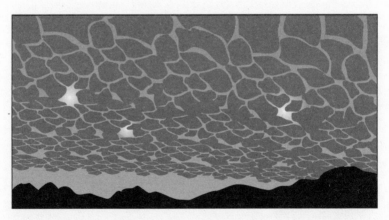

Stratocumulus clouds are low and layered and can cover the entire sky except for some brief glimpses of blue breaking through. In winter they bring with them stable weather with only a slight chance of rain. And, as you'd expect, the more blue you can see, the better the weather will become.

St Swithin's Day

There's one piece of weather lore that most of us are aware of – if it rains on St Swithin's Day, 15 July, we'll be in for 40 days of rain. Here's the full verse associated with the day:

> St Swithin's Day, if it does rain,
> Full forty days, it will remain.
> St Swithin's Day, if it be fair,
> For forty days, t'will rain no more.

So how true is the thousand-year-old prediction? The Met Office claims to have put the theory to the test on 55 separate occasions and they've never seen 40 days of similar weather follow St Swithin's Day.

The story arose from St Swithin, a bishop of Winchester from Anglo-Saxon times. His dying wish was that he would be buried in a common graveyard, where 'the rain will fall on me and the feet of ordinary men pass over my head'. And so it was for nine years until the local monks decided that such a lowly grave was inappropriate for a pious man and moved his earthly remains to an ornate shrine in Winchester Cathedral on 15 July 971. As the ceremony took place, a massive storm is said to have broken above the city and it didn't stop raining for – you guessed it – 40 days.

Although as the Met Office has proved, 40 days of consistent weather is unlikely, the general conditions of late June and early July do usually determine the general outlook for the rest of summer. If the weather at this time is coming from the north, you'll be looking at pleasant, dry conditions but if it's blowing in from the south, things will be much more unsettled. This is probably why our European neighbours have similar legends to our own St Swithin. For example, if you see rain in Germany on 7 July (Seven Sleepers Day), bad weather is predicted for the next month or two, while a storm over France on St Gervais' Day, 19 July, will be followed by 40 days of foul conditions.

How to avoid being struck by lightning

Deaths from lightning are fortunately rare in the UK – the chance of being struck is about one in three million. Around one in five of those unlucky souls are killed, so that's two people per 10 million each year – but, even so, it's not worth taking the risk. Lightning bolts can deliver around 300 kilowatts in a couple of milliseconds. They can travel for 60 miles, at speeds of around 14,000 mph, raising the temperature of the air around them to 30,000°C – that's five times hotter than the surface of the sun.

The best way of avoiding a strike is ensuring that you're not vulnerable in the first place. Here are some tips:

Keep count. If you can hear thunder then there's a chance you could be hit by lightning. Count the seconds between seeing a flash of lightning and hearing a clap of thunder. If it's less than 30 seconds then the risk of getting struck is high.

Park your vehicle. If you're driving, park somewhere safe, keep your windows tightly wound up and try not to touch the steering wheel, gear stick, pedals or doors. If the car is hit by lightning any of these may act as a conductor.

Turn off your mobile. The metal in the phone can conduct electricity. If you're indoors, avoid using the phone and remove headsets, unless it's an emergency. In bad storms it's also worth unplugging electrical appliances too.

Put down your umbrella. This might sound crazy in the middle of a thunderstorm, but it's better to get soaked than be hit by lightning. The metal in the umbrella could easily act as a conductor. The same applies to fishing rods and golf clubs.

Get out of the open. You don't want to be standing in an open, exposed space in the middle of a thunderstorm. Get to shelter, ideally a building, car or bus but avoid making for telephone boxes or porches, as well as tall objects such as isolated trees, electricity pylons, fences, sub-stations, mobile-phone masts or telegraph poles. A clump of shrubs cut at the same height is your best bet, a ditch even better. The idea is to get as low as possible.

Split up. If you're with a group of people, make sure there's a distance of at least 5 metres between you. Lightning can be attracted by a large group and passed between you.

Stay out of water. If you're in a boat – or even worse, swimming – get to the shore as soon as possible: water is one of the best conductors of electricity. If you're at home it's best to avoid taking a bath, doing the washing or the washing up in a thunderstorm. If lightning strikes your house, it may travel down the metal pipes to the water.

Take the brace position. Crouch down on the floor, keeping your feet together and your head between your knees. If your skin tingles or your hair stands on end, it's likely that lightning is about to strike very close.

Make sure the danger has passed. If you have to move on, or go out, make sure you leave 30 minutes after the last rumble of thunder before continuing on your way. The BBC Weather Centre tells me that over 50 per cent of deaths relating to lightning happen AFTER the thunderstorm has passed.

What to do if someone is struck by lightning

1. Call for help.

2. Check for a pulse and see if the person is breathing. It will be safe to touch them as the human body retains no electric charge after being struck by lightning.

3. If necessary and you know some first aid, begin CPR (and artificial respiration).

4. Check for burns and apply first aid if neccessary. There will likely be two burn-injury areas, where the bolt first entered their body and where it left them, more than likely the soles of their feet.

5. Try not to move the person if at all possible. They may have suffered broken bones. Loss of hearing or sight is also a common outcome.

Other tricks of the meteorological trade

Here are some other signs to watch out for:

> If there are bees in flight, you're usually in for good weather. Like most insects they don't like the wet, and aren't able to fly in strong winds so they usually head back to their hives or nests if conditions are worsening.

> Remember the old adage 'Red sky at night, shepherd's delight. Red sky in the morning, shepherd's warning'? There's some truth in it. If the sky is red at dawn it means there is high humidity in the higher atmosphere, indicating that rain is on its way. However, if it's the slightest bit pink in the evening, rain isn't likely for the next day or two.

> If you wake up to a rainbow then you're more than likely in for rain. Again this is a sign of humidity in the atmosphere. If you see one in the evening though, you're OK – the humidity won't be strong enough to bring on rain.

> Another early-morning sign of poor weather to come is a lack of dew on the grass. If your lawn is slick with dew you're usually in for a dry day.

> Keep an ear out for birds. If you can't hear much in the way of birdsong, like the bees they've taken shelter and a storm is probably brewing. Also, if you see seagulls landing on a beach, bad weather is on the way. Gulls would much rather land on water, but hate choppy seas. There's another old saying that matches this observation – 'Seabirds, stay out from the land, we won't have good weather while you're on the sand.'

> If daisies start to close their petals, then the humidity in the atmosphere is rising and it may soon start to rain.

> Similarly, pinecones close up when conditions are humid and open in dry weather.

> Have you ever heard someone comment that it 'smells like rain'? What they're actually picking up is the fact that all plants start emitting stronger fragrances as the humidity rises. It's more fragrant

in spring or summer when there's a higher concentration of flowers and musty in autumn thanks to old grass and fallen leaves.

> A circle around the moon at night is a sign that there's more moisture in the air, meaning you might have rain overnight or the next day.

British birds of prey

Do you know what makes one species a bird of prey as opposed to another? After all, seagulls eat fish but aren't classed as a bird of prey. The answer lies in the other name for a bird of prey – raptor. This comes from the Latin word *repere*, meaning to seize. And in the case of birds of prey, they seize their food with their feet rather than their beak (which, in the case of most raptors, are pretty ferocious too).

British birds of prey are made up of three main families:

Pandionidae

> Osprey (*Pandion haliaetus*)

Accipitridae

> Common buzzard (*Buteo buteo*)

> Rough-legged buzzard (*B. lagopus*)

> Honey buzzard (*Pernis apivorus*)

> Golden eagle (*Aquila chrysaetos*)

> White-tailed or sea eagle (*Haliaeetus albicilla*)

> Goshawk (*Accipiter gentilis*)

> Hen harrier (*Circus cyaneus*)

> Marsh harrier (*C. aeruginosus*)

> Montagu's harrier (*C. pygargus*)

> Red kite (*Milvus milvus*)

> Sparrowhawk (*Accipiter nisus*)

Falconidae

> Hobby (*Falco subbuteo*)

> Common kestrel (*F. tinnunculus*)

> Merlin (*F. columbarius*)

> Peregrine falcon (*F. peregrinus*)

There are also five main species of owls found in the UK (see pages 210–15).

The return of the red kite

Every time I drive along the M40 through the spectacular Chiltern Hills, I glance skyward for proof of a truly successful wildlife project – the sight of a red kite taking to the air.

Twenty years ago they were all but extinct in the UK, apart from a few in mid-Wales. For centuries, the red kite thrived as a scavenger, feeding on dead animals in rural areas and on food waste thrown into the streets of towns and cities. What went wrong? Well, our streets got a little cleaner without their help, landowners persecuted them, often wrongly accusing these mainly carrion eaters of wholesale attacks on their lambs and game birds, while taxidermists and egg collectors also took their toll. Britain's kites, once our most common bird of prey, disappeared from England in 1871 and from Scotland 30 years later.

Today, the skies over the Chilterns are full of these magnificent raptors with their distinctive forked tails. Numbers have risen from zero in 1990 to around 2,000 today. In fact, there's even the risk that the hills and valleys of south Buckinghamshire and Oxfordshire might become overcrowded with kites. Some have been taken from here to new areas to establish new colonies, so we now see red kites flying above Harewood in West Yorkshire, Rockingham in the East Midlands, Gateshead, Aberdeen, the Black Isle area of Ross and Cromarty, Stirling and Dumfries and Galloway along with those original survivors in mid-Wales.

Who could have predicted that when the RSPB and English Nature decided to import a few birds from Sweden and Spain in the early 1990s to see how well they would fare back in the UK?

I played a very minor role in their reintroduction myself. I flew to Madrid for *Countryfile* to collect one of them. My fellow passengers had quite a surprise when the box next to me issued a noise somewhere between a mew and a whistle.

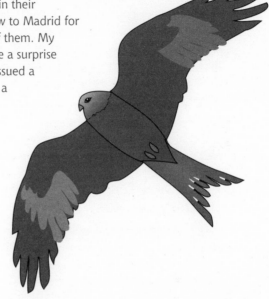

After a period of several weeks in quarantine, my kite, along with a number of others, was released in a clearing at Christmas Common, close to the M40 at Stokenchurch in Buckinghamshire. They made straight for the tops of the trees where they and their successors have remained ever since.

There is one drawback for people living in red-kite country. The birds are up to their old tricks, recorded among others by William Shakespeare – stealing ladies' underwear that is hanging out to dry. After a glorious return to our countryside, kites are once again nicking knickers to line their nests!

The plight of our birds of prey

They may be at the top of their own particular food chain, but our birds of prey are often victims of an even deadlier hunter – us. Every year, reports come in of raptors being illegally poisoned, trapped or shot, even though they have been protected by law since 1954 (other than the sparrowhawk, which was unprotected until 1961).

Between 2005 and 2009, there have been 121 recorded deaths by poisoning, including 83 buzzards, 23 red kites, six golden eagles, five peregrine falcons, two tawny owls and two sea eagles. Since the start of the millennium it's likely that, in round figures, 300 protected birds of prey have been poisoned and a further 100 shot, trapped or had their nests destroyed. The majority of cases occur in Scotland. And if one of those birds is a mother, it's the equivalent of killing her chicks as well. In species such as the peregrine, the male bird will attempt to continue feeding the young, but is often too small to deliver enough food.

In England the most threatened bird of prey is the hen harrier. The last figures, from 2008, show that a mere 17 pairs of hen harriers bred successfully even though there is enough available upland habitat to support around 300 pairs. Natural England claims that illegal killing and destruction of nests is the only possible explanation of the dangerously low numbers.

The perpetrators are said to be rogue elements of the game-bird industry and racing pigeon enthusiasts. That said, every gamekeeper, shooting enthusiast and pigeon fancier I've ever met condemns what's happening and denies having anything to do with it.

Unbelievably, there are still those who purposely go out to collect birds' eggs from the wild. This 'hobby' was pretty widespread until it was outlawed in 1954 by the Protection of Birds Act, which made it illegal to collect birds' eggs from wild nests. In 1981, the Wildlife and Countryside Act strengthened the law, so that egg collection became a crime. And in 2000 the Countryside and Rights of Way Act brought in custodial sentences for such offences.

If you're found with wild-bird eggs in your possession you could face fines of up to £5,000 and six months in prison *per egg*. While reported cases of egg collections are on the decline, there are still individuals willing to risk imprisonment just to add to their private collections and in so doing they pose yet another threat to the plight of our already endangered birds of prey.

The pros and cons of wind turbines

In April 2010, Great Britain reached an environmental milestone. Two new wind farms were opened out at sea in UK waters, meaning that for the first time we could generate 1 gigawatt (GW) of electricity from offshore wind turbines, enough to power 700,000 homes. I sailed out to one of them, off the Essex coast, and it was an impressive sight: over forty, each the size of the London Eye. And that's just the beginning – new turbines twice that size are being planned and one wind farm now on the drawing board could cover an area of the North Sea equal in size to North Yorkshire! As I write this, enough turbines to generate a further 4GW are in the process of being constructed with future plans to build enough to generate more than 40GW.

Wind is big business and is expected to be worth £75 billion by 2020, supporting over 70,000 jobs. There's a good reason for that optimism. Estimates show the UK has more than 33 per cent of the total European potential offshore wind-power resource, which, if it were harnessed, would power the entire country three times over.

But the big snag is that offshore wind farms are expensive. A gas-powered station costs £1 million per megawatt of stored capacity whereas wind farms cost the same as nuclear-power stations – a huge £3 million per megawatt. There are other downsides, too. The wind is variable and turbines only work when there is enough of it, unlike nuclear power, which can be generated 24/7. While many new offshore farms will be out of sight of land and out of earshot maintenance could be an issue; if something goes wrong during winter storms, it could be spring before engineers could get out to fix it.

It's no wonder, then, that alternative power companies so often look to our more accessible hills and fields to build their wind farms – and often that's where the battle begins. Over the past few years I've met plenty of people across the countryside furious that a wind turbine is being planned, or has already been constructed, on their doorsteps.

First, there is the issue of trucks carrying the parts to the site, putting stress on rural roads and then, when the turbine is up, the reality of living close to a huge, metallic windmill. Wherever they are erected they arouse fierce emotions. The remote village of Llanfynydd in South Wales went as far as to rename itself, albeit temporarily: Llanhyfryddawelllehynafolybarcudprindanfygythiadtrienusyrhafnauole means 'a quiet beautiful village, a historic place with rare kite under threat from wretched blades'.

Such opposition hasn't stopped Natural England hinting that we may soon see wind turbines built in our National Parks. Currently Britain has over 2,500 onshore wind turbines but plans to build a further 6,000 may mean the National Parks will have to play their part – a thought that has appalled campaigners.

So, as the battle lines are formed over that potential conflict, let's have a look at both sides of the argument.

Pros

> Britain is one of the windiest countries in Europe. What's more, the wind is free.

> The wind farms themselves produce pollution-free energy as no fossil fuels are burnt to generate the power.

> Wind farms don't need as much space as conventional power stations meaning that valuable agricultural land can be kept in production.

> The UK is largely reliant on foreign sources for fossil fuels and subject to volatile prices. More homegrown energy would mean more independence.

> While they are currently expensive, government estimates indicate that the nation's wind power will be cheaper than nuclear power by 2020. Supporters already insist that wind farms pay for themselves within 3 months of installation.

> Turbines will create jobs in currently depopulated areas.

> Locally owned wind farms can produce a valuable source of income for communities and farmers.

Cons

▶ Wind may be free, but it can also stop blowing and if that happens you're left with a turbine that's just standing idle.

▶ While the power generated is green, there will have been greenhouse gases emitted in the construction of the turbines themselves.

▶ Turbines are seen as unsightly eyesores. The problem is that to maximise airflow they often have to be erected high on hills meaning they can be seen for miles around, drastically changing the look of the landscape.

▶ Campaigners against wind farms complain that living under the shadow of the turbine can knock thousands off the value of their houses.

▶ Wind turbines are noisy and can generate a constant low-frequency hum that many find annoying at best and unbearable at worst.

▶ While the footprint of a turbine is relatively small, large foundations have to be dug and filled with concrete to support the structures. In most cases this can lead to trees being cut down and, some conservationist fear, a loss of vital habitat. Are they as green as we first thought?

▶ If placed in the wrong place wind farms can be a danger to bird life. This seems to be especially true when it comes to seabirds and birds of prey. There have been several reports of sea eagles being killed by blades in Norway and conservationists fear the same thing may happen here. However, the RSPB has spoken out in favour of wind turbines as long as they are sited appropriately, where birds are not endangered. In fact, the charity has gone so far as to say that wasting our potential for onshore wind farms would be 'disastrous'.

▶ There have been cases where sudden drops in air pressure around wind turbines have caused bats' lungs to overexpand leading to burst blood vessels and death.

CHAPTER FOUR

The Lowlands

The Right to Roam

Today, we have an unprecedented amount of access to our countryside. It seems so natural now, so much a part of country life, that some young people, out exploring the countryside for the first time, could be forgiven for thinking that it's always been the case. But the Right to Roam is a fairly recent development.

It was prompted by the decision in 1981 to sell off stretches of woodland that had been managed by the Forestry Commission, the government department responsible for the public forests and woodlands in Britain. Organisations such as the Ramblers became concerned. These entirely legal sales were being carried out without any mention being made of allowing public access. Places where people had enjoyed walking for years could, potentially, suddenly be closed off.

Four years later, the Ramblers launched the Forbidden Britain campaign, which set out to highlight the fact that there was no statutory right to walk across open countryside. Lobbying groups swung into action and mass trespasses the size of those witnessed back in the 1930s (see page 108) increased in frequency. Campaigners were steadfast and sure they would win – after all, it was pressure like this that helped create the National Parks several decades before.

In the 1997 General Election Labour's manifesto included the first commitment to open countryside from a major party and two years after they came to power work began to make good that promise. Many landowners were understandably concerned. Would open access to certain areas lead to confusion and clashes? And how would the proposals be policed?

On Monday, 31 October 2005, to the delight of walkers and ramblers everywhere, Westminster finally gave you and me the legal right to explore the uplands of England and Wales in the Countryside and Rights of Way Act 2000 (commonly known as the CRoW Act). Suddenly landscapes, both dramatic and tranquil, that were previously off-limits were open to all, from sweeping moorland, heath, downs and registered common land to majestic mountains and hillsides.

Colloquially, this breakthrough has become known as the Right to Roam, although that can be a bit misleading. It doesn't mean that you can just wander where you like. Only areas designated as 'open countryside' by the Act are legally accessible, meaning that you can't just walk on to private land claiming your right to be there. But there's a lot more open countryside than ever before: over 800,000 hectares (2 million acres) of land are now designated as Open Access, meaning that you can get off the beaten track and ramble, explore, climb and run where you please within the boundaries, which are marked on Ordnance Survey maps and waymarks with a special Open Access symbol. A waymark with a red line striking through the centre of the Open Access symbol tells you that you've wandered too far and you no longer have the legal right to pass that point.

In reality, landowners tell me, many walkers still keep roughly to the paths – maybe just straying off them for a few yards to appreciate a special view. After all, tramping across upland where the uneven ground is hidden under thick heather can be hard work!

You can find out about Open Access land by going to the Countryside Code web page (www.naturalengland.org.uk)

As you'd expect, there are some restrictions of what you can do on Open Access land. The following activities are prohibited by the CRoW Act:

❯ Driving or riding any vehicle across Open Access land

❯ Using a vessel or sailboard on any non-tidal water

❯ Bathing in any non-tidal water

❯ Walking with any animal other than a dog. Dogs must also be kept on a lead during lambing and the ground-bird nesting season (1 March–31 July) or at any time of year near livestock

❯ Lighting or tending a fire

❯ Intentionally killing or disturbing any wildlife

❯ Intentionally damaging or destroying any eggs, nests or plants

❯ Feeding livestock

❯ Hunting, shooting or fishing

❯ Using a metal detector

❯ Obstructing the flow of any drain or watercourse

❯ Neglecting to shut any gate, except where it is intended to be left open

❯ Engaging in any organised games, or in wild camping (see pages 125–6), hang gliding or paragliding

❯ Engaging in any activity for commercial purposes

These are general rules and in some cases the landowner may overrule them, allowing any or all of these activities on their land. Likewise, they also have the right to withdraw permission to allow any of these things without any notice at all. It's always wise before heading out to explore Open Access land to check what local restrictions apply. You may also find that some Open Access lands are closed at certain times of the year. The CRoW Act allows landowners and tenants to restrict access for any reason for up to 28 days a year, although the government advises that closures over weekends and during public holidays should be kept to the bare minimum.

Open Access in Scotland and Northern Ireland

Things are slightly different outside of England and Wales. The Land Reform (Scotland) Act 2003 and the Scottish Outdoor Access Code 2004 give right of access over most land and inland water throughout the country, provided that you act responsibly. This means that you can walk, cycle, ride horses and wild camp pretty much wherever you are in Scotland, although, as in England and Wales, this doesn't extend to private gardens or agricultural land. In Northern Ireland the situation is less good for walkers: at the time of writing there are no legal rights of access and no plans to introduce them.

Know the Country Code

With the foundation of the National Parks in the 1950s it soon became clear that there would have to be some way of informing inexperienced urban visitors about the ways of country life. The result was the Country Code, aimed well and truly at the visitor, with no mention of the responsibilities of the landowners. 'We regard the Country Code as a core around which will grow a body of information about the countryside,' declared the National Parks Commission in September 1951. 'As knowledge spreads, there should be much less of the damage often done by sheer thoughtlessness in well-intentioned people. By all these means we hope there will be a deepening respect and friendliness between countryman and townsman.'

The Code remained largely untouched, with the odd tweak here and there along the way, until the Countryside and Rights of Way Act 2000 introduced the Right to Roam. The new law required a long-overdue update of the Code and, in consultation with the National Trust, National Farmers' Union, the RSPB and the Ramblers, the Countryside Agency unveiled a new Countryside Code in July 2004. At its heart was the central theme that 'showing respect for other people makes the countryside a pleasant environment for everyone – at home, at work and at leisure' and for the first time, the Countryside Code wasn't just aimed at the public. Landowners were targeted as well, with some key advice for them.

The Countryside Code – advice for the public

As with the original code, the advice is all pretty much common sense, though it's worth reading the detail:

Be safe: plan ahead and follow the signs

▶ Before heading out into the country, make sure you've checked the latest up-to-date maps or guidebooks. Check too whether the land you're preparing to explore is Open Access (see page 145).

▶ Make sure that you've got the right equipment for exploring the countryside. In most cases, especially when you're heading into remote or hilly areas, your essentials should include: a waterproof jacket and preferably waterproof trousers, good walking boots or shoes with solid treads and firm ankle support, good-quality socks to protect your feet from painful blisters, a spare fleece or jumper (remember that wearing several light layers keeps you warmer than one heavy one) and a waterproof rucksack, containing at least a litre of water and enough food for the duration of your walk.

▶ Make sure you let someone know where you're going. Part of the joy of escaping to the countryside is to turn off that mobile phone and leave the world behind you. However, you may not see anyone for hours and if you do turn your phone on again, the chances are you'll struggle to find a signal. If, heaven forbid, something goes wrong, will anyone know where you're likely to be?

▶ Check the weather conditions before you leave and prepare for all eventualities. You'd be amazed how quickly the weather can turn on you in open countryside – as we've found out time and time again when filming *Countryfile*.

▶ Learn the signs you'll see in the countryside and make sure you know how to read a map (see pages 151–3).

Leave gates and property as you find them

▶ Often as you walk through the countryside you are walking through someone's place of work and your actions can affect their very livelihood. You need to respect landowners who have given you access to their land.

▶ Usually a farm gate will be closed to secure livestock, but there are cases when they're left open so that the animals can reach food and water. Make sure that you leave any gate as you find it or follow any instructions you find on signs.

▶ If you walk through crops, follow a path whenever possible or stick to the edges.

▶ Make sure you use gates, stiles or gaps where provided. Don't just clamber over walls, crash through hedges or try to vault fences. You could easily damage them, increasing the likelihood of a farmer facing the headache of escaped animals.

▶ Never disturb historic or ruined sites. Remember that our heritage belongs to every one of us, not to individuals.

▶ Never touch farm machinery.

Protect plants and animals, and take your litter home

▶ Does the point about litter even need explaining? Unfortunately, in many cases it seems it does. Dropping litter is not only selfish – why should anyone have to look at the rubbish left by someone else? It can be a danger to wildlife and can spread disease. Take it with you and, whatever you do, don't bury it. And if you see someone else has been irresponsible and dropped litter, why not pick it up and take it with you, thereby helping clear the countryside and giving yourself a pat on the back to boot.

▶ Make sure that you never pollute any waterway you come across.

▶ Don't start a fire and watch where you're dropping cigarette butts. If for any reason you feel the need to boil water for coffee on the go, then invest in a portable stove, but once again take care when dealing with naked flames in the countryside.

▶ Never pick wild flowers or plants. For a start, it's illegal without the permission of the landowner and, secondly, other people deserve to enjoy their beauty as much as you.

Keep dogs under close control

▶ Legally, you must control any dog you're walking with so that it doesn't disturb or scare farm animals. If you're on a public path, this doesn't necessarily mean putting it on a lead but you have to be sure that you can control it. On most areas of open country and common land, dogs must be kept on a short lead between 1 March and 31 July when ground-nesting birds have eggs and young and all year round if you're near farm animals. Remember, farmers have the legal right to destroy a dog that either worries or injures their livestock, so it's not worth taking any risk. For more about walking with dogs around livestock see pages 89–90.

▶ Remember to clean up after your dog and ensure it's regularly wormed to protect it as well as other people and animals.

▶ At certain times, dogs may not be allowed at all on some areas of Open Access land. Such restrictions will usually be marked on signs.

Consider other people

▶ Stick to speed limits when driving in the countryside and always slow down for horses, walkers and livestock, giving them as much space as possible.

▶ If you come across farm animals that are being moved or gathered, keep out of the way and follow any instructions given by the farmer.

▶ Respect the fact that this could be someone's home. Never block gateways or driveways with your vehicle.

▶ If you're riding a bike along a bridleway, remember that by law you need to give way to walkers or horse riders.

The Countryside Code – advice for land managers

Know your rights, responsibilities and liabilities

▶ Landowners are asked to keep rights of way clear and not obstruct people's entry on to Open Access land. It is against the law to discourage the right of way over public access land by means of misleading signs. Members of the public are encouraged to report any suspect signs to the local authority.

❯ While the Ordnance Survey's 1:25,000 Explorer maps show public rights of way and Open Access land, there are cases when the data might be out of date or in rare cases incorrect. It is the landowner's responsibility to check the legal status of any rights of way on their land.

Make it easy for visitors to act responsibly

❯ Landowners are encouraged to give clear, polite guidance whenever needed and to get rid of any agricultural waste properly, so that visitors don't think dumping their litter in the countryside is the norm.

❯ Landowners are responsible for the upkeep of public-access paths, signs, gates and stiles on their property.

Identify possible threats to visitors' safety

❯ Landowners are asked to consider whether there is anything on their property, man-made or natural, that may be hazardous to the general public. If so, they are asked to draw the risk to the public's attention as clearly as possible.

❯ It's advised that landowners avoid using electric fencing alongside public access while barbed wire can be especially dangerous for children. Plain wire is usually recommended.

❯ Landowners are asked not to allow animals that are likely to attack to roam freely where the public has access. The landowner may find himself or herself liable for any harm they cause.

Understanding signposts and waymarks

To help navigate where you can walk or ride, highway authorities are required to erect signposts whenever a footpath, bridlepath or byway leaves a 'metalled road' (usually one that has been covered in tarmac). The only reason this wouldn't happen is if a parish council decided that such a sign isn't necessary, although such cases are rare. Each is identified by a coloured arrow for ease of navigation and you may see the arrows, usually in the same colour coding, fixed to posts, stiles and even trees, along the course of the route. The coloured arrows designate different types of use.

Yellow arrow waymark = a footpath

This is a path that is only used for walking. Usually these are neither surfaced nor lit and are nothing more than just tracks.

Legally you are allowed to take a 'natural accompaniment' such as a pushchair or pram, while wheelchairs, both manual and powered, are fine as long as you're following the usual regulations. However, many footpaths aren't suitable for any wheeled vehicle, whatever the size.

Be aware that not all footpaths are public rights of way. Some, known as permissive routes, are only open to the public because the landowner has given specific permission and they can be withdrawn from public use at any time. Sometimes you'll find that permissive routes are closed for just one day of the year, so that landowners can protect themselves from claims that the path is actually a right of way. The law assumes that if a path remains open to the public without a break for 20 years it automatically becomes a public right of way – but it doesn't work the other way: if no-one has used the path in 20 years, it doesn't suddenly become private. In legal circles the saying is: 'once a highway, always a highway'.

Blue arrow waymark = a bridleway

A bridleway is a path open to walkers, cyclists and horse riders. There are a couple of other rules to bear in mind. The first is, if you're on a bike, you're required to give way to both walkers and horse riders, and second, horse-drawn carriages or motorcycles aren't allowed.

It's worth bearing in mind that bridleways aren't always surfaced, so if lots of horses pass that way, pedestrians may find them difficult to walk along – in more ways than one!

Red arrow and Plum arrow waymarks = byways

Red arrow byways are open to all traffic, including walkers, cyclists, horse riders, horse-drawn carriages and motorised vehicles. Plum arrow byways are Restricted Byways and cannot be used by motorised traffic. Both types of byway may be unsurfaced so can quickly become muddy.

🔔 = National Trail

The fourth symbol you might see on a signpost is a lone acorn, the official symbol of the National Trails. There are 15 long-distance walking routes in England and Wales, totalling around 2,500 miles. Each trail is watched over by a National Trail Officer who ensures it is kept to agreed standards. Much of the actual maintenance work is undertaken by the local highway authority along with landowners and an army of volunteers.

The father of the National Trails was journalist Tom Stephenson who, in 1935, wrote an article for the *Daily Herald* entitled 'Wanted: A Long Green Trail'. Stephenson had been inspired by the 2,175 mile Appalachian Way in the United States and started to campaign for a British equivalent. His route – which he named the Jubilee Way in honour of the King of the time, George V – would stretch from the Peak District to the Cheviots, on the Scottish border. 'Whatever the cost, it would be a worthy and enduring testimony', Stephenson wrote, 'bringing health and pleasure beyond computation, for none could walk that Pennine Way without being improved in mind and body, inspired and invigorated and filled with the desire to explore every corner of this lovely island.' It would take over thirty years for Stephenson's dream to become a reality but in 1965 the Pennine Way was officially opened. I remember the late Barbara Castle telling me how, as a young politician, she had campaigned for it and was one of the first walkers to tread its path. Now, 12 million people use the National Trails network every year.

The National Trails of England and Wales

Trail	Length (miles)	Location
Cleveland Way	110	North Yorkshire
Cotswold Way	102	South West England
Glyndwr's Way	135	Mid Wales
Hadrian's Wall	84	Northern England
North Downs Way	153	South East England
Offa's Dyke Path	177	England/Wales border
Peddars Way/ North Norfolk Coast Path	93	Eastern England
Pembrokeshire Coast Path	186	South West Wales
Pennine Bridleway	130	Northern England
Pennine Way	268	Peak District to Scottish Borders
The Ridgeway	87	Central England
South Downs Way	100	Southern England
South West Coast Path	630	South West England
Thames Path	184	Southern England
Yorkshire Wolds Way	79	North and East Yorkshire

The Long Distance Routes of Scotland

Scotland's equivalent of the National Trails are the Long Distance Routes:

Great Glen Way	73	North Highlands
Southern Upland Way	212	South Scotland
Speyside Way	63	North East Scotland
West Highland Way	95	West Highlands

Ave number of days to complete on foot	Start	End
9	Helmsley, North Yorkshire	Filey Brigg, North Yorkshire
7	Bath, Somerset	Chipping Campden, Gloucestershire
9	Knighton, Powys	Welshpool, Powys
7	Wallsend, Tyne and Wear	Bowness-on-Solway, Cumbria
14	Farnham, Surrey	Dover, Kent
12	Sedbury Cliff, Gloucestershire	Prestatyn, Denbighshire
8	Knettishall Heath Country Park, Suffolk	Cromer, Norfolk
15	St Dogmaels, Pembrokeshire	Amroth Castle, Pembrokeshire
8	Middleton-by-Wirkworth, Derbyshire	The trail loops in the south Pennines
16	Edale, Derbyshire	Kirk Yetholm, Scottish Borders
6	Overton Hill, Wiltshire	Ivinghoe Beacon, Buckinghamshire
8	Winchester, Hampshire	Eastbourne, East Sussex
56	Minehead, Somerset	Poole Harbour, Dorset
14	The source of the Thames, 2 miles north of Kemble, Gloucestershire	Thames Barrier, London
5	Hessle, East Yorkshire	Filey Brigg, North Yorkshire
6	Glasgow, Central Scotland	Fort William, Highlands
20	Portpatrick, Dumfries and Galloway	Cockburnspath, Scottish Borders
5	Buckie, Moray	Aviemore, Highlands
7	Fort William, Highlands	Inverness, Highlands

How to navigate naturally

Over the last couple of years, more and more people have been packing away the compass, shutting off the GPS and learning to navigate the way our ancestors did, by observing the natural world around us. This hobby, which has grown in popularity in the UK, is mainly thanks to explorer Tristan Gooley, the only living person to have both flown and sailed solo across the Atlantic, and who has set up Britain's first natural-navigation school.

Getting it right takes time and practice, and novices should never venture out without some kind of man-made backup. But next time you're out in the countryside, try these experiments to start your own journey towards becoming a natural navigator.

1. Look to the sun

The stars have helped man navigate for millennia so why not start with our own? The sun is the best way of working out the direction you're facing. First of all, as every schoolboy knows, it rises in the east and sets in the west. So if you're walking in the morning, get into the sunshine and stand a stick on its end pointing upwards. The shadow it casts will be to the west. Likewise if you do this in the afternoon the shadow it casts will point to the east. If the sun is right overhead at midday then the shadow will be at its shortest and directly in front of the stick, pointing north, as in the UK the sun is always slightly due south at midday. So, not only can the sun tell you where the points of the compass are, you can also roughly work out what time of day it is with a simple stick.

Of course this is only estimation and the angle of the sun changes throughout the year. In the middle of winter, for instance, it rises in the southeast, and that position changes to pure east in spring and autumn and northeast in midsummer.

2. Look to the trees

Schoolboy-lesson number two. Trees need sunlight to grow. So, armed with that knowledge, look for an isolated tree growing on its own. With a little training you'll be able to spot which side of the tree gets the most sunlight, because the foliage is thicker on that side. As the sun is largely in the south in the sky over the UK, the bushier side of the tree will generally be facing south. It's also likely that the stem of the tree will bend slightly – in some cases dramatically – to the source of light, which for us is the south. You'll notice that the branches on the side exposed to more light stretch out towards it, while on the dark side they'll grow in a more vertical direction.

The wind can also have an effect on trees. While breezes blow branches in random directions, the prevailing wind will have a longer lasting effect, and so an exposed tree is shaped against the direction of the wind. You need to know the direction of the prevailing wind, but in the UK that's not a problem – it's the southwest. This means that exposed trees will often seem to lean slightly, as if their extremities have been combed over, from southwest to northwest. In other words if you're facing a tree that is leaning towards the right, the left will be southwest.

3. Beware the moss

By this time you'll probably be remembering that old country saying 'moss grows on the north side of trees and buildings'. A valuable tool for the natural navigator? Sadly not. It's true that moss does grow on the north side of trees and buildings. Unfortunately, it also grows on the south side. In fact, it isn't fussy at all – as long as it's getting moisture it'll grow anywhere it can. It could be that the one side is rougher, which means it will retain water or that it's nearer to the ground, which also retains moisture, providing a great environment for moss.

So unless the moss is on a surface that is really, really smooth and considerably above ground level, the chances are that it could be pointing in any direction, but if those conditions are met, you may well be looking at something pointing north. There must be easier ways of working out what's due north?

4. Lick that finger

This one only works if you know which direction the wind is blowing from at that precise time. If you know, for example that the wind is blowing from the west, lick your finger and hold it up – the side that turns cold will be the west. It's an oldie but a goldie if you want quickly to orientate yourself.

5. Clear as muddy puddles

One thing the countryside has plenty of is mud and often pathways are broken up by muddy puddles, which, when you become more adept at the art of natural navigation can also tell you a story. Look at the path you're walking. Is one side drier than the other? Then the chances are that the wetter side hasn't felt the warming rays of the sun yet. Depending on the time of day and the position of the sun in the sky, you may be able to work out the direction you're travelling. Time to get that stick out again. Oh, and try to remember the good old prevailing wind too. The southwesterly wind often blows litter and leaves to the northwesterly point of the puddle.

6. Look at buildings too

All right, this doesn't seem particularly natural but if you pass a church it's worth keeping in mind that most British churches were built with the altar at the east end. Work out where the altar is and that's likely to be east. Here's another tip, although not as foolproof: many early graves were also aligned to face east so when 'the trumpet shall sound and the dead shall rise' (1 Corinthians, 15:52) the bodies were facing in the right direction!

There are a couple more good ways of determining east if you find yourself in a rural town, or even village, that has some kind of industrial heritage, such as a factory. As the prevailing wind is from the southwest the poorer and less desirable places to live were often downwind of the chimneys. Of course these days you can also keep an eye out for satellite dishes. In the UK they mostly point in a south-southwesterly direction to the position of the satellite that delivers digital TV to millions of British living rooms.

Did you know . . . ?

Only six of Britain's 2,500 species of moths eat clothes. The most voracious is the common clothes moth (*Tineola bisselliella*) although it's not actually the moths that leave those tale-tell holes – it's the larvae that are to blame. Usually, they'll be happy munching through bird nests but can sustain themselves on natural fibres such as wool. If the clothes are particularly dirty or sweaty all the better. The problem has lessened with the growth of man-made fibres although if you've expensive cashmere in your wardrobe, watch out!

How to tell the difference between a moth and a butterfly

There are 56 species of butterfly in the UK and around 2,500 species of moth. Apart from their beauty, these creatures are important key indicator species. If their numbers start to fall, it's a sign that the environment is taking a nosedive. Unfortunately, it seems that in the UK, as all around the world, that's exactly what's happening.

Britain's five rarest butterflies

Species	Scientific name	Decline
Duke of Burgundy	*Hamearis lucina*	45% over 31-year period
Pearl-bordered fritillary	*Boloria euphrosyne*	74% over 34-year period
High brown fritillary	*Argynnis adippe*	40% over 32-year period
Wood white	*Leptidea sinapis*	90% over 33-year period
Lulworth skipper	*Thymelicus acteon*	78% over 18-year period

Duke of Burgundy butterfly

It's hard to imagine a summer's day in the British countryside without butterflies but how can you be sure you're seeing the right thing? Here are six steps to differentiating between a butterfly and a moth.

Step 1 What's the time?

If you've spotted an insect with colourful wings during the day it's more than likely a butterfly. Moths are nocturnal and can be spotted flapping around lights at night. It's not that easy though. Some species of moths do come out in the day, such as the Mother Shipton (*Callistege mi*), chimney sweeper (*Odezia atrata*) and speckled yellow (*Pseudopanthera macularia*).

Step 2 Look at the antenna

Are the antenna long and skinny? Do they end with rounded clubs? Then it's a butterfly. If the antenna don't have the clubs at the end and look feathered, then it's a moth.

Step 3 See how it's resting

If the insect lands nearby does it rest with its wings closed together or opened wide? If they are held together, it's a butterfly, whereas moths tend to spread their wings out.

Speckled yellow moth

Step 4 Check out its wings

Both moths and butterflies have four wings – two forewings and two hindwings. Although this tip isn't 100 per cent foolproof, a butterfly's wings are largely more colourful than a moth's, which tend to be duller. There are some exceptions to the rule though. The cinnabar moth (*Tyria jacobaeae*), for example, has bright red wings.

If you look very closely you'll also be able to make out that a moth's forewings and hindwings are joined together with a hook, whereas in butterflies the two sets of wings aren't connected.

Step 5 Examine its body

The body of a moth is usually plump and fuzzy whereas a butterfly's is smoother and more skinny.

Step 6 Has it come from a cocoon or a chrysalis?

This is often a long shot, but sometimes you're lucky enough to find the insect's cocoon. Moths have cocoons, which they spin around themselves using silk, leading to a softer – and sometimes dirtier – surface. The butterfly's chrysalis is made of hardened protein and appears shiny and almost metallic.

Wild food

Foraging for wild food is becoming increasingly popular. After all, it's largely free. While countryfolk have been doing it for years, there is some concern that the growing numbers of people heading out to harvest hedgerows or scour forests for a free feast are taking food desperately needed by wildlife. But, if you're responsible – and follow some basic safety tips – foraging for food is a fun way to while away a few hours and come home with a tasty treat.

The man credited with introducing the concept of foraging to the wider public is the eminent naturalist and writer Richard Mabey, in his 1972 book *Food for Free*. Years later, he showed me just where to look, what to pick and (perhaps more importantly) what to leave alone. These tutored trips became a series of films for *Countryfile*, which were some of the most enjoyable, in every sense of the word, that I have ever made. To this day, I can't resist nibbling a few leaves of wild garlic whenever I spot it.

Dos and don'ts when foraging

Don't think that because one part of a plant is good to eat every other bit is too. For example, in spring the flowers of the elder (*Sambucus nigra*) can be used to make delicious cordial and, later in the year, the berries make wonderful wine or jam. However, while boiling up the elderberries gets rid of the natural toxins present in the raw berries, the leaves, roots or bark of the elder should never be eaten, cooked or otherwise.

Do always take an illustrated guide to flora so you know exactly what you're eating or, even better, take along someone who knows what they're doing. Check the leaf, berry colour and shape, flower and season to make sure that you identify the plant correctly. You can also check in books on poisonous plants before anything reaches the cooking pot.

This is obviously just as important when you're picking mushrooms (see pages 228–9).

Don't eat something if you're not 100 per cent sure what it is.

Do wash your foraged food well, whether you've collected it at home or while out and about it.

Don't eat any fruit that looks bruised or mouldy. Also avoid any plants that look as if they are dying. If they're yellowed or discoloured it could just be that the surrounding soil isn't that nutritious, but it may be that weed killers have been sprayed on them.

Do try to choose leaves and berries as near as possible to the middle of a clump of plants or well off the ground level as foxes and dogs often use the edges of bushes for ... well, I'm sure you get the idea!

Don't eat anything you find on busy roadside verges, on industrial sites or where you can clearly see that the ground has been covered by ash or oil.

Do just forage the foliage, flowers, berries and seeds. Remember it's illegal to uproot wild plants without permission.

Don't let children harvest or eat wild food on their own and make sure you know what they've picked before you let them pop it in their mouth.

Don't pick more than you need. It's all too easy when you go foraging to get carried away and cram your containers with as much free food as possible. First, you'll be hard pushed to find enough recipes to use up all your haul while it's fresh; second, and more importantly, you could be denying other foragers and wild animals the pleasure of finding food on their travels.

Do stay within the law. Usually, if you pick fruit from hedgerows on a public right of way you'll be OK, but don't be tempted to trespass on someone's land to bag a tasty morsel.

Ten common plants that make for a good hedgerow harvest

Once you've got the rules under your belt, here are some things to look for:

Acorn
(*Quercus robur and Q. petraea*)

Best in: October–November

What does it look like? (Hands up those who don't know that!) The nut of the oak tree is greeny brown in a scaly cup (for more tips on identifying oaks see page 192).

Where? Woodlands and forests

Uses? Once soaked in water and dried, you can grind the nut down to make an alternative to coffee or flour. Acorns can also be pickled.

Blackberry
(*Rubus fruticosus*)

Best in: August–September

What does it look like? Most of us have picked wild blackberries at some point in our lives. The brambles have short, sharp thorns and white or pink flowers in spring. The berries themselves are made up of subdivisions or 'druplets'.

Where? Hedgerows, along pathways and lanes.

Uses? Where do you start? Crumbles, cakes, jams, jellies, steamed puddings and gin.

Burdock
(*Arctium lappa and A. minor*)

Best in: March–April

What does it look like? There are two varieties of burdock, one with large kidney-shaped leaves (*A. lappa*) and the other with smaller triangular-shaped leaves (*A. minor*). You often find the spiky-haired fruits caught in your clothes or your dog's coat after a good walk.

Where? Woodland and hedgerows.

Uses? The roots can be cut to matchstick size and stir-fried as an alternative to shoots.

Dandelion
(*Taraxacum officinale*)

Best in: April–May

What does it look like? Do you really have to ask? One of Britain's most recognisable flowers with bright yellow flowers that turn into balls of fairy-like seeds at the end of their life.

Where? Lawns and meadows.

Uses? Young, raw leaves can be used in salads. They taste a bit like chicory and, of course, with burdock form the basis of a sweet, old-fashioned fizzy drink.

Garlic mustard or Jack-by-the-hedge
(*Alliaria petiolata*)

Best in: April–May

What does it look like?
Green kidney-shaped leaves and white flowers with four petals.

Where? Hedgerows and riverbanks at the foot of trees.

Uses? Young leaves can be used raw in salad for a mild, garlic-like kick while slightly older leaves can be cooked for flavouring. Be warned though, the older the leaves the more bitter they become.

Nipplewort
(*Lapsana communis*)

Best in: June–July

What does it look like?
Stiff stems, triangular leaves and yellow flowers with clusters of around ten petals.

Where? Hedgerows and along country lanes.

Uses? Raw leaves can be used in salad as an alternative to lettuce.

Rosehips
(*Rosa* spp.)

Best in: September–October

What does it look like? It depends of the variety. The fruit of the dog rose (*Rosa canina*) is oval and has no sepals (the part of the flower that protects a flower when it's in bud). Others, such as the field rose (*R. arvensis*), are rounder.

Where? Hedgerows and bushes.

Uses? Deseeded the red flesh of the rosehip can be used to make jam, jelly, syrup and wine. Never eat a whole rosehip though.

Sloe
(*Prunus spinosa*)

Best in: September–October

What does it look like? A sloe is dark purple with a slightly dusty look to the skin, rather like a small damson. The blackthorn bush itself is a dense, prickly shrub with dark, almost black bark and white flowers.

Where? Hedgerows, woods and forests.

Uses? The flesh of the fruit is used to flavour gin (sloe gin from a hip flask is my favourite winter warmer) and to make a jelly to accompany roast duck or lamb.

Sweet chestnuts
(*Castanea sativa*)

Best in: October (before the squirrels get them!)

What does it look like?
The fruit of the sweet chestnut tree (see page 195). Three brown nuts can be found within every spiky fruit. Don't mix it up with the inedible conker of the horse chestnut.

Where? Woodlands.

Uses? Follow the old song and roast them on an open fire (or in your oven if that's easier). Some folk also make a chestnut purée to use as an alternative to butter.

Wild strawberry
(*Fragaria vesca*)

Best in: June–July

What does it look like?
A creeping plant, pretty much similar to the cultivated variety you can get for your garden, with red fruit that are a good deal smaller than the ones you buy in the shops.

Where? Woodland, grassland and hedgerows.

Uses? Exactly like cultivated strawberries – lovely with cream and sugar!

Six things to do with a stinging nettle

I'm sure everyone reading this has brushed against a stinging nettle (*Urtica dioica*) and soon realised how it got its name. That sting – caused by a potent cocktail of toxins that are injected into your skin if you break off one of those hypodermic needle-like hairs – is actually a highly effective defence mechanism that stops most grazing animals from eating the nettle, except for sheep and goats who don't seem to mind.

Although the nettle is regarded as a weed it has a host of benefits. It supports over 40 species of insects, including red admiral and tortoiseshell butterflies whose larvae feed on its leaves, and one large nettle can produce up to 40,000 seeds for hungry seed-eating birds. They can be pretty good for us too, so cast aside your bad memories of sore arms and legs and grasp the nettle (wearing gloves of course).

1. Make a nice cup of tea

Pick off small, young leaves from the tip of the nettle – the older and bigger the nettle leaves get, the more bitter they taste. Give them a good wash to remove any lingering dirt or insects. Be careful as you do this as at this stage the nettle can still sting you. Boil the leaves in water, until it starts to go slightly green and strain out the leaves, which by now will have lost all their sting. Add sugar and lemon to taste.

Nettle tea is particularly good for hayfever sufferers, reducing the reaction to pollen, especially if you use local nettles in the brew.

2. Amuse the kids

Here's a fun science experiment. Drop a slice of lemon into a cup of green nettle tea and the colour will miraculously change. Depending on the pH level and acidity of the water it will go bright pink.

3. Make nettle soup

For something a touch more substantial why not try soup? First fry off some chopped onions in butter, but don't allow them to go brown and pop in a load of washed, young leaves. Let them wilt in the heat before adding 900ml vegetable stock and a diced potato or two. Add a little pepper and simmer for 20 minutes. Add some crème fraîche or milk depending on the consistency you want and blitz with a blender. You're left with a tasty green soup reminiscent of spinach, which is perfect served with a dash of cream.

4. Brew your own nettle beer

Free beer from a weed? Sounds too good to be true but nettles actually have a long history in the brewing world. Before hops became a standard ingredient, nettles were used to flavour beer. If you want to have a go, put about 1kg young nettles into a pot and boil in 2.4 litres water for 30 minutes. Strain through a sieve and dissolve 450g caster sugar in the liquid. You can also add the juice from either a lemon or orange at this point, if you wish.

Let the mixture cool to lukewarm and add 15g brewer's yeast and 25g cream of tartar. Give it a good stir and then leave in a warm place, covered with a tea towel, to ferment for three days.

Then all you need do is skim off any scum that has gathered on the surface and pour into sterilised bottles. Keep the bottles stored in a cool place and about a week later you'll be able to take your first sip.

5. Feed your plants

It isn't just us humans who can benefit from a sip of nettle tea every now and again. Our plants can too. Stinging nettles are packed with nitrogen – especially in spring before they flower when they are young – as well as iron, sulphur and magnesium. With a little effort they can be brewed into a nutritious – and free – fertiliser. Pop on some thick gloves and gather your nettles, crushing the stems and leaves. Drop the mangled nettles into a bucket, weigh them down with a brick or something similarly heavy and fill the container with water, to cover all of the nettles. Put the bucket aside for about four weeks to let it stew and then strain out and discard any remaining organic matter. The fertiliser you've made will need to be diluted to around one part liquid to 10 parts water.

There is only one drawback. As the nettles rot, the bucket will get a bit smelly so make sure it's tucked away somewhere. The slight stink is worth it though as your plants will love it.

6. Treat yourself

For a plant that most people think of as a nuisance, stinging nettles have a surprising number of medical benefits. As an anti-inflammatory, the juice of nettles can help treat gout and arthritis and, being a diuretic, can help your kidneys clear out any toxins.

Ask first

Believe it or not, nettles are classed as a wild flower so you shouldn't just head out into woods or sidings and start digging them up without the permission of the landowner – remember they're extremely good for wildlife. However, ask around and you'll soon find a gardener happy enough for you to come and harvest their weeds for them, or even give you cuttings to plant in your own garden.

A (baker's) dozen things you didn't know about British orchards and apples

1. The apple was probably brought to Britain by the Romans. The original apple, *Malus sieversii*, would have grown on the slopes of Tien Shan mountains, on what is now the border of China and Kazakhstan, where it can still be found today. In fact, the name of Kazakhstan's capital, Astana, means 'city that is rich with apples'.

2. You could eat a different variety of apple each day for six years and still not munch your way through the list of apples we can grow in this country. In total you're looking at 2,300 British apple cultivars.

3. British apples have a whole host of eccentric names such as the Arlingham Schoolboys, Beauty of Bath, Cornish Gillyflower, Peasgood's Nonesuch, Devonshire Quarrenden, Hangy Down, Philbert Nut Bush, Polly White Hair, Sheep's Nose, the Oaken Pin, Star of Devon, Sweet Lark, d'Arcy Spice, Ten Commandments and even Slack-ma-Girdle.

4. The traditional orchard is in trouble and Britain is losing them at an alarming rate. Research from Natural England shows that England alone has lost 63 per cent of its orchards since 1950. Wales is faring even worse – between 1958 and 1992 the decline was 94 per cent. England's worst-hit county is Kent, which has lost 92 per cent of its orchards in just under 60 years, while Devon saw 89 per cent grubbed up in the same period.

5. The decline is in part due to the large number of apples that are now imported. Supermarkets sell 70 per cent of all apples in the UK yet according to Friends of the Earth only 35 per cent of those are home grown. From over 2,000 varieties to choose from, supermarkets stock around 25, although independent greengrocers do better, stocking 51 British varieties.

6. At the moment the most popular apple is the Braeburn, originally bred in New Zealand. We munch through 100,000 tonnes of Braeburns every year. Next in the top of the crops is the Gala, also from New Zealand, the Australian Granny Smith and the French Golden

Delicious. It's only when you get to number five in the apple charts that you find an apple variety from the UK – Cox's Orange Pippin.

7. Half a trillion apples are produced worldwide every year, around 55 million tonnes' worth. Around half of that planet-wide harvest comes from China. Britain, on the other hand, produces around 200,000 tonnes a year, which equates to 63 per cent of our entire fruit industry.

8. The global marketplace has taken its toll on our orchards, with imported fruit flooding in from places like Chile and China, where labour is cheaper. The land that was once used for small British producers has been handed over to developers or is being used for different produce. There's another reason our orchards have dropped off. We've grown accustomed to being able to eat apples all year around. The British apple season, however, is a few short months from September – and though picked fruit can be kept much longer in cold store, to me the taste isn't quite the same. There's nothing better than a British apple straight off the tree.

9. Orchards are great places to spot wildlife throughout the year. In spring, when that wonderful fragrant blossom bursts into life, the orchard is a hive of activity with beetle larvae such as the noble chafer beetle (*Gnorimus nobilis*) feasting on the decaying wood – apple trees are relatively short lived and so provide vital dead wood for invertebrates and home for birds such as the lesser spotted woodpecker (*Dendrocopos minor*). Bats flit around apple trees in the summer, attracted by the insects that have laid their eggs in the bark and are sipping the sweet nectar of the blossom. When the apples fall in autumn, those that aren't picked as windfall provide sustenance to small mammals such as voles and insects such as wasps and hoverflies, who in turn attract a return visit from the bats. Then as winter hits, parasitic mistletoe begins to creep around the older trees, its white berries providing a snack for the mistle thrush (*Turdus viscivorus*) as the year wanes away.

10. Since 1990, 21 October has been designated Apple Day in the UK. It started, not in the countryside, but in London's Covent Garden when wildlife campaigner Angela King and university lecturer Sue Clifford put up a stall and gathered 100 varieties for passers-by to taste. One year later, 50 events sprang up around the country,

from pruning classes to markets. These days there are well over 600 events every year, all independent and all with the love of the humble British apple at their heart.

11. The apple is steeped in folklore. First, of course, is the fact that Eve used an apple to tempt Adam. Although, she didn't. The Bible doesn't say what the forbidden fruit was – in likelihood it would have probably been a fig. Traditionally in England the apple was seen to be the work of the gods not the tool of the devil. The burning or grubbing up of an orchard would have been sacrilegious to our ancestors who used to hold wassailing ceremonies in orchards early every year to wish the spirits of the trees well and see off any evil goblins who might disrupt the harvest later in the year. Wassailing festivals still take place throughout the UK, especially in the West Country.

12. While wassailing alone may not be able to save the British orchard, more practical schemes have been set up with that intention. The National Trust has committed £500,000 to restore, plant and maintain traditional orchards, while, on a local level, community orchards have sprung up. Groups of locals, determined not to let orchards die out, have bought, planted or leased traditional orchards that they maintain as a community project. I saw one in action in Herefordshire, where several hundred people have shares in a medium-sized orchard. They tend the trees, pick the apples and make their own cider.

13. I have three apple trees in my garden but that doesn't make it an orchard – technically, I'd need five or more to qualify. One of them is quite rare – an Ecklinville Seeding, developed in Northern Ireland more than two centuries ago. When I was doing a *Countryfile* item about unusual apple trees, I took along an apple and a leaf, and an expert identified it for me from a huge encyclopedia, purely about apples. My Ecklinville Seedling produces large yellow cooking apples that bruise easily, especially when they fall from a tall tree like mine, so they aren't commercially viable. But they make wonderful apple pies and it's something of a mystery how, generations ago, this Irish tree found its way into an Oxfordshire garden.

The rise of English wine

For years, British wine, to be fair, has been seen as a bit of a joke, the poor relation of our European neighbours' offerings and not something to serve to your friends. Over the past forty years that's all changed, with wine connoisseurs viewing our home-produced plonk with far more favourable eyes and taste buds.

Part of the problem comes with the term British wine, which doesn't mean wine made from grapes grown in Great Britain. Instead, this rather deceptive term indicates a wine made from imported, concentrated grape juice that is fermented and bottled in the UK. Such offerings are cheap, largely made from poor-quality ingredients and the result can put people off trying wine from these shores ever again. So if you see British wine on the label, put the bottle back and look for one labelled English or Welsh wine, which is the real deal – it comes from grapes grown in our own vineyards.

Today, Britain boasts more than 400 vineyards, producing white, red and rosé wines, both still and sparkling. Those in the know say that the rising number of vineyards has a lot to do with rising temperatures, especially in southern counties such as Kent, Sussex, Berkshire, Cambridgeshire, Essex and Hampshire. With the average temperature predicted to rise by between 1 and 5 degrees Celsius during the next hundred years (at the moment it's a degree lower than the Champagne region of France) vineyard success on a large scale is finally within our grasp. About 90 per cent of the wine we produce is white although production of red and rosés is increasing as the years roll by.

Main varieties of white grapes grown for wine in the UK

- Auxerrois
- Bacchus
- Huxelrebe
- Kerner
- Madeleine Angevine
- Müller-Thurgau (also known as Rivaner)
- Optima
- Orion
- Ortega

- Phoenix
- Pinot Blanc
- Pinot Gris
- Reichensteiner
- Regner
- Rivaner

- Rülander
- Schönburger
- Seyval Blanc
- Siegerrebe
- Würzer

Main varieties of red grapes grown for wine in the UK

- Dornfelder
- Dunkelfelder
- Pinot Meunier
- Pinot Noir

- Regent
- Rondo
- Triomphe

Hunting and shooting

The countryside is full of contentious issues, but the ban on hunting foxes with hounds is the one that has dominated the headlines for many years – and led to two mass marches on London by hunting supporters. No matter where you are, be it city or village, everyone has an opinion. I can't begin to count the hours that I've spent reporting on the issue for *Countryfile*: it is one story that isn't going to go away. Let's take a look at the history of the ban on hunting, including the battle that raged between the Commons and the Lords – taking up 148 hours and 6 minutes of parliamentary time between 1997 and 2005 – what the ban actually entails and the arguments on both sides of the debate.

Key events in the ban on hunting

2 May 1997

Tony Blair's Labour Party wins the General Election. Its manifesto had stated that: 'We have advocated new measures to promote animal welfare including a free vote in parliament on whether hunting with hounds should be banned.'

5 November 1997

Labour MP Michael Foster publishes a bill to ban hunting with dogs. When it passes its second reading in the Commons, a rally of 250,000 pro-hunting supporters organised by the Countryside Alliance marches on London – which *Countryfile* reported in a live programme. After the bill runs out of parliamentary time, Mr Foster withdraws it.

18 July 1999

Prime Minister Tony Blair makes the surprise announcement on BBC1's *Question Time* that fox-hunting will be banned before the next General Election.

21 July 1999

Mike Watson, a Labour MSP, announces that he will put forward a member's bill in the Scottish Parliament to ban hunting with hounds in Scotland.

11 November 1999

Home Secretary Jack Straw announces that former civil servant Lord Burns will lead an inquiry into the effect a ban on fox-hunting would have on the rural economy. Lord Burns, a former Treasury mandarin, allows *Countryfile* to accompany him during much of his investigation. His report makes no definite recommendations (its purpose was to compile unbiased information) but it does include the comment that hunting 'seriously compromises the welfare of the fox'.

7 July 2000

Jack Straw puts forward a bill with three choices for MPs: a total ban on all hunting, the creation of a new, stricter licensing authority that would regulate hunting, or no change to the law whatsoever. Local referendums are also considered.

8 December 2000

The government's Hunting Bill comes before Parliament.

17 January 2001

MPs vote to support a ban on hunting with hounds (399 to 155 votes). Proposals to allow licensed hunting are rejected (382 to 182 votes).

22 February 2001

The outbreak of foot-and-mouth disease brings a total, blanket ban on any hunting.

26 March 2001

The House of Lords throws out the hunting ban by 317 votes to 68. They vote 249 to 108 to leave hunting as it is. The coming General Election means that the Hunting Bill runs out of parliamentary time.

17 December 2001

The foot-and-mouth crisis over, legal hunting can recommence.

13 February 2002

The Scottish Parliament bans hunting with hounds in Scotland.

18 March 2002

The Commons votes to ban hunting with hounds by 386 votes to 175.

19 March 2002

Members of the House of Lords once again overturn the ban (331 votes to 71), but now favour stricter licences.

22 September 2002

Some 400,000 demonstrators march through London as part of the Liberty and Livelihood protest against a hunting ban – once again, *Countryfile* cameras cover the event live.

30 June 2003

MPs vote for a complete ban for the third time, 362 votes to 154.

21 October 2003

The House of Lords votes against a complete ban, proposing a system of regulated hunt. The bill runs out of parliamentary time again.

15 September 2004

A fourth vote on the ban sees MPs support it 356 votes to 166. On the same day pro-hunting demonstrators manage to bypass Commons security and break into the parliamentary chamber.

17 November 2004

When the Lords once again throw out the ban with 188 votes to 79, the Commons Speaker Michael Martin invokes the Parliament Act. The Hunting Bill is pushed through to law.

8 February 2005

The Countryside Alliance goes to the Appeals Court to argue that the use of the Parliament Act makes the Hunting Act unlawful. They are ruled against on 16 February 2005.

18 February 2005

The ban on hunting with hounds comes into force.

2010

Fox hunting is still legal in Northern Ireland. The Conservatives had promised a free vote for MPs on fox-hunting but under the coalition government this looks unlikely to occur.

The hunting ban explained

In accordance with the Hunting Act 2004 it is against the law to:

▶ Hunt a wild mammal with a dog.

▶ Knowingly permit a dog that belongs to you to be used in unlawful hunting.

▶ Knowingly permit land that belongs to you to be used in unlawful hunting.

▶ Knowingly let your land be used for and participate, facilitate or attend a hare-coursing event.

Potential penalties if you're found guilty of illegal hunting:

▶ A maximum fine of £5,000.

▶ The potential risk of forfeiting any vehicle, hunting article or dog used in illegal hunting.

However, you can defend yourself by proving that you believed that the particular hunting activity in which you were involved was exempt from the Hunting Act.

When it comes to legal hunting, you can:

▶ Go trail hunting, following an artificially laid scent.

▶ Use no more than two dogs to flush out wild mammals to be shot in order to protect livestock, property, biological diversity, wild birds or game birds.

▶ Recapture a wild animal that has previously escaped or been released.

▶ Flush out a mammal in connection with falconry.

▶ Stalk a wild and injured wild animal in order to kill it to relieve its suffering.

Arguments for and against fox-hunting

For: Hunters argue that foxes are pests that need to be controlled. It is estimated that 25,000 foxes per year were killed before the Act came into force. To counter arguments against the killing of foxes by hunting, hunters argue that foxes are not necessarily saved by the ban as more are now shot annually.

Against: After hunting was briefly banned during the foot-and-mouth crisis in 2001, the Mammal Society published a report that asserted that there had been no increase in fox numbers in that time. Research has also shown that, as territorial animals, new foxes soon move into areas vacated by a dead fox and that the fox population is self-controlled.

For: Fox-hunting helps farmers whose stock is being threatened by foxes. Hunters insist that killing with hounds is more humane as the fox dies almost instantaneously; poor shots leave a fox wounded and facing a long, agonising death.

Against: If foxes do have to be controlled for farming, they can be dispatched by expert pest-controllers. Hunting causes stress to the quarry, even if it eventually escapes.

For: Fox-hunting is a traditional sport. It was argued that a ban would lead to many country dwellers losing their jobs and packs of hounds being put down. The Countryside Alliance reckoned between 6,000 and 8,000 people would be affected either directly or indirectly.

Against: There has been no clear evidence that this has happened. Some huntsmen have been made redundant, but hunts using an artificially laid scent are taking place across the country. In fact, while no definite numbers are available for the number of people attending hunts, anecdotal evidence seems to indicate they are more popular than ever.

For: According to pro-hunt organisations, hunts help conserve the countryside.

Against: Anti-hunting groups insist that wildlife areas can be disturbed or even destroyed as a hunt passes through them.

British shooting seasons

A number of birds and mammals in the UK can be legally shot, whether for sport, as a measure of control, or for the pot. However, to make sure that they are able to breed successfully at certain times of the year, legally enforced close seasons were introduced to give the quarry a period when they are not disturbed. Below are the open-season dates for the main game species in the UK:

* The hare is a special case. Although it's classed as a pest and therefore has no close season in England, Scotland and Wales, it is illegal to sell the meat between 1 March and 31 July. Also, if the shoot takes place on moorland or unenclosed land then individual landowners may enforce their own close seasons.

Species

Blackgame or black grouse
(not currently found in Northern Ireland)

Common snipe

Coot/moorhen

curlew

Duck & goose
(below the high watermark of ordinary spring tides)

Duck & goose–inland

Golden plover

Grouse

Hare*

Jack snipe

Partridge

Pheasant

Ptarmigan (only found in Scotland)

Woodcock

Woodcock (only found in Scotland)

Did you know . . . ?

In England and Wales it is illegal for game to be shot on a Sunday or on Christmas Day. It's also illegal to shoot wildfowl in the following places on a Sunday: Anglesey, Brecknock, Caernarvon, Carmarthen, Ceredigion, Cornwall, Denbigh, Devon, Doncaster, Glamorgan, Great Yarmouth County Borough, Isle of Ely, Leeds County Borough, Merioneth, Norfolk, Pembrokeshire, Somerset, North and West ridings of Yorkshire.

In Scotland shooting game is legal on both Sundays and Christmas Day although it is customary that no-one actually does. However, it is against the law to shoot wildfowl on a Sunday or on Christmas Day.

In Northern Ireland pest birds (such as crows or magpies), game in season, rabbits and deer may not be shot on Sundays or Christmas Day.

England, Scotland and Wales	Northern Ireland
20 August–10 December	—
12 August–31 January	1 September–31 January
1 September–31 January	Protected at all times
Protected at all times	1 September–31 January
1 September–20 February	1 September–31 January
1 September–31 January	1 September–31 January
1 September–31 January	1 September–31 January
12 August–10 December	12 August–30 November
1 January–31 December	12 August–31 January
Protected at all times	1 September–31 January
1 September–1 February	1 September–31 January
1 October–1 February	1 October–31 January
12 August–10 December	—
1 October–31 January	1 October–31 January
1 September–31 January	—

183

Open seasons for deer

Species	Sex	England and Wales
Red	Stags	1 August–30 April
	Hinds	1 November–31 March
Fallow	Bucks	1 August–30 April
	Does	1 November–31 March
Sika	Stags	1 August–30 April
	Hinds	1 November–31 March
Roe	Buck	1 April–31 October
	Does	1 November–31 March
Red/sika cross-breed	Stags	1 August–30 April
	Hinds	1 November–31 March
Chinese water deer	Bucks	1 November–28/29 February
	Does	1 November–31 March
Muntjac*		1 January–31 December

Northern Ireland	Scotland
1 August–30 April	1 July–20 October
1 November–28 February	21 October–15 February
1 August–30 April	1 August–30 April
1 November–28 February	21 October–15 February
1 August–30 April	1 July–20 October
1 November–28/29 February	21 October–15 February
—	1 April–20 October
—	21 October–31 March
1 November–28/29 February	1 July–20 October
1 November–28/29 February	21 October –15 February
—	—
—	—
—	—

*Although the muntjac has no statutory close seasons, the British Deer Society recommends that only immature or heavily pregnant females are culled so that no young muntjac deer are orphaned at a time when they are dependent on their mother's milk.

Mammals with no close season

The following are classified as pests and therefore can be controlled all year round in all four countries using legally approved methods:

▶ Feral cat

▶ Fox

▶ Grey squirrel

▶ Mice (except dormice)

▶ Mink

▶ Rabbit

▶ Rat

▶ Stoat

▶ Weasel

CHAPTER FIVE

Woodlands

Why are there so many conifers in Britain?

After the terrible conflict of the First World War, Britain's woodland resources were at an all-time low. Our forested areas had been declining steadily since the Middle Ages and had been further decimated by the demands of the Industrial Revolution. During the Great War, dwindling stocks of wood quite literally supported our trenches but supplies had almost dried up – by then, less than 3 per cent of Britain was covered by woodland and we were dependent on imports.

In July 1916 Prime Minister Herbert Asquith appointed a special committee to investigate new ways of developing our woodland resources. The result was the Forestry Act, which came into force on 1 September 1919, and out of which came the formation of the Forestry Commission, a government-funded organisation with responsibility for woods throughout the United Kingdom. In particular, they were charged with the urgent re-afforestation of the country.

With agricultural land at rock-bottom prices, the new Commission was able to buy up huge swathes cheaply and within a decade around 138,000 acres of new forests had been planted, with a further 54,000 acres being created on private land using Commission grants. And, largely, those new trees were conifers, because the firs, pines, spruce and western red cedar grew far quicker than our native hardwoods: pine species can be cropped after about 20 years whereas oak generally does not provide good timber until 60 years. The dense, regimented conifer woodlands provided, among other things, much needed pit props for the coal mining industry, which in those days was still a thriving one.

But times change and needs change, and the past ten years have seen the conifer fall from favour. The Forestry Commission has pledged to fell tens of millions of conifers over the next century, making our woodlands lighter and, ultimately, more attractive and accessible. They will be thinned gradually, thus increasing the light levels required by native species such as hazel, ash, beech and oak to grow. The forests of the future will be brighter, because a lighter canopy of trees means flowers such as the primrose and bluebell can flourish, as well as a haven for woodland species including the nightingale, dormouse and many butterflies.

But before we write off the conifer, let's remember one thing. Whereas we entered the 20th century with only 3 per cent of our land covered by woodland, we entered the 21st century with 11 per cent, thanks mainly to the work of the Forestry Commission. In the past twenty years alone Britain's woodlands have expanded by an area three times the size of Greater London.

And we Brits are a perverse lot. I remember the local protests when the Commission planted a conifer forest across a ridge in Buckinghamshire. 'Foreign trees destroying our landscape' was the cry. But when the time came to fell them, protests were equally loud against the destruction of green hillsides!

How to read a leaf

The best way to start identifying trees is to examine their leaves, so a good tree detective will need to know how to find their way around a leaf. This is what you're looking for:

The surface

The flat surface of a leaf is known either as the lamina or blade. The top (or adaxial) surface is often different to the lower (or abaxial) side. It could be a different colour, or appear more veiny or hairy.

The shape

The different shapes found in leaves are described by a number of Latin words:

Acicular – needle-like

Cuneate – broad at the tip and tapering back towards the base

Deltoid – triangular

Lanceolate – longer and lance-like, broader at the base than the tip

Ovate – egg-shaped

Cordate – shaped like an inverted heart

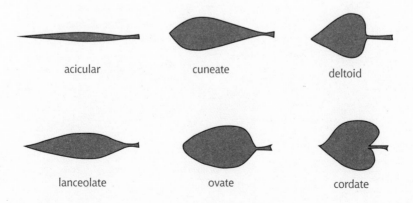

acicular   cuneate   deltoid

lanceolate   ovate   cordate

The stem

The primary vein that runs down the centre of the leaf is called the midrib.

The stalk

Leaves are attached to a plant's stem by a stalk known as a petiole and the angle at which it meets the stem is called the axil.

The edge

One of the most important methods of identifying leaves is to look at the edge, known as the leaf margin. There are three main types of margin:

Entire – a smooth edge

Toothed – a saw-like edge

Lobed – having one or more large indentations that divide the leaf into pointed or rounded lobes

The tip

The end of the leaf furthest away from the stem is called the apex. These can be sharply pointed (acuminate), rounded (obtuse) or even appear to have been cut off abruptly (truncate).

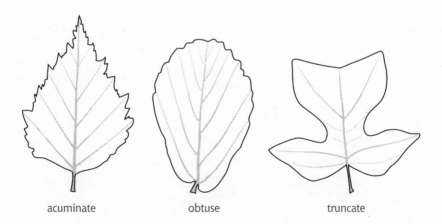

acuminate   obtuse   truncate

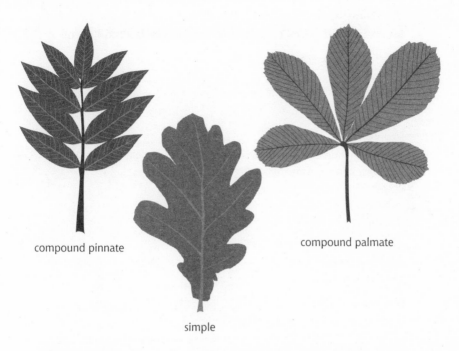

compound pinnate

compound palmate

simple

The structure

If the leaf's blade or surface is undivided – meaning that any lobes or teeth it may have don't extend as far as the midrib – it's known as simple. A compound leaf, on the other hand, is made up of several leaflets which all join to a single stalk. A palmate compound leaf has all of its leaflets joining at a central point, like your fingers join your palm, while a pinnate compound leaf has pairs of leaflets sitting opposite each other along a stem with a single leaflet at the tip.

Once you've mastered the leaf, identification becomes a lot more straightforward, especially when you start looking at buds, twigs and the bark for confirmation. Getting to recognise the height and overall shape of the crown (leaves and branches) of a mature tree can also help you work out what you're looking at.

Identifying our main broadleaved and coniferous trees

Ash (*Fraxinus excelsior*)

Height: Can be up to 45 metres tall.

General shape: An open, dome-like crown.

Leaf: A pinnate compound leaf with around four pairs of leaflets with one at the tip. The leaflet's margins are toothed and the lower surface hairy. Ash leaves are among the first to fall in autumn.

Bark: Silver grey and develops ridges with age.

Flowers and fruit: Small green flowers clustered near the tips of twigs. In late winter and early spring also look out for black buds at the edge of shoots.

Oak – Three varieties: sessile (*Quercus petraea*), pedunculate (*Q. robur*) and holm (*Q. ilex*)

Height: Can be up to 36 metres tall.

General shape: Spreading tree with a dense, domed crown.

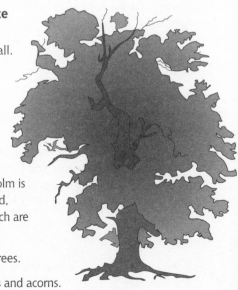

Leaf: A simple leaf with a lobed margin, between five and seven lobes per side. The holm oak, which is found throughout southern England, is an evergreen species. Holm is an archaic word for holly and indeed, young holm leaves have spikes, which are lost as they get older.

Bark: Grey and fissured in older trees.

Flowers and fruit: Produces catkins and acorns.

Beech (*Fagus sylvatica*)

Height: Can be up to 40 metres tall.

General shape: Large, domed crown.

Leaf: A simple leaf that is toothed slightly at the end of each vein. Almost lime green at first with slight hairs on the margin, the leaves darken over time as the hairs disappear.

Bark: Smooth and silver grey.

Flowers and fruit: Small yellow flowers and brown nuts within a green, prickly husk.

Birch – Two varieties: silver (*Betula pendula*) and downy (*B. pubescens*)

Height: Can be up to 26 metres tall

General shape: Birch have long, elongated and airy crowns.

Leaf: Simple and triangular with rounded corners and a toothed margin. The leaves of the silver birch are less rounded and more serrated along the margin.

Bark: Reddish while young becoming silver grey over time. As the downy birch ages, horizontal lines of grey appear on its bark.

Flowers and fruit: Drooping yellow catkins and upright green flowers.

193

Lime – Three varieties: small-leaved (*Tilia cordata*), large-leaved (*T. platyphyllos*) and common (*Tilia x europaea*)

Height: Can be up to 46 metres tall.

General shape: Both the small- and large-leaved lime have dense, domed crowns while the common lime has a tall, elongated crown.

Leaf: Simple, triangular leaf (except for the small-leaved, which is more heart-shaped) with toothed margins. The common lime has small white hairs in the angles of the vein on the lower side while the hairs on the small-leaved are brown. The upper surface is darker than the lower.

Bark: Grey and fissured.

Flowers and fruit: Yellowy white with five petals and sepals hanging with fruit like a small bunch of grapes.

Sycamore (*Acer pseudoplatanus*)

Height: Can be up to 35 metres tall.

General shape: Spreading, oval crown.

Leaf: A large, triangular simple leaf with five lobes, rounded teeth on the margin and hairs on the lower side.

Bark: Smooth and pinkish grey, flaking as it ages.

Flowers and fruit: Yellow, clustered flowers that form those familiar helicopter seeds we all played with as children.

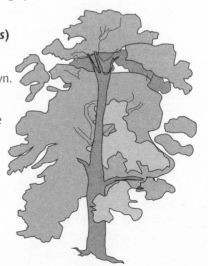

Horse chestnut (*Aesculus hippocastanum*)

Height: Can be up to 25 metres tall.

General shape: Thick, domed crown. The spread of its low, sweeping branches can be almost as wide as its height.

Leaf: A large, compound leaf with five to seven leaflets, serrated, toothed margin and prominent vein system.

Bark: Grey-brown and prone to flaking.

Flowers and fruit: Spiky pink-spotted white or pink flowers that form clusters known as 'candles'. These eventually form spiked fruit that contain every schoolboy's autumnal delight – the conker!

Sweet chestnut (*Castanea sativa*)

Height: Can be up to 35 metres tall.

General shape: Dense, oval crown.

Leaf: Long, thin and pointed, with a serrated, toothed margin. Prominent veins.

Bark: Silvery purple while young, becoming brown and fissured with age.

Flowers and fruit:
The sweet chestnut is monoecious, meaning it has separate male and female flowers on the same tree. The long, yellow catkins are male and the green rosettes are female. The edible nuts are contained in cases with finer prickles than the horse chestnut.

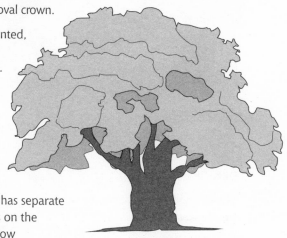

Hazel (*Corylus avellana*)

Height: Can be up to 6 metres tall.

General shape: Shrub-like, with multiple stems, spreading out like an upside-down pyramid.

Leaf: Simple with a toothed margin and hairy stalk and lower side.

Bark: Young stems have peeling, bronze bark while older stems become a paler shade of brown.

Flowers and fruit: Yellow catkins, often called 'lambtails', and pink small flowers. The edible nuts are produced in clusters of up to five hazelnuts, each one contained in a green husk.

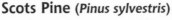

Scots Pine (*Pinus sylvestris*)

Height: Can be up to 36 metres tall.

General shape: A conical, airy evergreen that, over time, develops a flat top.

Leaf: Simple needles with a smooth margin.

Bark: Pink coloured on young trees, becoming greyer into old age.

Flowers and fruit: Small, crimson female flowers develop into cones two years after being fertilised.

Yew – Two varieties:
common yew (*Taxus baccata*), and
Irish yew (*T. baccata fastigiata aurea*)

Height: Can be up to 25 metres tall.

General shape: The common yew is broad and dense while the Irish yew grows into a more pronounced, upright column.

Leaf: Simple green needles with smooth margin, arranged on either side of the twig. The Irish yew's needles are blacker in colour, curve slightly and are arranged all around the twig.

Bark: Red and prone to peeling.

Flowers and fruit: Yellow flowers on male trees, green on females. Bright reddish-pink fruit.

Dutch elm disease

In 1967 a consignment of rock elm (*Ulmus thomasii*) logs arrived in Britain from the United States. It seemed innocent enough, but the imported timber harboured a virus that had already been wiping out elms on the other side of the Atlantic for twenty years. A strain of Dutch elm disease – known as *Ophiostoma novo-ulmi* – immediately began its insidious work in the forests of Great Britain. The first sign of trouble was the fact that leaves were beginning to turn yellow halfway through summer. By the mid-eighties approximately 25 million elms has been killed by the pathogen, which is spread by bark beetles.

Some elm colonies have survived. In 2003, the Natural History Museum began to survey the survivors, finding 207 hangers-on in the first two years of the study. This, of course, threw up questions. How had the trees survived the plague? Had they developed a resistance to the disease or was their bark repulsive to the beetles that unwittingly brought about the mass destruction?

It is hoped that answers may follow a new project to repopulate Britain's elm trees. In spring 2010, 250 schools received a sapling taken from one of the surviving elms, the first batch of young trees distributed by The Conservation Foundation as part of The Great British Elm Experiment. Each sapling will be constantly monitored to chart its progress and watch for any signs of Dutch elm disease. In the past the elm was a well-loved tree throughout Britain's lowlands. Perhaps one day it will be again.

Other serial tree killers

Sudden oak death

In 2002 an infection known as *Phytophthora ramorum* was discovered in a UK garden centre. First reported in California in 1995, the pathogen proceeded to wipe out 80 per cent of the State's tanoak trees and is known to infect around twenty species.

In part the problem is caused by rhododendron, camellia and viburnum species, which carry the spores responsible for sudden oak death. Many projects are already under way to burn and remove infected rhododendrons and fell trees that have already fallen foul of the effects of the alga-like fungus.

Horse chestnut bleeding canker

At least half of Britain's 470,000 horse chestnut trees are suffering from so-called bleeding canker. At first the infection, related to sudden oak death, was only found in the south of England, although as the 'noughties' drew to an end cases were reported from across England and Wales. Sore-like marks form on the bark where the infection first strikes, causing the tree to 'bleed' sap from the wound. Over time the tree's growth becomes stunted and it is increasingly susceptible to other infections.

Why we shouldn't get rid of dead wood

On 16 October 1987 a monumental storm hit Great Britain. We all awoke to the news that approximately 15 million trees had been blown over, 12 million within forests and the remainder in the parks and gardens of South East England. I pulled back the bedroom curtains to discover that a large Canadian oak in the next-door garden wasn't there anymore – it lay horizontal behind a high bank of bushes. But this blackest of storm clouds had a very particular silver lining.

The force of nature gave us a powerful reminder about the importance of dead wood. Foresters struggled to clear up the debris but in places where the timber was left as it fell, biodiversity blossomed. It was soon obvious that our tidy, managed woodlands were often ultimately stifling.

Death has as much a part to play as life in a successful ecosystem and dead wood is no exception. Here's why:

> ❯ It provides essential nutrients for many bacteria and fungi, which break down the structure of the wood thereby making it available for other life forms, primarily invertebrates. It is estimated that around 1,700 species of bugs, insects and invertebrates depend on the existence of dead wood for their survival. Perhaps the best example of dead-wood insects is the stag beetle. The female lays her eggs in dead wood – ideally oak. When the young hatch into larvae, they immediately burrow into the wood to feast on its decay and develop into adults over the next three years.

> In turn, the invertebrates provide nourishment for many woodland birds including willow tits, woodpeckers, tawny owls, redstarts and nuthatches and many of our species of bats.

> It isn't just about food. Dead wood provides shelter for a large number of animals including voles, woodmice and shrews.

> Dead organic matter is also believed to be an important carbon sink, vital in the fight against global warming.

So next time you're out on a country walk and see an unsightly lump of abandoned, rotten wood – don't complain. It's probably breathing new life into its surroundings.

Coppicing trees

Have you ever walked through a wood during winter only to find a section of trees have been cut down? It seems strange. In a world where we're fighting against deforestation, why would we allow such destruction to happen?

The answer is simple – what you're looking at is the foresters' equivalent of being cruel to be kind. The practice is known as coppicing, one of the oldest forms of woodland management. Our earliest ancestors discovered that carefully cutting most of our native broadleaf species down to its stump after the last leaf had fallen would cause it to sprout a large number of long, fast-growing stems with few or no side branches. Hazel, ash, field maple, oak and willow all respond well to coppicing.

Coppicing different species produces many different products:

> hazel – used for walking sticks, thatching spars, bean sticks and hurdles (woven fence panels)

> oak – used for lathes, fencing material, tiles and gates

> ash – used for tent pegs and tool handles

> sweet chestnut – used for stakes, hedge stakes, walking sticks and fence posts

> willow – used for baskets and (these days) garden sculptures

By the 13th century, the majority of British woodlands were managed as coppice and the practice only began to decline in the 1850s when the products traditionally produced by the coppice workers could be mass-produced on an industrial scale. Today, as forestry practices no longer emphasise conifer production, coppicing as a form of broadleaf-woodland management is undergoing something of a revival.

The next time you stroll through woodland, have a look for the signs of coppicing. Trees are cut down near to ground level, usually at a slight angle so that rain water can drain off easily and not cause rot. Although some older trees are left standing to encourage diversification of wildlife, sunlight can now reach the ground, often for the first time in years. Seeds lying dormant in the soil are triggered into germination. You may have walked that way a hundred times and not known that foxgloves, wood anemones and wild garlic were hiding beneath your feet, ready to burst into life, creating a carpet of colour.

Over time the new shoots from the stump – known as a stool – will grow, competing for light until the stronger stems put the weaker into shade. Where there was once a single trunk there are now many, creating a new canopy that eventually blocks out the sun, causing the flowers of the forest floor to die back again until the coppice workers return to harvest the same spot and the circle begins once more.

The coppicing period depends on the intended use of the wood and the species: fast-growing willow is harvested every 1–3 years, hazel every 6–8 and sweet chestnut every 20–40 years.

Four species that particularly benefit from coppicing

Pearl-bordered fritillary (*Boloria euphrosyne*)
This species of butterfly is so closely associated with hazel woodland it became known as the 'woodman's friend'. Fritillaries lay their eggs on the new carpet of flowers around coppiced trees before the encroachment of brambles means they have to move on to a new spot.

Nightingale (*Luscinia megarhynchos*)

Ever so slightly larger than a robin, this secretive, bush-loving bird arrives in the south of Britain during April, filling our woodlands with their melodious song until late May throughout day or night.

Willow warbler (*Phylloscopus trochilus*)

This little green-grey backed bird constructs its nest on the ground, weaving grass, rotten wood, roots and moss into small domes. They are particularly attracted to woodland containing birch and willow.

Common dormouse (*Muscardinus avellanarius*)

One of Britain's most endangered animals, the dormouse has seen its numbers fall by 39 per cent since 1992, making it vulnerable to extinction. Dormice particularly favour oak and hazel woods as they need to fatten up on a diet of nuts and berries to prepare them for their winter hibernation.

The bluebell bluffers' guide

Become an instant expert about one of our most popular flowers:

1. The bluebell is found in deciduous woodlands, meadows, hedgerows and on cliffs. There are three main varieties of bluebells in Britain:

▶ **The common or native bluebell (*Hyacinthoides non-scripta*)**
Violet-blue in colour and possessing a strong, sweet scent, our native bluebell has a distinctive flower spike that droops down.

▶ **The Spanish bluebell (*H. hispanica*)**
In 1680 a new variety of bluebell was introduced to our shores as an ornamental plant. Hailing from Portugal and Spain, the blooms of the Spanish bluebell are larger than the native bluebell and can range in colour from pale blue to pink and even white. An incredibly vigorous plant, *H. hispanica* can grow just about anywhere, which meant that by 1909 it had already escaped to the wild along verges, hedgerows, wasteland and railway cuttings.

▶ **Hybrid bluebell (*H. x massartiana*)**
By 1963, the aggressive Spanish bluebell had crossbred with our native species. The hybrid shares characteristics with both of its parents, making identification and therefore control difficult.

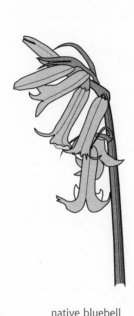

native bluebell   Spanish bluebell

2. The patriotic Victorians claimed that the flower bloomed on St George's Day (23 April) and that its colour represented the blue waves where Britannia ruled supreme. In truth, you're likely to see the first shoots in January, before spreading trees block sunlight; the flower itself ready to bloom between early April and late May.

3. Britain is believed to be the home of between 25 and 50 per cent of the Earth's total population of bluebells.

4. According to the conservation charity Plantlife, one in six British broadleaf woodlands is contaminated by either the Spanish or hybrid bluebell.

5. Bluebells are a favourite source of early nectar for hoverflies, bees and butterflies. In order to extract the nectar, bees bite a hole at the bottom of the bell.

6. Over the years, bluebells have also been known as crawtraes (or crow's toes), bloody fingers, dead men's bells, fairy thimbles, wild hyacinths and Granfer Griggles.

7. Back in the 13th century monks used bluebells to treat leprosy while in Wales it was also a popular 'cure' for tuberculosis. In the 16th century the sap from the bluebell bulb was used to glue feathers to arrows while gentlemen could stiffen their ruffs with its starch. Even as recently as the 19th century bluebell glue was used widely in bookbinding as toxins from the highly poisonous bulb deterred silverfish.

8. The bluebell was associated with Beltane, the ancient Celtic festival that marks the start of summer. They were a taboo flower as they were believed to be the property of the fairy world. If you disturbed or damaged the blooms, the fairies would be so furious that they would ensure that you were lost in the woods for all time. Bluebells near oak trees were particularly protected by pixie folk. Pick one of these flowers and the little people known as oakmen would wreak their revenge by stealing your chickens, cattle or even children.

   It was also dangerous to have bluebells in your garden in the time of the witch-trials of old. The blue blooms were said to be grown by witches for trade with fairies and were seen as evidence of dabbling in the dark arts.

9. Bluebells are a protected species. It is illegal to sell bluebell bulbs or seeds, even if they are growing on your own land, unless you have a special licence. Conservationists recommend that, when buying bluebells for your garden, you only go to reputable suppliers who can assure you that the bulbs are legally sourced native flowers.

10. A mature bluebell bulb – around six years and up – can be cut into smaller bulblets that will grow into new individual plants. Cut the tip off the bulb and then slice into segments ensuring that a piece of the basal root plate remains in each section. You can then pot them up ready for planting in late summer, when the bulbs are dormant.

Nature's pollution detectors

Lichens are everywhere. In the city they flourish on pavements and walls while in the country they're smothered over fences, gravestones and, more often than not, trees.

Amazingly, they are also two lifeforms for the price of one. In every lichen a fungus forms a thallus – a protective covering – for an algae that in turn provides essential nutrients for the fungus. Together they act as one, in perfect harmony, and are remarkably resilient, covering 8 per cent of the Earth's total land mass.

Lichens are also rather handy as they can tell us a thing or two about the quality of the air. Back in the 1970s the sudden absence of certain lichens from our cities rang alarm bells – scientists started to investigate what was killing them off. The answer was acid rain, a problem that prompted European governments to pass Clean Air Acts.

Today boffins use lichens as a yardstick of air quality all over the country. For example, if we need to find out if the air has been tainted by nitrogen-based pollutants such as ammonia, which is often found in areas where agricultural fertiliser is heavily used, or with nitrogen dioxide, which is common near busy roads, then, as an initial indicator, look to see what lichens are found nearby. Some genuses, such as the beard-like *usnea* or the bushy *evernia*, are incredibly sensitive to nitrogen so will be repressed if there is too much in the air. However, the bright yellow cushion-like *xanthoria* or black-whiskered *physcia* thrive in nitrogen-rich environments.

Clever, eh? And I bet before now you've hardly given them a second glance.

Woodland wildlife: winners and losers

The nightingale (see page 202) has all but vanished from our woodlands. It's topping the list of woodland birds that are declining in the UK, many of which spend their winters in West Africa where habitats are shrinking. The most recent figures come from the Common Bird Census, a survey by the British Trust for Ornithology (BTO), which gathered data on 49 key species between 1967 and 1999. Here are those birds on the up and those in trouble:

Thriving woodland birds

   1. Collared dove (*Streptopelia decaocto*) – up 1052%

   2. Stock dove (*Columba oenas*) – up 359%

   3. Woodpigeon (*C. palumbus*) – up 344%

   4. Jackdaw (*Corvus monedula*) – up 311%

   5. Black-billed magpie (*Pica pica*) – up 292%

   6. Eurasian nuthatch (*Sitta europaea*) – up 226%

   7. Green woodpecker (*Picus viridis*) – up 180%

   8. Carrion crow (*Corvus corone*) – up 180%

   9. Blackcap (*Sylvia atricapilla*) – up 161%

   10. Winter or northern wren (*Troglodytes troglodytes*) – up 139%

So why are birds such as the collared dove and woodpigeon doing so well? It's largely due to the gradual increase in winter-crop planting, which gives them the advantage of a valuable source of food while their migrating neighbours head back over to Africa.

nightingale

Declining woodland birds

1. Nightingale (*Luscinia megarhynchos*) – down 95%

2. Common starling (*Sturnus vulgaris*) – down 91%

3. Linnet (*Carduelis cannabina*) – down 89%

4. Lesser redpoll (*C. cabaret*) – down 85%

5. Spotted flycatcher (*Muscicapa striata*) – down 83%

6. Lesser spotted woodpecker (*Picoides minor*) – down 82%

7. Whitethroat (*Sylvia communis*) – down 81%

8. Willow tit (*Poecile montanus*) – down 77%

9. Yellowhammer (*Emberiza citrinella*) – down 77%

10. European turtle dove (*Streptopelia turtur*) – down 76%

What's wrong with grey squirrels?

Few creatures get such a mixed reception from us as the grey squirrel. It's a regular sight in our gardens and parks, and many people are captivated by its cute antics, and by its amazing agility and sheer cleverness as it gets food from near impossible places. But to others it is a menace – 'a rat with a bushy tail and good public relations'.

The grey squirrel (*Sciurus carolinensis*) was introduced to Britain from North America in the last decades of the 19th century. At the time it was seen as a charming, engaging creature but soon gained a new reputation, that of the bully of the squirrel world and the mortal enemy of our own native red (*S. vulgaris*).

The greys are bigger than the red, are prolific breeders and can cause damage to trees by quickly stripping bark away. They often raid bird tables – digging holes in our lawns to hide the food they've pinched – and are known to build their nests (or dreys) in roof spaces, stripping insulation or beams in the process.

However, their biggest impact is on their red cousins. It soon became clear that wherever the greys invaded, red numbers would dwindle. At first it was believed that the greys were actually killing the reds, although this wasn't the case. They simply outcompeted the reds at every turn, eating seven times more food per hectare than our native species. As if that weren't enough, the greys unwittingly brought with them a deadly weapon: a lethal squirrel pox, to which, ironically, they are largely immune. It is believed that when the greys mark their territory with scent the virus is passed on to their red neighbours.

Red-squirrel numbers are currently down to around only 120,000, with all but 15,000 of them north of the border in Scotland. Some experts fear the species may even become extinct within ten years. By comparison, countrywide the grey-squirrel population has hit 2.5 million.

So is the only way of saving the reds systematically to cull the greys? Even Prince Charles has joined the rallying cry to eradicate what he classes as an 'alien species'.

But getting rid of them is easier said than done. One place where eradication has worked is the island of Anglesey, off the northwest coast of Wales. Back in 1998 only 40 red squirrels were left, facing 3,000 invading adult greys. Extinction seemed certain until a local conservation group, Menter Môn, stepped in, led by woodland ecologist Dr Craig Shuttleworth.

His plan was simple – trap and kill greys, not just on Anglesey but also on the nearby mainland to stop them reaching the island via the bridges or even by swimming across, and then re-introduce reds. I went to check out the results, and they are spectacular. 'We now have more than 300 reds on Anglesey,' Craig told me. 'They are back in habitats where for decades only greys could be found.' We checked traps set by Menter Môn in a woodland and in each of the three we found reds. When Craig set them free they darted into the undergrowth and straight up the nearest tree. Had they been greys, they would have been dispatched. 'Of course I don't hate greys,' he said, 'but they are in the wrong place at the wrong time. Though we have not eradicated them completely from Anglesey, at least the reds do now have a fighting chance of survival.'

grey squirrel

Such intervention projects can be controversial, with campaign groups like Animal Aid arguing it is wrong artificially to control wildlife populations. Yet because of the work of Craig Shuttleworth and his colleagues, Anglesey is now one of the few long-term refuges for red squirrels in the UK.

But a nationwide cull would be costly and difficult to coordinate, and many animal-welfare campaigners believe that efforts should be made to develop a vaccine for the pox or to attempt to control the grey population with contraception.

The last few years have also brought a glimmer of hope for the reds. Some areas of Merseyside saw around 90 per cent of their red squirrels fall victim to the virus but now numbers have, surprisingly, stabilised. Scientists from Liverpool University are wondering if this could be the beginning of a breakthrough and are checking to see if any of the surviving reds have begun to build up immunity. Let's hope they'll soon be off the endangered-species list.

How to distinguish between Britain's five main owl species

Once upon a time, the owl was a bird to be feared. From Chaucer and Shakespeare to Hammer Horror and *Scooby Doo*, these nocturnal hunters have long been the harbinger of doom and terror. Families in the 16th century would quake if an owl's cry were heard during the birth of a child, fearing a life of misery, while it was commonly believed that an owl hooted every time a girl lost her virginity.

Despite these misgivings the owl is now one of our most beloved birds and is increasingly difficult to spot. Stealing a glance at an owl in the wild is no longer something to dread, but a real privilege. And how else would Harry Potter get his mail delivered at Hogwarts?

So, how can you tell which owl you've just seen?

Little owl
(*Athene noctua*)

At roughly the size of a starling, the dumpy little owl lives up to its name and is the smallest in Britain. First introduced to the country in the 19th century from mainland Europe, it has been known over time as the little Dutch owl, little grey owl and Spanish owl.

With a rather stern stare, thanks to prominent white feathers forming 'eye-brows' above its yellow eyes, the little owl's grey-brown wings and upper parts are dappled with white spots while its breast is pale and streaked with grey.

While you may be able to spot one during daylight perched on a branch or post, your best chance is to catch a sighting at dusk while it hunts. Don't look to the sky, though, as it mostly stalks its prey by running or hopping along the ground.

The little owl can mostly be found on agricultural land and in woods throughout England and Wales. Listen out for a mewing 'ki-ew' or a rather mournful 'wooop' from the male, especially during courtship, which occurs between March and April.

Barn owl

(*Tyto alba*)

One of Britain's most iconic birds, the barn owl was once a regular companion for country folk but now all too rare, largely due to changes in agriculture. Intensive farming methods have vastly reduced the numbers of small mammals that the barn owl hunts, while barns – popular roosts for them, hence their name – have been increasingly converted into houses. As the barn owl flies quite low along hedgerows and walls, it is also now particularly at risk from trucks and other traffic and has become a victim of road kill in the last half century. Overall the total barn-owl population has plummeted from 12,000 pairs in the 1930s to around 4,000 today, although there are some encouraging signs that the trend is being reversed and, thanks to increased conservation, numbers are increasing.

Often the first indication you have that a barn owl is near by is its screeching cry. In flight, they make for a heart-stopping, if eerie sight, spotted at twilight sweeping slowly close to ground level along field edges, riverbanks and railway verges. Their white chest often confuses novice 'birders' into thinking they're witnessing a snowy owl, although there's no mistaking that white, heart-shaped face.

Tawny owl
(*Strix aluco*)

Ask anyone to impersonate an owl and they will probably respond with an instant 'Twit twoo', which could be due to the way an owl call is characterised in thousands of spooky scenes in films and television dramas. What they're actually doing is imitating the calls of a pair of tawny owls. The female calls out 'kew-itt' and the male replies with a 'hoo-hooooo'.

This tubby, chestnut-brown bird is Britain's most common owl, but that doesn't make them any easier to see. Around the size of a woodpigeon – although their metre-wide wingspan makes them appear far bigger in flight – they roost in hollow trees and hunt at night, dropping suddenly on their intended prey, which usually consists of beetles or small mammals such as voles.

At present there are around 20,000 breeding pairs in Scotland, Wales and England, although there are some concerns that their numbers have started to decline.

Short-eared owl
(*Asio flammeus*)

The short-eared owl is both diurnal and nocturnal, hunting by day and night across open countryside and marshy habitat. Usually the short-eared owl is seen but not heard as they are largely silent save for a sharp clap as their wings meet beneath their body in flight and the odd low cry of 'boo-boo-boo-boo'. With heavily spotted buff-brown plumage, your best chance of spotting these solitary birds is in Scotland and northern England, although numbers do swell in coastal areas of south and east England, bolstered by European visitors. Between 1,000 and 3,500 pairs are thought currently to nest in Britain.

Long-eared owl
(*Asio otus*)

If you've ever spotted one of these elusive 'horned' hunters, then you've been lucky. Rarely out in the day and at night almost completely silent, the long-eared owl prefers to nest in isolated conifer plantations. It is identified by those distinctive tufts of feathers that raise when the bird is alarmed or agitated, and its deep orange eyes that keep lookout for its diet of mice and voles. On the rare occasions they are heard, the long-eared owl cry is a soft 'hoo-hoo-hoo-hoo'. As they are so secretive, estimating numbers is difficult, although current surveys indicate that there are between 1,400 and 4,800 pairs of these superbly camouflaged birds currently breeding in Britain.

The problem with our deer

There are six species of deer found in the UK:

➤ Red (*Cervus elaphus*) and roe (*Capreolus capreolus*) are both indigenous species.

➤ Fallow (*Dama dama*) were probably introduced by the Romans

➤ Sika (*Cervus nippon*), muntjac (*Muntiacus reevesi*) and Chinese water deer (*Hydropotes inermis*) arrived in Britain during the past couple of centuries, having been introduced to private parks from where they subsequently escaped. The muntjac, our smallest deer, isn't just a country dweller; it's also become something of a city slicker and according to the British Deer Society in some urban areas is almost as common as the fox.

Britain's deer are becoming victims of their own success. There are now around 2 million deer in the UK, the highest population for a thousand years, and they're causing no end of trouble.

First is the environmental damage. With their ferocious appetites, deer snack their way through woodland, stripping off bark and threatening the very life of trees. They're also fond of ground-nesting birds' eggs and grazing on the vegetation on woodland floors, which increases the plight of already endangered small mammals like dormice and also puts at risk native flowers such as bluebells.

There's another major problem. Increasing numbers of deer are coming into disastrous contact with motor vehicles as they wander across woodland roads. Over the years I've had several narrow escapes – the closest being while driving in Scotland at dusk when a huge stag appeared from nowhere a few yards ahead. Luckily for us both, it dashed into the forest.

The worst time for accidents is during the autumn rutting season. The toll is tragic: every year around 74,000 accidents are logged involving deer and vehicles; according to figures I've seen, between 15 and 20 people are killed, a further 1,100 are seriously injured and 700 suffer minor injuries at a cost of £32 million, in medical terms, and £17 million, in damages to vehicles.

Many deer are not killed instantly – they have to be put down at the roadside. More than 10,000 are severely injured annually, often managing to escape into the woods where many suffer long and agonising deaths. Luckier ones are treated by rescuers from organisations like the RSPCA.

So, what is being done? Over the last few years there have been increased calls for deer control. You can, of course, throw up high wire fences, but these are expensive and simply move the problem on to different areas, and, if they really want to, deer can clear a 1.8-metre fence.

Scientists are attempting to create an immuno-contraceptive drug to control their rate of breeding, but how do you apply it? Dart guns are expensive and, of course, it doesn't help reduce the current population.

roe doe

Is the only real solution to control the numbers by shooting deer? Obviously, that option is opposed by animal-rights supporters but in many areas now, there does seem to be too many deer for the good of the species or the environment. I once spent some time with a professional deerstalker on a Scottish estate. He would identify his target – usually an older female, or hind, – and stay with it, crawling through the heather downwind of her. Only when he had a clear shot, and she was totally unaware, would he squeeze the trigger. I was in awe of his skills.

One of the fears is that if something isn't done, less talented shots will take matters into their own hands, with awful consequences for their targets.

How to drive safely through deer hotspots

1. Be particularly wary during the rutting season (October–December) where deer have other things on their minds than road safety.

2. Take care in the dark. The deadliest hours are from sunset to midnight and just after sunrise. Particular blackspots include the A9 in Scotland, the A14 through Cambridgeshire and Suffolk and the M4 between South Wales and London.

3. Reduce your speed in known deer territory.

4. When possible do not swerve to avoid a collision – this could be even more hazardous because you could career into a ditch or crash into another vehicle.

5. If you do hit a deer, contact the police immediately, but do not approach it – a large, wounded animal is potentially very dangerous.

6. If you spot an injured deer on or by the road, call the RSPCA advice line on 0300 1234 999.

Ticks and Lyme disease

If you've ever spent much time in woodland where deer are present there's a good chance you've been – or know someone who has been – bitten by a tick. These little insects, which look like tiny spiders, lurk in long vegetation ready to hurl themselves at any warm-blooded mammal. At the moment they make the jump on to you they might only be the size of a pinhead, but after they've gorged themselves on your blood they can swell to something resembling a coffee bean.

The main problem with ticks is that they can pass on Lyme disease, which can affect horses, dogs and us humans. Not every bite brings Lyme disease but the longer the tick remains connected to its host the higher the risk. Early symptoms, which can develop within weeks of a tick bite, include fever, headache, chills, muscular and joint pain, blurred vision and swollen lymph glands. If the disease is not identified, more serious complications may develop within months or even years including arthritis, meningitis, Bell's palsy and memory problems.

Tick hotspots

> Exmoor
> The Lake District
> The New Forest
> Salisbury Plain

> The South Downs
> The Scottish Highlands and Islands
> Wiltshire, Berkshire and Thetford Forest
> The North York Moors

How to reduce the risk of tick bites

> Avoid high grass and vegetation, especially when deer are near.

> Wear long trousers tucked into your socks and long-sleeved tops in areas that may be infested with ticks.

> Wear light-coloured clothing that makes it easier to find ticks.

> If you've been in a tick hotspot, remove your clothes as quickly as possible, brushing them down and washing them to prevent ticks being brought into your home.

> Check your body every day for ticks, especially in folds of skin such as behind your knees and elbows.

> Check children every day, especially around the neck and in their hair.

> Check pets' fur to avoid ticks being brought into the home. There are also a number of drops, sprays and collars available to lessen the risk of ticks jumping on to your pets.

Dos and don'ts if you find a tick embedded in your skin

> **Do** try to remove it immediately.

> **Don't** follow the old advice of smothering them in oil, petroleum jelly or stabbing ticks with lighted cigarettes or matches. Other than the fact you might burn yourself, you'll more than likely cause the tick to regurgitate the contents of its stomach straight into your bloodstream, increasing the risk of infection.

> **Don't** try to pluck them out with your fingers. Use either fine-tipped tweezers, as close to your skin as possible, trying hard not to squeeze their body, or use one of the commercially available tick-removing tools.

> **Do** seek medical attention if any part of the tick is left in your skin after you've detached it. Sometimes head or mouth parts can remain in your flesh, causing pain and discomfort.

> **Don't** just throw the tick on the ground once it's out. It might attach itself to another victim.

> **Do** throw the tick into an open fire, flush them down the toilet or crush them in a sealed bag.

> **Do** wash your hands immediately afterwards.

How to buy your own wood

The past ten years have seen an increasing number of people buying their own woodland. For some it's an investment and a place to relax while others want to learn traditional woodland crafts. But how do you go about buying a wood of your own and what can or can't you do in it when it's yours?

How do I find a wood to buy?

The internet has developed into a great resource for the would-be woodlandowner. There are a number of sites you should check out on your search for that perfect plot:

www.woodlands.co.uk
Woodlands.co.uk buys up woods, which it then splits into smaller plots and sells on. You'll find loads of info about buying your own wood here, as well as a bustling online community of woodlandowners.

www.woodlandowner.org.uk
A place to buy and sell woods and learn more about woodland management, uses and resources.

www.woods4sale.co.uk
Another site offering woods for sale across England and Wales.

Is it very expensive?

Depending on your wood's location you should be able to pick up a 10-acre plot of woodland for well below the price of an average house, although if you're looking at buying any land within the M25 you should expect to pay a lot more.

The only other costs will be solicitor's fees, which are similar to what you would pay when buying a house, and negligible land-registry charges.

If you are planning to keep your wood in the family, provided you own it before you die, it won't trigger any inheritance tax.

Grow your own wood

Some conservation organisations, such as the Woodland Trust, have expressed concern that the trend of splitting established larger woods into smaller lots may fragment their biodiversity, because individual owners have different ideas about how their plots should be managed.

One alternative is to create your own wood by buying a plot of agricultural land, planting local, native broadleaf trees and sowing wildflowers around the nursery. Within 15 years your field will feel very much like a real wood.

Grants for tree planting are also available from the Woodland Trust, the Tree Council and the Forestry Commission.

Before buying a plot to plant a wood you need to check:

▶ that it isn't already a valuable habitat, which may result in your having to pay for a botanical survey from an ecologist to assess the impact of planting trees.

▶ that you don't need an Environmental Impact Assessment from the Forestry Commission. This may be required if you're looking to plant over 12 acres in a non-sensitive area or 4 acres in a natural park, Area of Outstanding Natural Beauty or particularly scenic area.

▶ that there are no rights of way across the land, either public or private, e.g. the right to cross the land to run water pipes through it or reach farmland.

▶ whether there are any records of landfill or tipping, which may cause contamination. The Environment Agency will be able to help you with this.

Are there annual charges?

Not really. Woodlands don't come under either business rates or council tax. If your woodland adjoins marshland or river you may have to stump up for agricultural-land-drainage charges, but these cases are rare. Main rivers, for example, are managed by the Environment Agency so if your wood is beside one of these, you won't incur any charges.

Can I build in my wood?

It's very difficult to get planning permission in woodland. In some cases shelters and stores are permissible but you have to be able to prove that they're there for forestry purposes and should always inform your local authority.

What about camping?

Well, it'll be your private land so it's up to you. Up to three caravans are also permitted in private woodland as long as the site isn't used for human habitation for more than 28 days in a year.

Are there any other restrictions?

You'll need to maintain any public rights of way or footpaths that go through your land. When it comes to felling, it's up to you how many trees are cut down but if you want to clear more than 5 cubic metres every month, you'll need to obtain a felling licence from the Forestry Commission.

All of this changes, however, if your woodland includes a Tree Preservation Order, which protect trees for amenity or environmental benefits. If that's the case, then you'll need to contact the Forestry Commission before any work is carried out. If you don't, you could face a fine of up to tens of thousands of pounds.

Gathering firewood

As we all search for alternative ways to heat our homes more people are turning back to wood-burning heaters and one of the reasons given is that firewood is often free. While this can be the case, there are a couple of things you need to remember:

➤ Always ask permission. Before taking wood from a site you need to check with the landowner that it's OK. Although wood may seem to be just lying around, waiting to be taken, it's still their property. Finding out who owns it is easy if you're on National Trust or Forestry Commission land – just check with the local office. It can be trickier if you're on private land – remember even if you're on a public footpath the chances are you're walking through someone else's property. The rule of thumb is, if you're not sure who owns it, don't take it.

➤ Never take every single scrap of wood. You need to responsible. After all, other people might be collecting wood in the area and don't forget that the fuel for your fire is a precious habitat for the insects that live in old wood and the birds that feed on them. Clearing woodland certainly has benefits – promoting new growth, for example – but stripping it out completely helps no-one. (See pages 199–200 for more on the importance of dead wood.)

How to prepare your firewood

The last thing you want to do is to chuck your newly gathered firewood straight on the fire. More than likely it will not burn and if it does the clouds of foul smoke produced won't be pleasant – and neither will your neighbours when they catch up with you. There's no instant fix with gathered firewood, but there are some simple guidelines.

1. Dry the wood out thoroughly

Your firewood needs to be dried out or seasoned. Newly gathered firewood, which is known as green wood, is still 45 per cent water. If burnt while still green it will be hard to light, give out little heat as the fire struggles to evaporate all that moisture, and belch out excessive amounts of smoke. You need to get its moisture content down to around 20 per cent before burning, which is why you need to let wood dry for several months before using it.

2. Cut it to length

It's time for a little strenuous work, cutting your wood to the right size for your wood-burner, usually around 8cm shorter than your firebox. Most models will take lengths around 48cm but check first if you have a small wood-burner.

Remember, the bigger the log, the longer it will take to dry.

3. Let's split

Your wood will season quicker if larger logs are split into widths no more than 15cm.

4. Let the sun do the work

Pile your wood somewhere where the sun can start to evaporate the moisture locked within the wood, ready for the wind to whisk it away. Try not to stack the logs too close together, otherwise the air cannot circulate. Ideally, you should get your wood stacked and ready by March or April so you have the full benefit of the spring and summer sun. Popping the logs on a palette will help the airflow considerably.

Some people cover their stack with plastic sheeting or corrugated sheets to protect it from the rain, but again don't wrap it too tightly. You still need the air to get through so try to keep the sides open to the elements.

5. Wait

After about six months your wood will be ready to burn although the longer you can leave it, the better it will be, especially for very dense hardwood, such as oak.

Which firewood should you choose?

Apple – A great choice if you can get it. Burns nice and slowly, giving a good amount of heat with hardly any flame. The smell is lovely too.

Ash – Will actually burn pretty well when green but, as with other woods, it's best to wait until the logs are completely dry. Gives off a strong flame throughout the burn and plenty of heat. Easy to split the logs, too.

Beech – Almost as good as ash, but best avoided when green.

Blackthorn – A great wood that burns slowly, giving off some good heat with hardly any smoke.

Cedar – A good choice with the potential for long-lasting heat. Also burns with lots of atmospheric pops and crackles. It needs to be well dried, though.

Hawthorn – One of Britain's most traditional firewoods that used to be gathered into faggots, or bundles, before drying. You can see why, as it gives a lot of heat over a long period.

Holly – Only really any good after it's been seasoned for a year or more. When ready it burns quickly but doesn't give too much heat.

Oak – An excellent firewood, burning hot and slow, as long as it's been properly seasoned for at least two years. Don't be tempted to try it before because you'll have little in the way of heat and lots of choking smoke.

Pine – Good flames, but watch out for spitting embers. Season it well and you'll be rewarded with a fantastic odour.

Yew – A nice slow burn with an amazing amount of heat.

And which should you avoid?

Alder – Doesn't last long, and even then gives out little heat.

Chestnut – Not really worth it. Not much in the way of flame or heat but is prone to shooting out embers.

Elder – In days gone by, burning the wood of the elder tree was seen as incredibly unlucky, and was tantamount to welcoming Satan into your house. While I can't vouch for that, Elder isn't the best to burn. It extinguishes quickly after giving off an acrid smoke.

Laburnum – Acrid smoke from a poisonous tree. Never, ever use.

Poplar – Not popular at all with wood-burners. Atrociously low-heat output and thick, suffocating smoke – even after seasoning.

Willow – Hardly any value when burning. Has to be exceptionally well seasoned and then produces scarcely any heat or flame. Best kept for weaving!

Going on a fungi forage

One of the joys of autumn is seeing all the weird and wonderful mushrooms shooting up through the decay of the woodland floor or the bracket fungi that attach themselves to tree trunks. Everywhere you look there's a new colour, texture and smell to experience.

For some there's a new taste as well. The growth in popularity of 'food for free' has led to more people grabbing a basket and heading to the hedgerows and woods to find a tasty snack. But collecting mushrooms is a risky business and every year you're guaranteed to read headlines about an unfortunate forager who has picked the wrong variety and poisoned themselves.

If you do fancy a foray into the world of edible wild mushrooms there are a few essential rules you need to remember at all times.

> Only ever eat a mushroom when you are 100 per cent sure that it's edible. If there is any doubt that you haven't identified it correctly, then don't risk it. Of the 16,500 species of fungi in the UK, more than 50 are poisonous and the deadly effects aren't always instantaneous. Eat a death cap (*Amanita phalloides*), for example, and you'll only start having ill effects after it's ruined your liver. Usually, you'll be dead within six days of consuming a death cap.

> The problem is that many of the safe varieties have almost identical toxic doppelgangers. Field mushrooms (*Agaricus campestris*), for example, are the spitting image of the poisonous yellow-staining mushrooms (*A. xanthodermus*) and the pretty chanterelle (*Cantharellus cibarius*) has a poisonous double in the false chanterelle (*Hygrophoropsis aurantiaca*).

> Sign up for a foraging course and go out with an expert rather than heading out on your own.

> Take a good, well-respected field guide with you, but don't just rely on pictures.

▶ Never believe old folklore about poisonous mushrooms. (See the old wives' tales on page 230.)

▶ Make sure you have landowners' permission to pick fungi on their land and, remember, foraging for mushrooms isn't allowed on National Trust properties.

▶ Never allow children to gather mushrooms.

▶ Never mix edible fungi with questionable varieties.

▶ Before you eat a new mushroom make sure that you keep a small portion clearly labelled in a fridge. It can then be used to identify the offending fungus if there is a negative reaction.

▶ Never eat raw wild mushroom. Some mushrooms only become edible once they're cooked.

▶ When trying a new mushroom, only eat a small amount at first to make sure your body can cope.

▶ When experimenting with a new find, it's best not to wash it down with booze. Some fungi can cause bad reactions when taken with alcohol.

▶ Be a responsible forager. Never take more mushrooms than you need as you could be depriving the local wildlife of a snack.

▶ Use a knife to cut them off at the base, rather than just ripping them out roots and all.

Five old wives' tales about poisonous mushrooms

1. Poisonous fungi will always blacken a silver spoon

The reality: there isn't a single toxic mushroom that obeys this 'rule'

2. Poisonous fungi are made safe by cooking

The reality: cook a death cap and it will kill you just as easily as it would have done raw.

3. Poisonous fungi are always a devil to peel

The reality: the beechwood sickener (*Russula mairei*) peels easily. It also gives you unbearable abdominal cramps and stomach upsets.

4. Poisonous fungi are always brightly coloured

The reality: the destroying angel (*Amanita virosa*) is pure white and is utterly lethal.

5. Poisonous fungi are toxic to insects

The reality: death caps are quite often riddled with larvae. Just because it can't hurt them doesn't mean it can't hurt us. After all, we are quite different to insects.

CHAPTER SIX

Waterways, Wetlands and the Coast

River access

The first-ever episode of *Countryfile* went out on 24 July 1988. It would be another year before I joined the programme, but I still remember watching the very first report – on clashes between canoeists and anglers over rights of access on British waterways. More than twenty years later it's still a hot potato. As with many aspects of country life, tempers fray and debates soon become heated whenever the subject is mentioned. But let's try to break it down into simple facts.

> There are approximately 43,000 miles of rivers in England and Wales.

> The British Canoe Union (BCU) claims that only 5 per cent of that total mileage has rights of access for non-motorised boats and canoes.

> The public has no legal rights to navigate non-tidal waterways in the UK. There is a legal right to navigate tidal waters, although this depends on the presumption that the Crown owns the riverbed beneath the water. There have been cases when the tidal riverbed has been proved to be under private ownership.

▶ Even when you do have the right to navigate a non-tidal waterway, you shouldn't assume that you have the right to moor on the banks or use the adjoining land to either gain access or leave the river. That could still be private land and attempts to moor there may be seen as trespassing.

▶ The situation is different in Scotland. The Scotland Land Reform Act 2003 gave the right to paddle on inland waters, as long as it is done responsibly and your canoe doesn't interfere unreasonably with other interests. On lochs, canoeists are requested to keep a safe distance from anglers, while on rivers they are to await a signal from the angler to proceed if there is a line in the water.

▶ Anglers point out that they pay for fishing rights on private land and are also required to invest in an annual rod licence. This scheme raises £22 million for the Environment Agency, which ploughs the funds back into replenishing fish stocks and environmental projects.

▶ Conversely, canoeists believe that they should be allowed to navigate any waterway for free, as long as their presence doesn't affect the ecology of the area. They argue that, unlike anglers, they don't remove anything from the river, don't need the banks to be cleared or fish stocks to be maintained. In their minds, if walkers or riders aren't expected to pay for the paths they use, why should canoeists be expected to pay for rivers?

▶ BCU claims that there are around 2 million canoeists currently in the Britain, contributing around £700 million to the economy. Meanwhile, the Angling Trust says that there are around 3.8 million British anglers and that freshwater anglers contribute around £3.5 billion.

▶ It's not just canoeists campaigning for access to non-tidal rivers. Many wild swimmers also believe that they should have the right to swim anywhere they like, as long as it is safe, and especially when there is a footpath alongside a river.

The ten longest rivers in Great Britain

River	Country	Source	Mouth	Length
1 Severn	Wales, England	Plynlimon, Wales	Severn Estuary	220 miles
2 Thames	England	Thames Head, Gloucestershire	Thames Estuary	215 miles
3 Trent	England	Knypersley, Staffordshire	Humber Estuary	185 miles
4 Tweed	Scotland, England	Tweed's Well, Scottish Borders	North Sea	155 miles
5 Nene	England	Arbury Hill, Northamptonshire	The Wash	148 miles
6 Great Ouse	England	near Syresham, Northamptonshire	King's Lynn, Norfolk	143 miles
6 Wye	Wales, England	Plynlimon, Wales	Severn Estuary	135 miles
7 Tay	Scotland	Loch Tay, Scottish Highlands	Firth of Tay	117 miles
9 Spey	Scotland	Loch Spey, Scottish Highlands	Moray Firth	107 miles
10 Clyde	Scotland	Lowther Hills, south Lanarkshire	Firth of Clyde	106 miles

Country bridges

One of the earliest problems our ancestors faced was crossing any expanse of water. Today the countryside is full of crossings, from simple stepping-stones and fords to causeways and bridges. Here are some of the most common ways to get across the water.

Fords

The earliest way of crossing a river was to find a ford, a place along the river's path where the waterway spread wide enough – and shallow enough – to cross safely. Over time some fords were paved to save travellers from getting stuck in the mud.

By paying special attention to placenames you can still spot where fords were located in days gone by. The most obvious example is Oxford, which derives its name from 'a ford used by oxen'. In Cornwall, fords were known by the words *rit, ret* or *rid* so that Redruth gained its name from two words: *rid* for a ford and *rudh* meaning red – the ford where the water ran red, thanks to the nearby tin mines. In Wales, you need to look out for the Welsh for ford – *rhyd* – tacked on to the front of words such as Rhyd-Ddu in Gwynedd, meaning the place of the black ford.

Sometimes placenames reveal how dangerous a ford could be. There is a spot near Whitfield Gill in Wensleydale known as Slape Wath, which literally meant slippery ford. This was particularly treacherous as it formed part of the Wensleydale Corpse Way, the route villagers had to take when carrying their dead to remote churchyards for burial. In the 15th century one group of mourners actually lost their relative's body while crossing the River Wharfe. The grieving family could only watch in horror as their dearly departed was washed away.

Clams

In this context a clam is a wooden footbridge. One of the simplest ways of crossing water was to create a footbridge by throwing a tree trunk across the two banks of a stream. A clam certainly gave Trowbridge in Somerset its name – from *treow* or tree-bridge.

The trouble was even the best clam could be almost as dangerous as a ford and was useless if you wanted to take a cart across. Bridges needed to be built.

Clapper bridges

Bridges had, in fact, been built since prehistoric times and medieval craftsman turned to the same design used by their Stone Age ancestors. A clapper bridge is thought to either take its name from the Anglo-Saxon *cleaca*, meaning bridging the stepping stones, or the Latin *claperius* meaning a heap of stones. Either way the early clapper bridges quite simply consisted of planks of wood laid across piles of rocks or stepping stones. There are still many places – such as Elbridge in Kent or Thelbridge in Devon – that take their name from *thel brycg* or plank bridge.

Over time, stone slabs took the place of the wood. One of the most famous is the Postbridge Clapper over the East Dart in Devon, with its four slabs of granite resting on two piles of stones spanning 13 metres from one side of the river to the other. The first recorded mention of the Postbridge Clapper dates from 1655, although sometime in the 1820s a local farmer is said to have taken it upon himself to tip the slabs into the

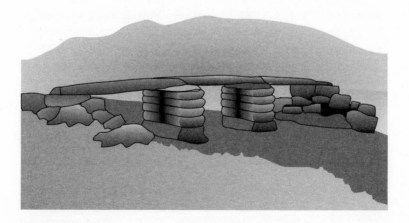

river, intending to create a dam to form a lake for his ducks. The vandal didn't get far and the first slab ended face down on the riverbed. Thankfully the bridge was rebuilt in 1879 and still stands today.

In some parts of the country clapper bridges also became known, rather grandly, as Cyclopean bridges, alluding to the monstrous one-eyed Cyclops of Greek mythology who enjoyed building structures of stone.

Packhorse bridges

As trade routes started to form across England, packhorse bridges started to spring up – narrow, humped bridges often no wider than the horses that used to trot over them, laden with bags, wool and pedlars' wares. If these bridges had any parapet walls at all, they would be very low so as not to impede the horse's load. Many of these bridges are still in use to this very day and it was not until the days of the drovers – who used to drive great flocks or herds of animals across the countryside – and the coming of more wheeled traffic that the need arose for more substantial crossings.

The stone bridge

Some of our oldest bridges were built by monastic houses eager to encourage trade between communities as well as to assist pilgrims along their way.

You can usually tell how old a bridge is by the width of the arches. Narrow pointed arches are older, usually from medieval times, when the monastic architects had yet to master wider spans. Instead they relied on a succession of repeated smaller arches. Over time the arches begin to widen from a maximum of 8 metres, around the year 1200, to the 23 metres of the mid-18th century. There's another clue to look out for: bridges from the later medieval period included v-shape spaces along the parapet so that pedestrians could tuck out of the way of oncoming traffic. Many a country walker still makes use of these when they find themselves sharing a narrow bridge with a car.

Since the Industrial Revolution iron and concrete began to be used increasingly in bridge construction.

Enjoying Britain's canals

For a relatively short period of time, canals were the lifeblood of our industry, transporting valuable cargo across the country. The first-ever canal in England was actually built by the Romans in the second century. The Car Dyke connected the Witham and Nene rivers through Lincolnshire and was probably used as a form of drainage to improve the quality of the surrounding agricultural lands.

However, the canal in its more familiar form came to Britain with the 3rd Duke of Bridgewater, who had visited the 150-mile long Canal du Midi in France during the 18th century. The Duke owned a number of coal mines northwest of Manchester and wanted to find a direct route into the city to take his fuel to market. The Bridgewater Canal opened in 1759, kicking off half a century of frantic canal building and introducing us to the word 'navvies'. The navvies were the labourers, also called navigators, who undertook the work. Over time navigators was shortened to navvies.

The end of the canal bonanza was heralded in 1830 by the arrival of the railway and the navvies shifted from digging canals to laying track. Today, very little cargo is carried by canal – it's all on goods wagons and lorries – and the waterway network has been transformed into one of our major leisure facilities.

Canals are enjoying a great renaissance with more miles being restored every year than were being built two centuries ago. No longer are they derelict eyesores, the dumping place for shopping trolleys and much worse. Restoring and reopening canals creates a sense of pride in the surrounding area – and property prices along their banks rise accordingly.

For many people, a gentle holiday in a canal boat – working the locks, stopping at pubs along the way, getting a unique opportunity to admire wildlife and scenery – is hard to beat. Here are just a few of my favourite canals:

Oxford Canal – for a spot of peace and quiet

My local canal meanders for 77 peaceful miles from the university city to join the Midlands canal network near Coventry. It was one of Britain's earliest canals and is surprisingly winding, more like a river, following the contours of the lands through vales and valley bottoms. Later engineers made canal routes straighter, using embankments and cuttings, and carried them up and over higher ground by building locks. Once, 'the Oxford' was a major trading route between the south and the Midlands, transporting coal and paper. I know an elderly couple who were born and brought up on working boats and their little cottage near Oxford is packed with brightly painted mementos of those days. Now, the canal is busy with pleasure boats and these days Tooley's Boatyard in Banbury (established in 1790 and well worth a visit) builds luxury craft – a far cry from the workaday boats of old.

Regent's Canal – for an instant escape from the daily grind

You don't always have to head out of London to find some tranquillity. Regent's Canal is one of the capital's best-kept secrets, stretching the 9 miles between Paddington and Limehouse Basin, on the Thames. You can hop on your bike and take in some of the best urban landscapes the city has to offer, from London Zoo at Regent's Park to the hustle and bustle of Camden Market.

Originally opened in 1801, the Canal had one last burst of revival during the Second World War as horse-drawn longboats helped ease the burden on the struggling railway network. By the 1960s commercial traffic had all but disappeared but the towpath has become a popular cycling route.

Kennet and Avon Canal – for a spot of exercise

Facing your first lock on a canal trip is challenging but fun. Imagine what it would be like to come up against the Caen Hill flight between Rowde and Devizes on the Kennet and Avon. The canal runs from the Severn Estuary to the River Thames at Reading and gave the canal builders many headaches largely due to the steep inclines along its route. This particular flight was the last section of the Canal to be built and consists of no fewer than 16 locks, one after another, up steep hillside. It's actually part of a bigger system that comprises 29 locks that rise 72 metres in just 2 miles. Traversing that lot would certainly keep you fit.

The Caen Hill flight did give its engineer John Rennie a particular headache. Usually locks include a chamber, known as a pound, which has gates at both ends to control the level of water. As he needed to cram so many locks into such a small area, Rennie couldn't rely on the usual design and so had to create side ponds to store the water the loch needed to operate, thus giving the system its distinctive look.

Leeds and Liverpool Canal – for a change of pace

This was the canal that got me hooked as a child. I grew up in Leeds and Dad used to take me to the Five Rise flight of locks at nearby Bingley. I used to help with the gates (or at least that's how he made it look).

At 127 miles the Leeds and Liverpool is the longest in Britain and as it was built for larger barges, at 4 metres across it's one of the widest too. Connecting with the Aire and Calder Navigation in Leeds, it links the west and east coasts of northern England, traversing both wild moorland and the gentler fringes of the Yorkshire Dales.

It takes a good week to travel from one end of the Canal to the other, longer if you want to explore the many offshoots along the way. The one thing you can't do is rush. The maximum speed limit on a canal is 4mph. No longboats come with speedometers so the only way of telling if you're going too fast is to see whether you're causing a breaking wave behind the boat. Don't worry, if you are going too fast other canal dwellers will soon tell you.

Llangollen Canal – for a touch of history

In 21 years of *Countryfile* I've hardly ever been lost for words, but one of the rare occasions was when I took a narrow boat over the Pontcysyllte Aqueduct on the Llangollen Canal. It's a surreal experience, travelling 35 metres above the River Dee's valley in a 3.4-metre wide, 310-metre long iron trough. If your boat's deck bobs above the top of the trough it feels as if you're floating in the air.

It's easy to see why it's been one of the stars of Britain's canal system since it opened in 1805 and why it's now been classified as a World Heritage Site.

Lancaster Canal – for wildlife wonders

As it only has six locks, the Lancaster Canal is a favourite with novices. You'll also see quite a few birdwatchers along its banks too as the Glasson branch, opened in 1826 to connect the Lancaster Canal with the sea in the Lune Estuary, is a haven for tufted ducks, coots, moorhens, shelducks, great crested grebes and mute swans. As it's so close to the sea, the winter also brings in both yellow-legged and Mediterranean gulls.

Pocklington Canal – a secret gem

You can walk the entire length of the Pocklington Canal, in the Vale of York, but only about half the 10-mile stretch is navigable. Where nature has taken over the Canal provides a home for the rare bittern, otters and water vole.

Forth and Clyde and the Union canals – for engineering excellence

Most people write off canals as the stuff of history and, indeed, in the past they were the place where engineers faced some of their biggest challenges. But even today they are a springboard for creativity as shown at the junction of the Forth and Clyde and the Union canals in Scotland.

The two canals had once been connected by a system of locks, but these had been filled in when the canal industry began to falter. As more people wanted to travel the canalways for leisure a new connection had to be found. The answer came in the form of the Falkirk Wheel, the only rotating boat lift in the world. The 35-metre high structure was opened by the Queen in 2002 and ever since millions of people have flocked to see up to eight boats lifted into the air from one canal to the other. The system is so energy efficient that it only uses the same power to operate as you and I would need to boil eight kettles.

How do canal locks work?

A lock is a surprisingly simple bit of engineering. When planning a new canal the engineers would try to map a route that was as flat as possible. However, this wasn't always the case and as the surface of a canal needed to remain on the level, they were stepped to negotiate inclines. But how could you lift a barge from one level to another? The answer was the modern lock, first developed in Holland in the Middle Ages.

Here's how it works:

1. When you want to go up a lock, you approach the lock and open the lower gate, closing it again once you've steered the boat into the chamber (or pound) between the gates.

2. You then go up to the upper gates and locate the winding handle. Turning this opens the sluice so that the chamber gradually starts to fill with water from above. As the water level rises, so does your boat.

3. When the water level in the lock matches that of the top level, you can open the gates and continue on your way. Unless there is a boat waiting to go down, it's usual to jump out and shut the gates and the paddles behind you.

Descending a lock means reversing the process. Obviously before you do any of this, you need to check where the water level is in the first place. If you want to go up a lock and find it's still full of water you need to open the lower sluices to drop the water in the chamber down to your level and vice versa.

Did you know . . . ?

It's often said that Birmingham has more canals than Venice. It's true. In fact, the Birmingham Canal Navigations extend to just over 100 miles, including a waterway version of Spaghetti Junction. It's one of the most intricate canal systems in the world and our *Countryfile* office overlooks one of the basins.

The top 20 wildlife sightings on Britain's canals

In 2009 British Waterways, the organisation that cares for our historic canals, undertook a survey of the wildlife you're likely to spot:

1. Mallard
2. Canada goose
3. Swan
4. Moorhen
5. Starling
6. Bumblebee
7. Rabbit
8. House sparrow
9. Coot
10. Stickleback
11. Roach
12. Frog
13. Perch
14. Damselfly
15. Robin
16. Heron
17. Grey squirrel
18. Cormorant
19. Dragonfly
20. Pondskater

Watery wildlife: winners and losers

Crayfish vs Crayfish

It's like something out of a science-fiction film. An alien invader lands on our shores and begins to eat everything in its path. Armour-plated and incredibly dangerous, the invader will not rest until it's the dominant lifeform.

The problem is that this isn't fiction – it's fact and it's happening every day in Britain's waterways.

The American signal crayfish (*Pacifastacus leniusculus*) was first introduced to England in the 1970s, bred to feed farmed trout and to delight gourmets in top restaurants. It wasn't long before they escaped and started to colonise the country's rivers. Our own native white-clawed crayfish (*Austropotamobius pallipes*) didn't stand a chance.

The aggressive crustacean lays up to 275 eggs at a time in burrows nearly a metre long and feeds on plants, invertebrates, snails, small fish and eggs, out-competing the white-clawed crayfish. And if it can't find enough food to support them, it simply eats its own young. Armed with two massive pincers the signal can also march several miles across land in its search for new habitats.

And that isn't all. The signal carries a plague that literally eats our native crayfish from the inside out. *Aphanomyces astaci* is a parasitic fungus that can kill the white-clawed crayfish within weeks. At first the symptoms are behavioural – the usually nocturnal crayfish begins to be seen in the day, and as the disease progresses the infected creatures show signs of increased disorientation. However, the true horror of the crayfish plague is only revealed after death. While the dead crayfish outwardly may look perfectly normal, break open its shell and you'll find little other than the fungus.

It's estimated that in just two decades, we've lost around 95 per cent of the white-clawed crayfish population. So can anything be done?

There are a few conservation projects already in place, most notably the South West White-Clawed Crayfish Conservation Group, which has begun trapping the native crayfish and moving them to two sanctuaries, hopefully, safe havens from the relentless signal. The locations themselves are being kept top secret to avoid visitors tramping the plague spores to the new breeding grounds. If such schemes don't work, the British white-clawed crayfish could be facing extinction within thirty years.

How to trap crayfish

Another salvo against the American signal crayfish was launched in 2005 when the Environment Agency (EA) introduced a new set of by-laws that – under certain conditions – allow the trapping of any non-native crayfish in our waters.

If you fancy trapping your own aliens, here's what you need to do:

1. Obtain a licence from the EA. It's free, although the EA will want to know where you're going to set your traps. This is so it can work out whether such trapping is likely to affect adversely other species in your local waterway, including the white-clawed crayfish.

2. If the requirement is met, and your licence granted, you need to ensure that the waterway you plan to use doesn't run through private land. If it does, then check with the landowner first, getting their permission to trap the crayfish on their watercourse.

3. Buy a legal crayfish trap. Your local EA office will be able to give you advice on this to ensure that you don't get one with a mouth larger than 95mm in diameter. In some cases otters have been known to drown in illegal traps.

   Make sure you know how to identify the signal crayfish. The main difference is that the white-clawed crayfish grows to lengths of up to 12cm and if you flip them over they have pinkish-white undersides to their claws. The signal crayfish can grow up to 30cm and the underside of its claws is red.

   Remember, it's illegal to capture a native white-clawed crayfish which is protected under the Wildlife and Countryside Act 1981.

4. Once all permissions have been granted, set your traps, but remember that you need to check them every 24 hours.

5. If you catch a signal crayfish, it must be killed rather than returned to the water. It's actually illegal to put them back.

6. You'll need regularly to treat your traps with disinfectant to avoid spreading the crayfish plague. Fishermen should also clean any boots or nets before moving between rivers.

Other problem invaders

American mink (*Mustela vison*)

First imported for the fashion industry from Alaska and Canada in 1929, the American mink soon found its way off the fur farms and into the wild. Ruthless predators, mink are agile swimmers and feed on fish, shellfish, frogs, birds' eggs, rabbits and rats. They are also held largely responsible for the collapse of our native water-vole population (see page 249–51). The descendants of the escaped mink were also thought to be a reason behind the decline of the otter (see page 256), outcompeting Tarka in the wild. However, recent years have seen otter numbers rise and mink numbers falling. In the 1980s there were 110,000 in the wild, although today there may be fewer than 40,000. There is even evidence that in some cases otters are killing mink.

Japanese knotweed (*Fallopia japonica*)

Introduced to Great Britain by the Victorians as an ornamental from the slopes of Japanese volcanoes, the plant, with its bamboo-like stems and creamy flowers, was originally thought charming by 19th-century gardeners. However, another picture soon started to form as the weed from the Far East smothered everything else in the garden. Annoyed, the Victorians dug it up and dumped it in the countryside, thinking that was that. It wasn't. One hundred years later Japanese knotweed has conquered the UK.

Known back home as 'itadori', meaning strong plant, the weed can grow more than a metre in a month and needs only a piece the size of your fingernail to establish itself. Not only does it overcrowd and dominate habitats, it also causes havoc to developments, even cracking tarmac and concrete. And, as its roots go so deep, you have to be careful as spreading the weed is a criminal offence. It is thought that the removal of knotweed currently costs the UK economy £150 million each and every year. It's not just big business and developers that have to shoulder the burden – homeowners have found that having Japanese knotweed on their property immediately reduces the value of their house, while some banks even refuse to lend on properties in neighbourhoods where the plant has been discovered.

The problem is that while knotweed has plenty of predators back home in Japan it has none here. Until now.

Over the next few years a psyllid – a species of plant lice – known as *Aphalara itadori*, which is one of the weed's natural predators, is to be introduced to Great Britain. As the tiny insect spreads they will feed on the superweed's sap, stunting its growth and depleting its extensive root system. This is first time biocontrol – the introduction of a natural predator into an alien environment to control a pest species – has been carried out in the EU, and other countries will be watching carefully.

But isn't this a bit risky, introducing one alien agent to destroy another? Scientists maintain it's a safe bet, as the psyllid only snacks on Japanese knotweed. Either way, it's a long-term strategy. The biocontrol may take ten years seriously to affect the onslaught of knotweed.

Chinese mitten crab (*Eriocheir sinensis*)

Named after the soft hair-like bristles that covers its large claws, the mitten crab is considered a delicacy in Southeast Asia, but is causing havoc along the banks of the Thames. Spread around the world in the ballast of ships, the mitten crab has particularly hit areas in and around London and is thought to be moving west, occupying a niche opened by the decline of the native crayfish. It's a threat as it burrows deep into riverbanks, undermining their structure. Along some stretches of the Thames the riverbank has retreated 6 metres due to mitten crab damage.

The Natural History Museum has just completed a two-year project that concluded that the mitten crabs in the Thames were safe for human consumption so increased fishing and culinary use could help fight this particular invasion. It appears the gloves are off.

Floating pennywort (*Hydrocotyle ranunculoides*)

We didn't learn from the Victorians. Water or floating pennywort, which sounds delightful but isn't, was introduced to Britain by the aquatic nursery trade just over twenty years ago and is already a massive problem. In late summer, the fleshy-stemmed plant can grow up to 20cm per day, swamping entire waterways with dense mats of vegetation. Before you know it, fish are having to fight for oxygen and native plants are being crowded out. Navigation of affected rivers also becomes impossible, as boats struggle to break through the thick mattress of green.

The Environment Agency currently spends £120,000 removing the plant every year and the cost is rising.

Zebra mussels (*Dreissena polymorpha*)

Stripy stowaways that travelled to Britain's waterways on the hulls of ships, zebra mussels can grow up to 5cm long. At first it appeared that zebra mussels were doing a useful job of cleaning waterways by feasting on plankton. But all this was actually doing was allowing more sunlight to shine through and that encouraged the growth of clogging weeds. While British zebra mussels haven't reached the levels in America – the Mississippi in particular is plagued by thousands of them per square metre – they do cause problems along our canal system, jamming lock gates and sluices, and even blocking the intake pipes of power stations.

Water fern (*Azolla filiculoides*)

Also known as fairy fern, there is nothing ethereal about this waterway pest. Spreading like a spongy carpet across the water's surface, water fern blocks out the sun for the plants below and also lowers the temperature of the entire waterway, putting other life at risk. Free-floating and able to survive the coldest of winters, water fern also represents a potential risk for children and animals as it appears solid enough to walk on.

The fern does have a natural predator, albeit one only found in certain areas. Although it has never deliberately been released into the wild over here, the South African frond-feeding weevil (*Stenopelmus rufinasus*) has been spotted in Surrey and Cumbria, and has proved effective against the spread of the plant.

What you can do to help combat invasive plant species

▶ Never buy any of the following plants for your pond:

- Australian swamp stonecrop or New Zealand pygmyweed (*Crassula helmsii*)

- Curly waterweed or curly water thyme (*Lagarosiphon major*)

- Floating pennywort (*Hydrocotyle ranunculoides*)

- Parrot's feather (*Myriophyllum aquaticum*)

- Water fern (*Azolla filiculoides*)

- Water primrose (*Ludwigia grandiflora*)

▶ Always buy native plants such as:

- Water starwort (*Callitriche stagnalis*)

- Needle spikerush or hairgrass (*Eleocharis acicularis*)

- Water forget-me-not (*Myosotis scorpioides*)

- Greater spearwort (*Ranunculus lingua*)

- Arrowhead (*Sagittaria sagittifolia*)

- Frogbit (*Hydrocharis morsus-ranae*)

▶ When buying aquatic plants, always check that they don't contain even the smallest fragment of an invasive plant. Most only need a scrap to spread. Check with your supplier if you're not sure.

▶ If you already have these invasives in your pond, get rid of them, but don't just put them down the drain or throw them in the rubbish or compost. Ideally, burn them if at all possible.

▶ Never transfer plants, frogspawn or anything else between ponds. You may unwittingly spread invasive plants.

▶ If you see any invasive plants on sale, alert the provider of the threat they pose.

Ratty fights back

Kenneth Grahame's children's classic *The Wind in the Willows* began life as a series of bedtime stories and letters written for his son, whom he affectionately called Mouse. Inspired by the countryside around his home near the Thames and childhood holidays in Cornwall and Berkshire, Grahame filled his stories with all manner of colourful characters including the faddish Mr Toad, wise old Badger, timid Mole and, of course, the ever resourceful Ratty.

The interesting thing about Ratty is that he's not actually a rat at all, but a water vole (*Arvicola amphibius*) and sadly his kin have been in trouble for many years now. The small creatures are thought to be Britain's fastest-declining mammal, with a population that has shrunk by 90 per cent in just two decades.

The reasons behind the slump are manifold. Britain's largest voles construct burrows in grassy banks. Thanks to the trend for concreting the side of some major waterways and more intensive farming methods those banks have rapidly started to vanish from the countryside.

Then there's the fact that the water vole is at the very bottom of the food chain on our waterways. Stoats and weasels may have been the villains in *The Wind in the Willows*, but in the real world the water vole must watch out for otters, pike, polecats, herons and owls. Just like Ratty, the voles are quick-witted and past masters at making a quick getaway. If surprised by an otter, a vole will kick up mud from the riverbank to create a kind of smokescreen so it can escape into one of its tight burrow entrances. Usually, that's good enough as most of the vole's natural predators are too big to follow it inside. Unfortunately that's not the case for the American mink (see page 245), which can squeeze into the tightest of places. The introduction of the mink was the nail in the water vole's coffin, decimating the already fragile population.

The invasive mink isn't the only problem on the river. There's man too. The fact is that many people can't tell the difference between a brown rat and a water vole. Too often, when someone has been lucky enough to spot a rare water vole, developers, pest controllers and builders think they have a rat problem and so set rat poison, disturb their homes or even shoot them.

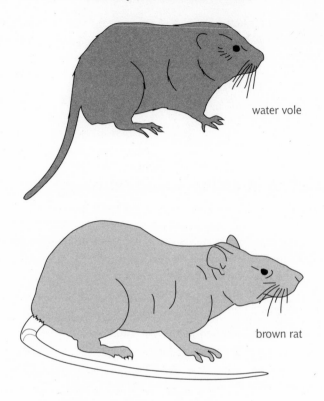

water vole

brown rat

How to tell the difference between a brown rat and a water vole

Brown rat	Water vole
Body length of up to 30cm	Body length of up to 20cm
Pointed nose	Blunt nose
Larger ears that stick up	Small hidden, rounded ears
Long, scaly, pink, hairless tail	Shorter furry tail
Grey/brown fur	Silky chestnut-brown fur

But all is not lost for Ratty. The species is now protected and anyone found disturbing its habitat or injuring a water vole can face a £5,000 fine. In some areas mink culls seem to have had a positive effect on water-vole numbers but the most encouraging result comes from the recent survey by British Waterways which showed that 89 water-vole sightings had been made in 2009, twice as many as the previous year.

Rewilding in action — the return of the beaver

In 2009, a Eurasian beaver (*Castor fiber*) swam in Scotland's waters for the first time in four centuries. Once a familiar sight in British waterways, the beaver was hunted to extinction for its thick waterproof fur, meat and even a secretion known as castoreum, produced in a gland under its tail, which was used for pain-relief.

The release of 11 beavers into the wild at Argyll is part of a five-year scheme to access a wider reintroduction – or rewilding – process across Scotland. The new incumbents were brought from Norway and then placed in quarantine for six months before being set free.

Rewilding is a controversial process and for people who live and work in beaver country the mammals are often like Marmite – either hated or loved and nothing in between. But what are pros and cons of rewilding beavers?

For

▶ For many conservationists beavers are a missing piece of the environmental jigsaw. They are known as a keystone species – one that affects the ultimate survival of other wildlife in the area. Beavers adapt the habitat and, it is said, introduce various benefits.

▶ The dams they build stabilise water levels, slowing rivers and helping to control flooding. They even purify the water, reducing sediment drift and aerating water that passes through the structures.

❯ The slow-moving water around beaver ponds attracts fish and then, in turn, fish-eating birds such as herons, goosanders and kingfishers as well as otters, which often move into areas with beaver ponds. The rotting wood in the beaver's dam also becomes a perfect habitat for invertebrates and therefore a perfect hunting ground for woodpeckers.

❯ Beavers naturally coppice trees. In one night, the nocturnal rodent is able to fell a tree with a 40cm diameter. The tree will grow back healthier than ever.

❯ They keep smaller streams flowing by swimming regularly through them.

❯ Other species can make use of beaver burrows. Otters often occupy abandoned burrows and water shrews and water voles often find shelter alongside beavers.

❯ It is believed that the rewilding of beavers will lead to an increase in tourism and therefore bring a financial boost to nearby rural communities.

Against

❯ Some experts question the sense of reintroducing an animal that has been absent from a location for over four hundred years. They say that the ecosystem would have moved on and changed over time and that rewilding beavers is no different to introducing an alien species to the environment.

❯ There have been cases when a beaver's dam hasn't been so beneficial to the surrounding countryside. In Estonia, beavers have been blamed for the destruction of a number of forests as well as the closure of drainage canals. This has even led to culling of the Estonian beaver population.

❯ While beavers do not eat fish, there are fears that their dams will block the passage of Scotland's migratory fish returning to spawn, including the native Atlantic salmon and sea trout.

❯ Beavers may spread a parasite (*Giardia lamblia*), that lives in the small intestine of many mammals and can affect humans, bringing on stomach cramps, unexplained weight loss and vomiting. In Canada the infection is even known as beaver fever. However, all beavers currently involved in legal reintroductions are quarantined for six months before release to ensure that they're not infected and are regularly checked in the wild to see whether they have picked up the parasite.

Whatever the arguments, there is something magical about seeing these creatures back in the wild. My first glimpse in Argyll came as dusk fell on the small loch I was exploring. As I peered into the mist that had begun to rise from the limpid water, two swam close to my canoe. I had been told that, while filming the project for *Countryfile*, there was a good chance of seeing them but I wasn't holding my breath. I've been assured many times on wildlife assignments that I would see this or that wildlife wonder and have been often terribly disappointed. (The usual comment is: 'You should have been here yesterday.') So this was a real thrill, but in all of these cases one mustn't let emotion obstruct the reality that rewilding is, and probably always will be, a highly contentious issue in the British countryside.

Comeback kings

Other species that rewilders want to see back on British soil and some recent successes include:

Wild boar (*Sus scrofa*)

Became extinct in Britain: Around the 13th century

Reason for extinction: Hunting

The great storm of 1987 had many effects, one of which was the destruction of the enclosures of captive wild boar in various parts of Britain. The boar escaped and re-established themselves, with breeding populations now believed to be thriving in Kent, Herefordshire, Dorset, Devon, Somerset and the Forest of Dean.

Grey wolf (*Canis lupus*)

Became extinct in Britain: 1743, when the last wolf was said to be shot in Moray, Scotland

Reason for extinction: Destruction of habitat and hunting

One of the most controversial rewilding targets, the reintroduction of wolves to Scotland is largely based on the need to control red deer. When the wolves vanished, the red deer had no natural predators and flourished, endangering other species such as capercaillie. However, there are fears that a new population of wolves would prey on livestock and even be a threat to humans, though there are very few reported cases of wolves attacking people.

Eurasian lynx (*Lynx lynx*)

Became extinct in Britain: Around a thousand years ago

Reason for extinction: Hunting

Considered by many as one of the best candidates for rewilding in Scotland, it is hoped that the lynx would predate on juvenile roe, red and sika deer as well as keeping fox numbers down. At least 450 lynx would be needed to establish a viable population although there would be some threat to sheep in the areas chosen for reintroduction.

Brown bear (*Ursus arctos*)

Became extinct in Britain: Unknown, but thought to be before the Roman occupation of Britain

Reason for extinction: Habitat loss and hunting

While a reintroduced population of bears would certainly bring in the tourists, the bear is one of species that is least likely to be rewilded in the near future. It is thought that a population of 250 would be needed for any project to be a success and even the vast expanse of the Scottish Highlands would struggle to support such numbers.

Great bustard (*Otis tarda*)

Became extinct in Britain: 1840

Reason for extinction: Changing agricultural practices and hunting

The world's heaviest flying bird has been the subject of a reintroduction programme on Salisbury Plain since 2004. Sheltered by the fact that the majority of this great swathe of southern England is off-limits thanks to its status as an MoD training ground, the birds have started to re-establish themselves. In 2009 the first great bustard egg was hatched in Britain since 1832.

I received permission to watch a group of these mighty birds through binoculars – to the envy, I'm sure, of many birders. I also met, close up, two of them in a pen as they were about to be released. Rather too close, in fact. One edged towards me then lunged at my leg, giving me a powerful peck. Very painful, but not many people can claim to have been attacked by Britain's rarest bird.

White-tailed eagle or sea eagle (*Haliaeetus albicilla*)

Became extinct in Britain: 1916

Reason for extinction: Hunting

Reintroduced to the Scottish islands of Rum and Mull since the mid-1970s, the white-tailed eagle, with its 2.5-metre wing span, is again a familiar sight in some areas of Scotland. Plans are currently under way to run a similar scheme in East Anglia, prompting fears that the predator's arrival in the skies over Suffolk would threaten flocks of sheep and even local birdlife such as lapwing and grey partridge.

Large blue butterfly (*Phengaris arion*)

Became extinct in Britain: 1979

Reason for extinction: Changes in agriculture and the reduction in number of grazing rabbits meant that a species of ant *(Myrmica sabuleti)* all but disappeared. No-one knew at the time that the large blue butterfly's lifecycle was completely dependent on this one particular ant species.

Large blues were imported by conservationists from Sweden and reintroduced into specially prepared land across the Southwest where grazing had been re-established. Today there are over thirty colonies supporting around 20,000 large blue butterflies.

Go otter spotting

The Eurasian otter (*Lutra lutra*) is Britain's most heart-warming conservation, success story. During the 1950s and 60s our otter population crashed from around 50,000 to dangerously low levels. It is commonly believed that the decline was largely due to organochlorine pesticides like aldrin and dieldrin, two insecticides that were introduced to help control agricultural pests. Being predators, otters were particularly vulnerable to the chemicals' effects, which became concentrated at the top of the food chain. They were also hunted – as a boy I can remember watching the local otter hounds in hot pursuit on the River Wharfe near Harewood outside Leeds.

By the beginning of the 1970s you only saw otters in zoos or wildlife sanctuaries. Then, things started to change. The hunting of otters for their pelts or for sport was banned in 1978 and under the Wildlife and Countryside Act 1981 they became a protected species. Kill an otter and you could face a £5,000 fine or even a six-month stint in prison. Controls on pollution were also tightened and reintroduction programmes sprang up in restored habitats throughout lowland Britain.

Eurasian otter

Today while the mammal, which is about the size of a small dog, is still vulnerable, it has staged a remarkable comeback. In the mid-1970s, when the Environment Agency carried out its first otter survey of England and Wales, viable otter populations were only found in 6 per cent of all the sites surveyed – all the others had disappeared. The latest survey, in 2000–2, shows they have returned to more than a third of those sites in England, and in Wales an amazing 71 per cent of sites showed otter activity. It is believed that there are now around 10,000 otters in Britain, a fantastic achievement considering they came so very close to extinction.

But how can you check out if your local river or canal houses a family of these shy but ferocious hunters? Here are some helpful tips:

1. Head out at either dawn or dusk. This is the time when otters largely feed and so you've got a better chance of spotting one. There are some exceptions to this rule. Coastal otters are active throughout the day and young cubs feed at any hour.

2. Find a waterway that would offer good fishing for the otter. As you'd expect fish is the mainstay of the otter diet, although they will happily eat frogs, small birds and crustaceans too. Every day an otter eats 15 per cent of its own body weight.

3. Leave your faithful friend at home. If an otter gets a whiff of dog it will run and hide.

4. Keep an eye out for otter footprints, which you may be able to find in soft mud. They are asymmetrical and between 42 and 80mm wide and 70mm long. Often you can only make out four of the toes – complete with slight webbing between them – but some footprints do show all five.

5. You may be able to find an otter's home – or holt. The entrances are often in riverbanks, or more usually beneath the roots of a tree. Conservation groups often construct artificial holts in areas where otters have returned to give them a helping hand.

6. Otters also sleep in resting places beside the river during the day, so keep an eye out for otter-sized depressions in the mud – known, rather nicely, as otter couches – where hardly any grass grows.

7. Use your nose. The best way of tracking an otter is to keep a nostril out for a smell like jasmine tea, lavender or even newly mown hay on the riverbanks. These are just some of the descriptions that have been given over time for the peculiarly sweet odour of fresh otter faeces (or spraint if you want to use the technical term). Generally about the size of a 10-pence piece, spraints are often left in quite prominent places, be that on tree roots, under bridges or on boulders or logs. Colour-wise the spraint will be tarry black, although some can be dark green, and full of fish bones.

8. Otters leave their spraints to mark their territory, which can be substantial. An otter can easily cover 24 miles in a single night, leaving around 20 spraints in total. Of course, in many areas, otters may still be competing with mink so how can you be sure you're not studying mink droppings? Easy. Mink scats are shiny, long, black and largely full of fur. They also smell absolutely dreadful.

9. Keep your ears pricked for a sharp, whistle-like call that the otters use as a sign of enjoyment rather than a territorial warning. Excited young otters in particular often squeal like this when playing.

10. Look out for bubbles on the surface of the water. When underwater, an otter will close its nostrils and air is forced out of its coat, causing a trail of bubbles.

11. If you are lucky enough to spot an otter swimming, there are a few signs that confirm you are indeed watching a playful *Lutra lutra* and not an American mink. When an otter swims, only its head breaks the surface of the water, leaving a v-shaped wake in the water, whereas you can see both the head and the back of the mink as it is swimming.

12. Another sure sign that you're watching an otter is that it will arch its tail and back before diving into the water.

13. Keep your distance. Seeing a wild otter is a real privilege, but you need to take great care not to startle the animal or disturb its environment.

An otter cull?

Otters can still be hunted in the UK but only by people granted a special licence – and so far that hasn't happened. But some sectors of the angling community have suggested that a cull of otters might one day be needed to help preserve fish stocks.

The problem seems to be that while otters have returned, their main meal has not. Eels were always a major part of an otter's diet and these slippery customers declined heavily while otters were absent. With a lack of eels, the recovering otters have turned to such fish as salmon, pike, trout and carp. Some anglers claim that fishing clubs are beginning to close as thousands of pounds worth of stock is decimated by hungry otters, while others are forced to drop their prices as they can no longer provide so many fish to catch.

Still-water angling sites are often the hardest hit and so anti-otter fencing may be the answer. This has led some to call on the government to help fund the defences, which can be expensive: fencing off a small lake costs in the region of £10,000. The argument runs that if the law protects the otter, then public money should be made available to protect an industry that is worth £3.5 billion a year, supports 2.6 million anglers and provides jobs in many rural areas.

Conservationists and angling organisations alike have called for more research into the problem and are eager to point out that any proposed cull would have be the very last resort. However, the fact that the subject has been raised at all, highlights the problems that every conservation and reintroduction project involves. Any change in a waterway, be it good or bad, affects everyone else who uses it.

The benefits of wetlands

People often joke that England is a wet country but the truth is that the land at least is drier than it's ever been. When William the Conqueror invaded he would have found great areas of the country partially flooded. The lowlands were a series of swamps, marshes, bogs and mires awash with wildlife, but a difficult place for human habitation. The hardy country dwellers who made this unforgiving landscape their home harvested the reeds, rushes and peat to make a living, or fished for eels that were once so plentiful that they were even used as currency (in 1301, for example, Glastonbury Abbey paid its £13 rent in 3,000 eels from the Stathe weir).

The largest area of wetland was the Great Fen Basin, which covered the lowlands of Norfolk, Suffolk, Cambridgeshire and Lincolnshire, an area of around 1,485 square miles. The Romans had expressed interest in draining this vast area, as did Queen Elizabeth I many centuries later, but in the 17th century the Duke of Bedford won the support of a number of investors and, employing Dutch engineers, began to reclaim the land. The Duke's men cut ditches and set up dykes that drained the water, giving access to more of the rich peat below and making the land available for arable farming. Four centuries later 99.9 per cent of the Great Fen Basin has been drained.

I've seen for myself the result of wetland destruction all around the UK. In upland areas like Plynlimon in the Cambrian Mountains of mid-Wales and the North York Moors, farmers were paid to drain peat bogs in the mid-20th century to make the land more suitable for sheep. Over the years, the thousands of ditches cleaved through the uplands expanded as the peat dried out. They became covered with vegetation, turning them into hidden death traps for sheep and danger zones for unwary walkers. Heavy rainfall, which occurs regularly in these areas, results in surface water sweeping in torrents through the ditches and down into valleys, adding considerably to the hazards of flooding.

Today 35,000 hectares (86,487 acres) of wetland remain in England. That's only 10 per cent of what existed just five hundred years ago and the majority of that drainage has taken place since the Industrial

Revolution. Figures from DEFRA show that 85 per cent of our lowland rivers have also been modified, either straightened to assist navigation, deepened or in some cases completely disconnected from their floodplain.

But all is not lost. Schemes like the Great Fen Project are planning to turn back the clock, re-creating these vital habitats. This lottery-funded project aims to create 3,700 hectares (9,000 acres) of new wetland habitat between Huntingdon and Peterborough, including farmland that will link together two existing National Nature Reserves, Woodwalton Fen and Holme Fen. A hundred years from now the surrounding countryside should look very different.

But why bother? Many farmers argue that re-creating wetlands takes away valuable arable and grazing land, so aren't these schemes just standing in the way of progress? Here are four reasons why wetlands are important:

1. They offer natural flood control

In times of floods a single acre of wetland can hold an amazing 6 million litres of water, which it slowly releases later in the season. When the terrible floods of 2007 hit Britain, Natural England was quick to point out that a programme of wetland re-creation, along with the restoration of peat bogs and free-flowing rivers, would be far more effective than tradition flood defences such as earth embankments and concrete. In basic terms, the countryside needs to be able to absorb water once again.

Wetlands – be they rivers, marshes or lakes – help slow down the relentless march of floodwaters and protect the cities. For example, the River Aire passes through extensive washlands as it snakes its way through Yorkshire. It's believed that this marshy territory – which alone can provide up to 25 million cubic metres of water storage when bad weather hits – saved Leeds when severe floods hit the North in 2000. Without them, my home city would have faced repair bills running into the tens of millions. In the South, there have been similar successes. By simply restoring the floodplains around the River Quaggy in southeast London, more than 600 homes and businesses have seen the chances of serious flooding drop from one every five years to one every 70 years.

2. They clean our water

Freshwater wetlands are Mother Nature's very own water-purifying system. As incoming water meets wetland, it slows down meaning that particles of pesticides, phosphates or heavy metals begin to settle to the bottom of the area. Over time, sediment buries the pollutants, removing them from the water so that it runs cleaner as it flows back into rivers and streams.

There are other ways that wetlands help filter the water. They are home to a lot of decaying organic matter, which attracts and binds pollutants, such as the heavy metals zinc, lead and magnesium, while microbes feast on pesticides and other impurities.

The need for clean water becomes clear when you think that it's estimated that, owing to increasing population and usage, the demand for clean water in London will outstrip supply by 2016.

Of course, this doesn't mean that we can use wetlands as dumping grounds for chemicals. While their purification powers are impressive, there is only so much pollution they can deal with before the balance is tipped.

3. They are proven carbon sinks

The Earth's remaining wetlands contain 771 billion tonnes of greenhouse gases and one-fifth of all carbon, trapped within its soggy soil. If wetlands continue to dry out and harden, either due to our own interference or the changing climate, that devastating cocktail could be released into the atmosphere.

4. They support a huge array of wildlife

Wetlands are incredibly important for a wide range of wildlife. They provide a home for midges, dragonflies, butterflies and moths, all of which are food for other species. Amphibians such as toads and frogs obviously flourish there as do many specialist plant species including the butterfly orchid, flag iris, marsh marigold and ragged robin.

Furthermore, Britain's wetlands are of vital importance to the world's population of waterbirds. We lie slap-bang on the major migratory routes for Arctic-nesting birds, which is why millions of waterbirds are attracted to our estuaries every winter. A recent survey by the RSPB showed that 225 British wetland sites host one of more species of overwintering birds in internationally important numbers and 85 hold an average of 10,000 or more birds.

Britain's top wetlands for wintering birds

Location	Region	Average number of birds (resident and migrant)	Species of international importance
The Wash	East England/ East Midlands	371,308	16
Ribble Estuary	North West England	238,160	16
Humber Estuary	Yorkshire and Humberside	217,805	12
North Norfolk coast	East England	206,703	8
Morecambe Bay	North West England	197,291	11
Thames Estuary	South East/ East England	186,302	12
Dee Estuary	North West England/ Wales	129,271	7
Solway Estuary	North West England/ Scotland	122,602	10
Somerset Levels	South West England	99,035	6
Breydon Water and Berney Marsh	East England	98,071	7

Our most successful British waterbirds

Surveys undertaken in 1997–8 and in 2007–8 indicate the following species have increased their numbers within the decade:

Little egret
(Egretta garzetta)

Population up 811 per cent

A relatively new arrival to Britain, the little egret first started to arrive in significant numbers in 1989 and first bred here in 1996, in Dorset. This striking, pure white, heron-like bird with its black legs and bright yellow toes can be seen all year round although their numbers increase in winter as birds fly over from the Continent.

Best places to see them:
Estuaries in Cornwall and Devon, Poole Harbour, Dorset and also becoming more common in East Anglia.

Whooper swan
(Cygnus cygnus)

Population up 135 per cent

Only three to seven pairs breed in Britain each year, although thousands fly in from abroad from October to November in large v-formations. Larger than the Bewick swan and distinct from the mute thanks to its yellow beak, most whooper swans mate for life, although just under 6 per cent of pairings can end in 'divorce'.

Best places to see them:
Across northern England, East Anglia, Northern Ireland and Scotland.

little egret

whooper swan

Black-tailed godwit

(*Limosa limosa*)

Population up 79 per cent

In the 17th century the black-tailed godwit was considered a delicacy and increased hunting meant that it stopped breeding in the British Isles altogether. That has changed over time and there are now between 44 and 52 breeding pairs in the UK. The godwit is often seen digging for crabs with its slender bill. In spring, its browny-grey winter plumage gives way to a rusty red flush on its chest and neck.

Best places to see them:
Southwest Wales, Southwest and east England and East Anglia.

Avocet

(*Recurvirostra avosetta*)

Population up 73 per cent

Famous these days as the emblem of the RSPB, the up-curved beak of the black and white avocet was once a familiar sight from the Humber to Kent and went by a number of local nicknames, among them yelpers, whaup and clinker. Numbers began to drop as people killed the birds for their feathers – which were often used in fishing flies – and collected their eggs for cooking.

By 1837, their numbers had dwindled to extinction as a breeding bird. During the Second World War, newly flooded military defences in Suffolk created ideal avocet habitats and in 1947, a century after their disappearance, they returned to breed. Today there are 877 breeding pairs in the UK.

Best places to see them:
The RSPB reserves of Minsmere and Titchwell in East Anglia and the Tamar Estuary in Devon.

black-tailed godwit

avocet

Greenland barnacle goose

(*Branta leucopsis*)

Population up 66 per cent

A medium-sized goose with white cheeks standing out against a long black neck and head, the barnacle goose is a social visitor to Britain. Flying in noisy packs, there are 1,000 breeding birds although their numbers are bolstered between October and March when as many as 68,000 geese swoop in from the Netherlands.

Best places to see them:
The Solway Firth and Islay in Scotland, as well as coastal areas of Northern Ireland.

Greenland barnacle goose

For peat's sake

Peat has always been valuable stuff. It is an accumulation of dead organic matter that can't fully decompose owing to extremely waterlogged and boggy conditions. Cut and dried, it became a major source of domestic fuel. Where other fuels were scarce, peat for burning could warm your home and fill your pockets, although extracting it from England's wetlands was cold, hard work.

The best peat is always the deepest and peat cutters spent days slicing blocks of the stuff out of the earth in pits that were constantly refilling with water. At its peak in the 13th century, peat cutting was a massive industry, especially across East Anglia. In the Norfolk Broads alone, it's estimated that the volume of peat removed by hand equates to 28,000 Olympic-sized swimming pools.

By the 14th century, water levels were rising and, in the face of alternative fuels that could be obtained more easily, the peat industry began to decline.

Unfortunately, today our peatlands are in trouble. In 2010 Natural England reported that around three-quarters of England's deep peat area is damaged, degraded or is being dried out for cultivation and for livestock grazing. While the hand-cut peat industry of old was largely sustainable, modern extraction methods are intensive and – as peat bogs grow at the rate of only a millimetre a year – remove peat at a rate that the planet can't replace.

This is particularly worrying as peat is an important carbon reservoir beneath our feet. Worldwide, peat only covers 3 per cent of the planet, but captures more carbon than all of the tropical rainforest on Earth.

England's peat reserves store 580 million tonnes of carbon and once peat starts to degrade it leaks back into the environment, helping to warm the planet. Natural England believes that every year our peatlands are now releasing just under 3 million tonnes of CO_2.

To put that into context, that's the equivalent of the average carbon emissions of over 350,000 homes.

However, this is one potential environmental disaster that the average man in the street can do something about. Over 2 million cubic metres of peat – about 70 per cent of all UK peat use – finds it way into our back gardens every year as our nation of enthusiastic amateur gardeners buys compost laced with peat. And as if stripping our own peat reserves wasn't bad enough, around 55 per cent of the peat we use is imported. Every year, for example, an area the size of 250 Trafalgar Squares is dug up in the Republic of Ireland for British gardens.

At present, 46 per cent of all compost sold in the UK contains peat although the government has called for peat-based products to be completely phased out by 2020.

Alternatives to peat include bark, wood waste and fibre, mushroom and coir (coconut husk) compost – and of course you could even start your own compost heap. It's certainly true that the majority of our garden plants don't even need peat to flourish, except for extremely specialist species such as carnivorous plants – but how many of us have those in our gardens anyway?

How well do you know your coast?

As Winston Churchill was fond of reminding us, we are an island people. There's something about our sea that stirs the soul and inspires us. Whether we just visit the seaside from time to time or live alongside the coast, it is our place of refuge, sustenance, reflection and a springboard to a world of possibilities. Our national passion for the sea is hardly surprising as no place in the British Isles is more than 75 miles away from it.

But how much do you actually know about the coast? Why not try out your knowledge with a little game of true or false.

The largest island in the United Kingdom is Lewis and Harris.

FALSE

OK, so that was a trick question. The largest island in the UK is Great Britain (the landmass made up of England, Scotland and Wales) at 83,698 square miles. Lewis and Harris comes in second at 841.3 square miles with the Isle of Skye third with 639.5.

There are over 6,000 islands in the British Isles (including Great Britain and all of Ireland), the smallest of which is Bishop Rock, 4 miles off the Isles of Scilly. This rock ledge is only 46 metres long by 16 metres wide and yet still manages to support a lighthouse.

No-one can agree on the exact length of the coastline of Great Britain.

TRUE

The problem is that if you take a map at, say, 1:2,500,000 scale and measure around the coastline using a piece of string and work out the length, you'll get a completely different length if you try the same trick with a map scaled at 1:10,000. Why? Because the larger the scale, the more detail it shows and the more detail it shows the more wiggly it gets (and that's not a technical term) and the more nooks and crannies you'd have to include. Just imagine how difficult it would be to measure the real thing. And this is even before you throw in the problem that the coastline is constantly changing thanks to erosion and drift (see pages 276–8)

Most people go for the Ordnance Survey estimate (which is the figure also used by the AA). This puts the length of the great British coastline, including all principal islands, at 19,491 miles. Of that, mainland England excluding the Isle of Wight, Lundy and the Isles of Scilly (never say the Scilly Isles – the locals will hate you for it!), makes up only 5,581 miles.

You have a statutory right of access to walk around the English coast.

FALSE (at the moment)

Recently Natural England reported that 87 per cent of us believed that the English seaboard was ours to explore freely, possibly thanks to confusion over the Right to Roam (see pages 144–6). At present that just isn't the case. Currently there is no access at all to 30 per cent of the coast. However, that is about to change because of the Marine and Coastal Access Bill 2009. This Act of Parliament includes plans to open a footpath that stretches along the entire Welsh and English seaboard, while protecting certain key environmental, farming and shooting areas. The first stretch, a 12-mile section starting in Weymouth, is set to open at the same time as the Olympic flame is lit in 2012. The footpath, known widely as the 'coastal corridor', is expected to be completed in 2020. The estimated cost will be £50 million in total to establish the path and if you walk just over 12 miles a day you will take around 225 days to walk the whole lot.

As always, things are slightly different in Scotland. The Land Reform (Scotland) Act 2003 means that you have the right of 'responsible access' to all land, shore and inland water for outdoor recreation.

You have a right to visit a beach.

FALSE

There isn't anything in the law that says you can pick up your bucket and spade and head to the beach for a spot of sunbathing. The fact that we can visit so many beaches is thanks to landowners and local authorities granting us permission. And that's why every year we make 174 million trips to seaside towns.

There are places along the coast where it is illegal to fish.

TRUE

Lundy Island, off the coast of Devon, was the UK's first No Take Zone. Fishing is banned. In fact, no living thing can be taken from the waters surrounding the 3-mile long island. That's not the only protection Lundy offers. Lundy is Britain's only Marine Nature Reserve and since January 2010 the only Marine Conservation Zone (MCZ), the equivalent of a National Park beneath the waves.

The National Trust is Britain's largest coastal landowner.

TRUE

The charity owns over 700 miles of English, Welsh and Irish coastline, including over a third of the coast of Devon and Cornwall.

The head of any dead whale found on the British coastline legally becomes the property of the king.

TRUE

Royal Prerogative 1324 states that this is the case, although the tail becomes the property of the queen.

Sustainable fishing

Modern trawlers are fifty times more efficient than the sail-powered boats used by Victorian fishermen – yet their counterparts today only manage to pull in half the amount of fish. So, why is that?

Simple. The fish just aren't there in vast numbers any more. The astonishing truth is that stocks of some of our favourite fish such as haddock, plaice, turbot and halibut have dropped by 94 per cent in the past 120 years.

Many conservationists have been concerned about overfishing for a long time and recently researchers from York University working with the Marine Conservation Society (MCS) have shown that in the 1880s Britain's trawlers hauled in 300,000 tonnes of fish a year, while these days they struggle to catch 150,000. The peak was in 1937, with 804,630 tonnes – including 442,353 tonnes of cod and haddock.

Back in the 1880s most trawlermen stuck to the waters round our shores – now they spend weeks out at sea, covering thousands of miles in search of elusive fish.

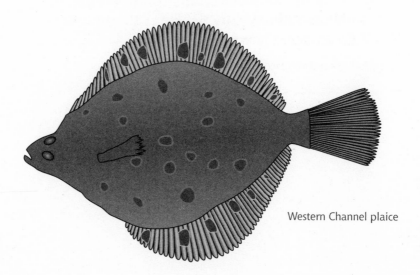

Western Channel plaice

Some fish to avoid

▶ Anchovy (from the Bay of Biscay)

▶ Cod, Atlantic (wild caught from all areas except the northeast Arctic, Iceland, and western English Channel, Bristol Channel, southeast Ireland and Sole Bank)

▶ Eel, European

▶ Haddock (from the Faroes and west Scotland fisheries)

▶ Hake, European (southern stock)

▶ Halibut, Atlantic (wild caught)

▶ Halibut, Greenland (from northwest Atlantic and Greenland, Iceland, west of Scotland and the Azores)

▶ Herring or sild (from west Scotland, west Ireland and Great Sole fisheries)

▶ Plaice (from the western English Channel, Celtic Sea, southwest Ireland and west of Ireland stocks)

▶ Plaice, American, or long rough dab

▶ Salmon, Atlantic (wild caught)

▶ Tiger prawn (except organically farmed)

There are calls for the EU's quota system to be even tougher to allow stocks in the North Sea to recover – no consolation for Britain's ever dwindling fishing fleet. But there are steps we can take to ensure we still have fish on our plates without threatening the oceans any further. Just make sure your order is from a sustainable source.

To help you make an informed choice, MCS produces a list of fish that it's OK to buy and fish to avoid, dependent on the current stock levels. To see the up-to-date list go to www.fishonline.org

Shifting sands and changing coasts

King Canute knew you couldn't hold back the tide and that's never been so obvious as today. Our coastline is constantly changing as the seas and winds rage against it. If you look closely at maps, you'll see that certain aspects of our coast looked very different 300, 200 or even 100 years ago. But what will they look like in the future? How will rising sea levels and climate changes affect our more recognisable coastal icons? As I mentioned earlier, the National Trust manages 700 miles of the coast and it identifies these ten landmarks as being most at risk:

1. St Michael's Mount (Cornwall)
In the early 1800s the causeway that links St Michael's Mount to the mainland was accessible for 6 hours a day at low tide. Today it's only accessible for four. By 2040 that might have dropped to one and then it could soon become a true island, while the harbour becomes increasingly threatened by flooding.

2. The white cliffs of Birling Gap (East Sussex)
The iconic white cliffs of the south coast are currently eroding on average by a metre a year. However, the National Trust has made the tough decision to let nature takes its course and has already started to demolish properties along the cliff edges.

3. Studland Bay (Dorset)

More than a million people a year enjoy the stunning 3-mile long Studland beach but the southern end is being lost at the rate of around 3 metres each year. Sea defences are now failing and have only pushed the problem further up the coast. These are now being removed.

4. Formby Point (Merseyside)

Part of the Sefton coast, one of Britain's largest sand-dune systems, Formby beach is losing 4 metres every year and if a major storm hits that can rise to 16 metres. The next century is expected to see the beach recede by at least 400 metres.

5. Porthdinllaen (Gwynedd)

This 18th-century fishing hamlet, set directly on a beach, constantly has to cope with flooding. Again, the National Trust is working to prepare its tenants in the village for the worst. While repairs are currently being made after recent damage, the time will come when Porthdinllaen is left to sink beneath the waves.

6. Farne Islands (off Northumberland)

Visitors flock to the Farne Islands to marvel at the 55,674 pairs of puffins and get close to the grey-seal colony. In future, they may find the crossing over the North Sea impossible, if predictions of increasingly stormy weather over the next four decades are correct. The more erratic conditions will also put at risk the thousands of seabird chicks that shelter among the 30-odd islands.

7. East Head (West Sussex)

The shingle spit at the entrance to Chichester Harbour has constantly shifted over the centuries. Now there is a danger that, unless a way can be found to work with the tide, the spit will be washed away, turning East Head into an island.

8. Blakeney Point (Norfolk)

Another shingle spit, Blakeney is a National Nature Reserve and an important habitat for birds such as the common tern, sandwich tern and little tern. The Environment Agency has, in the past, altered the course of local rivers to help protect the shingle, but the decision has now been made to let the waters do what they will.

9. Rhossili (Gower Peninsula, South Wales)

Rockfalls are now a common occurrence along this series of beautiful sandy beaches and the remains of an abandoned medieval village have already been covered by shifting sands.

10. Portstewart Strand beach and dunes (County Down)

Every year 100,000 holiday-makers head for Portstewart, but the dunes are rolling back inland all the time. Despite this, a new visitor centre is being built, albeit one that can be dismantled and relocated further inshore if needs must.

CHAPTER SEVEN

Climate Change and the Countryside

You can't open a paper or switch on the television without being confronted by climate change. You also can't help but wonder what our countryside will look like in the future. After all, some scientists are predicting that in just 70 years' time, the English countryside will be experiencing temperatures currently found in southern Europe, whereas other experts do not believe there will be such dramatic changes or that the warming of the planet has anything to do with the way we humans behave.

Personally, I do believe that climate change is happening and, yes, that will mean more periods of drought and of heavy sudden rainfall As our weather becomes more volatile, here are just a few ways in which scientists predict the countryside will be affected, although in some instances these are worst-case scenarios:

Britain will get wetter in winter and warmer in summer

One of the things most people don't realise is that, if predictions are correct, climate change could make Britain wetter than ever – for half the year at least. Country folk of 2080 could be used to heavier, harsher storms during the winter months and increased risk of flooding. The summers, on the other hand, could bring droughts and drier soils. I know farmers who are building their own reservoirs to cope with these expected conditions. Lush green pastures may be a thing of the past, replaced by dusty meadows of scrub, on which it will be more difficult – and costly – to raise livestock dependent on grazing.

Spring will spring sooner ...

According to studies of plant records of the Royal Botanic Garden in Edinburgh, by 2050 cherry and pear trees will burst into blossom as early as January and the official start to spring will have to be brought forward to before Valentine's Day.

That may be hard to believe after the long harsh winter of 2010, which made spring very late. But, as scientists never tire of telling us, that was a short-term weather condition – climate covers a much longer period. And climate records show that spring is already starting earlier than it did a hundred years ago.

But while an earlier spring seems a very nice prospect it does pose some potentially disastrous problems. Nature will desynchronise. The birds and insects that feed on plants won't be active until long after they are in flower and the cycle isn't likely to change as animal behaviour is linked to length of day rather than how hot it is.

... And so will summer

Researchers tell us that summer is starting 18 days earlier than it did half a century ago. A team from Sheffield University looked at temperatures and flowering plants, and found that summer temperatures averaging 14°C for three consecutive days now occur in early May rather than mid-June, and summer flowers such as geraniums and roses are coming into bloom earlier. And other research shows that autumn is starting later.

Our crops will change with the weather

Longer, drier summers and higher temperatures mean that farmers in the UK will be able to experiment with crops they never dreamed they'd be able to grow. I've heard that in my county of Oxfordshire the most popular crop could well become sunflowers. And already the growing season for plants in central England is a month longer than it was back in 1900.

These Mediterranean and other exotic crops are already growing on British farmland:

- Apricot
- Chilean guava
- Kiwi
- Nectarine
- Olive
- Peach

- Pecan
- Persimmon (Sharon fruit)
- Pineapple guava
- Szechuan pepper
- Tea
- Wine grapes (see pages 175–6)

Alien parasites and pests will flourish

It may sound like something out of a science-fiction film, but increased temperatures will mean that insects that have only thrived in hot countries will now be able to survive and flourish in Britain. This will impact on both livestock and humans as diseases that have been kept at bay by our milder climate in the past now get a foothold on British soil. The World Health Organisation is already warning that malaria may become a problem in the UK in the decades to come.

Our oldest trees will suffer

Oak trees, in particular, presently thrive in the British Isles as there is a year-round supply of water. If most rainfall occurs during a shorter winter season, oaks will struggle when faced with an irregular supply, as will beech trees, which need plenty of water to get through hot summers at present temperatures.

The English country garden will no longer be full of lupins, foxgloves and roses

Traditional spring bulbs, such as daffodils, snowdrops and bluebells, could also be doomed thanks to less moisture in the soil during spring. Aloe veras and cacti will take their place, alongside bamboos and palm trees, and every gardener could be faced with more aggressive weeds that grow 12 months a year.

Outdoor swimming pools could be warmed naturally, although would we be allowed to fill them during droughts?

Lakes and rivers will silt up due to increased soil erosion

For many anglers of the future, freshwater fishing will be a mere memory. For more about the increasing effects of erosion, see pages 53–5.

More people will suffer from hay fever

Current figures indicate that one in five of the British population has a pollen allergy. By 2030 that may have risen to over 50 per cent, according to researchers at the University of Worcester. The pollen season will lengthen and become more severe, while city dwellers will suffer most as pollution and poorer air quality make matters worse.

Wildlife will have to move home

Many creatures will instinctively move northwards, looking for somewhere a little cooler as the climate gets warmer. It will be far from easy, though, as much of the land they will have to cross has been developed. Wildlife 'stepping stones' will need to be created to help them on their way. For some species, like the snow bunting, which lives in the high Cairngorms, warmer temperatures could spell extinction. If all the snow disappears, so does the snow bunting.

CHAPTER EIGHT

So What is the Future of the Countryside?

Throughout this book we've explored the various landscapes that make up the great British countryside. However, I hope we've also discovered that the countryside is far more than just the scenery. As well as the fields, the hills, the woodlands and the waterways, it is also very much about the people. As we've seen, country folk have supplied the history, moulded the landscape into the myriad of forms it takes today and, for good or ill, their presence has deeply affected our wildlife.

It's still the case today. As I travel throughout the UK, reporting on rural affairs, it sometimes seems that the land we love is beset with problems. We've examined just some of the issues in these pages – threats to village life, the future of farming, conservation problems and, of course, the impact of climate change. But there's also an awful lot to celebrate about life in the UK countryside.

Wherever I go, I also hear about people rolling up their sleeves and getting involved, not content just to let events pass them by. If they believe their way of life is threatened, they fight for it. If they see their shop shutting down, they look for new ways to revive it. I've seen post offices and village stores springing up in pubs, halls and even churches as the community rallies round. Volunteers give up their time to help with conservation projects, to protect wildlife and preserve our heritage. Many of them are local but a large proportion head out from suburbia to do their bit to save the countryside they love.

Times are, of course, changing. Rural tourism is more popular than ever before. In 2001, when the countryside was all but closed down thanks to foot and mouth, the world looked grim, but from that crisis came a new birth for many. When we weren't allowed access, we realised how important our countryside actually is to us. Afterwards, tourism boomed, and while that has brought with it such concerns as how rural roads cope with increased traffic, it also brought huge benefits, as visitors pour cash into the local economy and farmers are able to diversify to help keep their livelihoods afloat.

Some of those same farmers are seeing their customers rediscover where their food comes from and the link from farm to fork is strengthening, slowly at first, but with growing momentum. There doesn't seem to be any turning back now and the profile of the countryside can only grow, especially with so much of our rural land now accessible to walkers.

All of which takes me back to the point I made in the introduction. I honestly believe that the more we explore our countryside, the more questions we ask and the more we understand, the more we'll want to get involved. Rural affairs will continue to be pushed up the national agenda rather than be left to slip away, and more work will be done to protect the countryside's beauty and riches.

So, please make use of what we've shared in this book to find out more about the great outdoors and embrace what you discover. Over the next few pages, you'll find a directory of just some of the organisations and associations that make a difference to country life so you can continue your journey of discovery.

Remember, it's your countryside.

CHAPTER NINE

Countryside Organisations

Sometimes it feels like you can't move for groups and organisations in the countryside! Here are some of the main ones along with useful contact details.

Animal welfare

Compassion in World Farming

A charity, founded in 1967, concentrating on animal welfare on farms.

River Court, Mill Lane, Godalming, Surrey GU7 1EZ
01483 521 950
www.ciwf.org.uk

League Against Cruel Sports

A charity set up in 1924 that campaigns against the perceived cruelty of animals in the name of sport.

New Sparling House, Holloway Hill,
Godalming, Surrey GU7 1QZ
01483 524 250
www.league.org.uk

Royal Society for the Prevention of Cruelty to Animals (RSPCA)

Founded in 1824 and given royal status by Queen Victoria 16 years later, the RSPCA is a charity that promotes animal welfare and prosecutes those found harming animals.

Wilberforce Way, Southwater, Horsham, West Sussex RH13 9RS
0300 1234 555
www.rspca.org.uk

Conservation

BTCV

A charity, set up as the British Trust for Conservation Volunteers in 1959, which runs volunteer courses, holidays and activities across the British Isles.

Sedum House, Mallard Way, Doncaster,
South Yorkshire DN4 8DB
01302 388 883
www.btcv.org.uk

Butterfly Conservation

A conservation charity that monitors and tries to assist the UK's butterfly and moth populations.

Manor Yard, East Lulworth, Wareham, Dorset BH20 5QP
01929 400209
www.butterfly-conservation.org

Campaign to Protect Rural England (CPRE)

Formed in 1926 in response to continued urban sprawl, CPRE campaigns to protect the countryside's green spaces and habitats as well as what they perceive to be key aspects of the rural areas, such as tranquillity and regional diversity.

128 Southwark Street, London SE1 0SW
020 7981 2800
www.cpre.org.uk

British Trust for Ornithology (BTO)

An independent scientific-research trust that studies British birds, including scientific surveys and bird ringing.

The Nunnery, Thetford, Norfolk IP24 2PU
01842 750050
www.bto.org

John Muir Trust

Found in 1983, the John Muir Trust protects wild places in Scotland. It currently owns over 25,000 hectares and is in partnership with various landowners of a further 50,000.

Tower House, Station Road, Pitlochry, Perthshire PH16 5AN
01796 470080
www.jmt.org

People's Trust for Endangered Species (PTES)

Set up in 1977 and previously known as the Mammals Trust UK, PTES raises funds to reverse the loss of our mammals in the wild.

15 Cloisters House, 8 Battersea Park Road, London SW8 4BG
020 7498 4533
www.ptes.org

Plantlife

Originally conceived as an 'RSPB for plants' Plantlife works to protect the UK's wild flowers, plants, lichens and fungi and their habitats.

14 Rollestone Street, Salisbury, Wiltshire SP1 1DX
01722 342730
www.plantlife.org.uk

The Tree Council

A charity that encourages – and provides grants for – the planting of trees in our towns and cities with an army of 8,000 volunteer tree wardens across the country.

71 Newcomen Street, London, SE1 1YT
020 7407 9992
www.treecouncil.org.uk

Royal Society for the Protection of Birds (RSPB)

One of the UK's largest conservation charities, with over a million members, the RSPB manages 200 nature reserves, researches the problems facing our birds and campaigns for their protection. It's less well known that the RSPB also concerns itself with mammals and insects.

The Lodge, Potton Road, Sandy, Bedfordshire SG19 2DL
01767 680551
www.rspb.org.uk

The Wildlife Trusts

There are 47 local Wildlife Trusts all over the UK, making up the UK's largest voluntary conservation organisation and managing 2,256 nature reserves.

The Kiln, Waterside, Mather Road, Newark,
Nottinghamshire NG24 1WT
01636 677711
www.wildlifetrusts.org

The Woodland Trust

A charity dedicated to protecting native woods, tree and their wildlife.

Autumn Park, Dysart Road, Grantham, Lincolnshire, NG31 6LL
01476 581111
www.woodlandtrust.org.uk

Wildfowl & Wetlands Trust (WWT)

Founded in 1946 by the late Sir Peter Scott – a man Sir David Attenborough has called 'the patron saint of conservation' – the WWT works to conserve our wetlands, operating nine visitor centres.

Slimbridge, Gloucestershire GL2 7BT
01453 891900
www.wwt.org.uk

Farming

Department for Environment, Food and Rural Affairs (DEFRA)

The government department dealing with agriculture, rural development, wildlife, animal welfare, food and the environment.

Eastbury House, 30–34 Albert Embankment, London SE1 7TL
08459 33 55 77
www.defra.gov.uk

National Farmers' Union (NFU)

The trade union for British farmers, founded in 1908.

Agriculture House, Stoneleigh Park, Stoneleigh, Warwickshire CV8 2TZ
024 76858500
www.nfuonline.com

National Farmers' Retail & Markets Association (FARMA)

A cooperative of farmers, local producers and farmers' market organisers, FARMA also advises and inspects farm producer outlets and markets.

12 Southgate Street, Winchester, Hampshire SO23 9EF
0845 45 88 420
www.farma.org.uk

Rare Breeds Survival Trust (RBST)

Founded in 1973 to help protect Britain's rarest native farm livestock.

Stoneleigh Park, Near Kenilworth, Warwickshire CV8 2LG
024 7669 6551
www.rbst.org.uk

Soil Association

Britain's largest certifier of and campaigner for organic food and farming.

South Plaza, Marlborough Street, Bristol BS1 3NX
0117 314 5000
18C Liberton Brae, Tower Mains, Edinburgh EH16 6AE
0131 666 2474
www.soilassociation.org

Linking Environment and Farming (LEAF)

An organisation promoting environmental responsibility in farming and the importance of public understanding of what's happening on the farm.

The National Agricultural Centre, Stoneleigh Park, Warwickshire CV8 2LG
0247 6413 911
www.leafuk.org

Fieldsports and shooting

The British Association for Shooting & Conservation (BASC)

Originally the Wildfowlers' Association of Great Britain and Ireland, BASC is the largest shooting organisation in the UK, boasting 129,000 members.

Marford Mill, Rossett, Wrexham LL12 0HL
01244 573 000
www.basc.org.uk

Countryside Alliance (CA)

Set up in 1997, the Countryside Alliance is primarily concerned with the support of fieldsports but also campaigns to protect other aspects of rural life.

The Old Town Hall, 367 Kennington Road, London SE11 4PT
020 7840 9200
www.countryside-alliance.org.uk

Game & Wildlife Conservation Trust

Primarily working with the shooting industry, the Trust, formally known as the Game Conservancy Trust, promotes the management of game and wildlife to improve biodiversity.

Burgate Manor, Fordingbridge, Hampshire SP6 1EF
01425 652381
www.gwct.org.uk

The British Falconers' Club

Britain's oldest falconry association, founded in 1927, dedicated to the preservation of the ancient art of falconry and the conservation of birds of prey.

Westfield, Meeting Hill, Worstead, North Walsham,
Norfolk NR28 9LS
01692 404057
www.britishfalconersclub.co.uk

The National Gamekeepers' Organisation (NGO)

Founded in 1997 by a group of gamekeepers concerned that their role in the countryside was not understood by the general public, the NGO is the national representative body for gamekeepers in England and Wales and strives to uphold standards in the profession.

PO Box 246, Darlington, Durham DL1 9FZ
01833 660869
www.nationalgamekeepers.org.uk

Landowners and government

Country Land & Business Association (CLA)

Organisation representing land, business and property owners in rural England and Wales.

16 Belgrave Square, London, SW1X 8PQ
020 7235 0511
www.cla.org.uk

Countryside Council for Wales (CCW)/Cyngor Cefn Gwlad Cymru (CCGC)

The Welsh Assembly government's conservation authority for Wales, advising on conservation and outdoor activities.

Maes-y-Ffynnon, Penrhosgarnedd, Bangor, Gwynedd LL57 2DW
0845 1306229
www.ccw.gov.uk

Environment Agency (EA)

The non-departmental public body of DEFRA, charged with protecting and managing the environment in England and Wales. The EA also administers rod licences for fishing.

National Customer Contact Centre, PO Box 544, Rotherham, South Yorkshire S60 1BY
08708 506 506
www.environment-agency.gov.uk

Forestry Commission (GB and Scotland)

The government department responsible for managing Britain's woods and forests and one of the country's largest landowners, managing 827,000 hectares (2,000,000 acres) of woodland. That's 1.4 billion trees' worth!

Silvan House, 231 Corstorphine Road,
Edinburgh EH12 7AT
0131 334 0303
www.forestry.gov.uk

Highways Agency

Part of the government's Department of Transport and responsible for maintaining our road network.

123 Buckingham Palace Road, London SW1W 9HA
0121 335 8301
www.highways.gov.uk

Natural England

The government's independent public body, formed by the amalgamation of the Countryside Agency, English Nature and the Rural Development Service in 2006. Natural England is responsible for protecting the natural environment and providing the means by which we can enjoy it.

1 East Parade, Sheffield S1 2ET
0845 600 3078
www.naturalengland.org.uk

Northern Ireland Environment Agency (NIEA)

Northern Ireland's equivalent of Natural England.

Cromac Avenue, Gasworks Business Park, Belfast BT7 2JA
0845 302 0008
www.ni-environment.gov.uk

Scottish Natural Heritage

Scotland's equivalent of Natural England.

Great Glen House, Leachkin Road, Inverness, IV3 8NW
01463 725000
www.snh.gov.uk

Heritage

Cadw

The Welsh Assembly's body charged with protecting and managing historic buildings, ancient monuments and historic parks and gardens.

Welsh Assembly Government, Plas Carew, Unit 5/7 Cefn Coed, Parc Nantgarw, Cardiff CF15 7QQ
01443 33 6000
www.cadw.wales.gov.uk

English Heritage

Originally the Historic Building and Monuments Commission for England, English Heritage is an independent public body that protects over 400 buildings and monuments.

1 Waterhouse Square, 138–142 Holborn, London EC1N 2ST
0870 333 1181
www.english-heritage.org.uk

Historic Scotland

The Scottish equivalent of Cadw and English Heritage, safeguarding the nation's historic building and landmarks.

Longmore House, Salisbury Place, Edinburgh EH9 1SH
0131 668 8600
www.historic-scotland.gov.uk

The Landmark Trust

A charity that rescues buildings of historic note and makes them available for holiday rental.

Shottesbrooke, Maidenhead, Berkshire SL6 3SW
01628 825925
www.landmarktrust.org.uk

National Trust

An independent conservation charity and one of the largest landowners in England, Wales and Northern Ireland. The Trust maintains 350 historic houses, gardens and monuments, which are open to the public, as well as farmland, islands, nature reserves and entire villages.

PO Box 39, Warrington, Cheshire WA5 7WD
0844 800 1895
www.nationaltrust.org.uk

The National Trust for Scotland (NTS)

An organisation similar to the National Trust, the NTS manages over 127 properties and 72,843 hectares (179,998 acres) of land in Scotland.

Wemyss House, 28 Charlotte Square, Edinburgh EH2 4ET
0844 493 2100
www.nts.org.uk

Waterways

British Waterways

A public corporation that acts as the navigation authority in England, Scotland and Wales, looking after the 2,000-mile network of rivers and canals in the three countries.

64 Clarendon Road, Watford, Hertfordshire WD17 1DA
0845 671 5530
www.britishwaterways.co.uk

The Waterways Trust

A national charity that works to promote greater public awareness and enjoyment of our inland waterways.

Llanthony Warehouse, Gloucester Docks, Gloucester GL1 2EH
01452 318 220
www.thewaterwaystrust.org.uk

Angling Trust

The new, independent governing body representing all game, coarse and sea anglers and angling in England. Includes a legal arm – Fish Legal – which fights pollution and damage to fisheries on behalf of member clubs.

Eastwood House, 6 Rainbow Street, Leominster, Herefordshire HR6 8DQ
0844 7700616
www.anglingtrust.net

Marine Conservation Society (MCS)

A charity that works to protect UK marine wildlife and environments.

Registered office: Unit 3, Wolf Business Park, Alton Road, Ross-on-Wye HR9 5NB
01989 566017

Scottish office: 3 Coates Place, Edinburgh EH3 7AA

www.mcsuk.org

Index

Acknowledgements

I would like to thank my good friend and colleague Cavan Scott for the tremendous amount of help he has given me in researching and compiling this book – I could not have done it without him. Thanks also to Andrew Thorman, Teresa Bogan, Andrea Buffery, Andrew Tomlinson and the rest of the *Countryfile* team for the support, advice and friendship they have given me over the years.